Rethinking Religious Education and Plurality

As Western society becomes increasingly plural in character, both in terms of conventional multiculturalism and the intellectual plurality of late modernity, schools must reassess the provision of religious education and look at how they might adapt in order to accommodate students' diverse experiences of plurality. This book offers a critical view of approaches to the treatment of different religions in contemporary education, in order to devise approaches to teaching and learning, and to formulate policies and procedures that are fair and just to all.

Beginning with a contextual overview of the religious, social and cultural changes of the past fifty years, the book goes on to illuminate and assess six different responses to the challenges posed by religious plurality in schools. Conclusions are drawn from the various positions explored, identifying what the character of religious education should be, how it should be taught and addressing the issues raised in policy, practice and research.

Drawing on a wealth of international research, including the author's own work, *Rethinking Religious Education and Plurality* argues for a plural approach to education and will be a valuable resource for students and researchers studying courses in religious education as well as teachers, education advisers and policy makers.

Robert Jackson is Professor of Education and Director of Graduate Studies at the Institute of Education at the University of Warwick where he is also Director of the Warwick Religions and Education Research Unit. He is Editor of the *British Journal of Religious Education*.

Rethinking Religious Education and Plurality

Issues in diversity and pedagogy

Robert Jackson

Routledge
Taylor & Francis Group

LONDON AND NEW YORK

First published 2004
by Routledge
2 Park Square, Milton Park, Abingdon, Oxon, OX14 4RN

Simultaneously published in the USA and Canada
by Routledge
270 Madison Ave, New York NY 10016

Routledge is an imprint of the Taylor & Francis Group

Transferred to Digital Printing 2009

© 2004 Robert Jackson

Typeset in Garamond by
HWA Text and Data Management Ltd, Tunbridge Wells

British Library Cataloguing in Publication Data
A catalogue record for this book is available from the British
Library

Library of Congress Cataloging in Publication Data
Rethinking religious education and plurality : issues in diversity
and pedagogy / Robert Jackson
     p. cm.
Includes bibliographical references (p.) and index.
  1. Religious education. 2. Religious pluralism. I. Title.

    BL42.J33 2004
    207´5–dc22   2003019826

ISBN 0–415–30272–2 (pbk)
ISBN 0–415–30271–4 (hbk)

To the memory of my parents, Hilda Jackson 1910–1990 and Leslie Jackson 1911–2000

Contents

Acknowledgements

I am grateful to all my colleagues in the Warwick Religions and Education Research Unit for their encouragement and in particular to Ursula McKenna for keeping me to deadlines and helping with references and to Ann Henderson, Eleanor Nesbitt and Elisabeth Arweck for suggestions and comments on some draft chapters. I am also grateful to my research students, past and present, for their work, some of which is discussed in the book. I am especially grateful to Julia Ipgrave for her translation of parts of the Debray Report and for her on-going research on dialogue in religious education. Members of the European Network for Religious Education through Contextual Approaches (ENRECA) and the International Network for Inter-religious and Inter-cultural Education have responded to presentations based on ideas in the book; Geir Skeie, Sissel Østberg, Heid Leganger-Krogstad and Wolfram Weisse have been especially generous with their time, ideas and suggestions. Thanks also go to colleagues working on the Council of Europe and Oslo Coalition projects discussed in Chapter 10 for their interest and encouragement, and to Tim Key and the Research, Analysis and International Division of Ofsted for aggregated inspection data which are referred to in Chapter 3.

I am grateful to sponsors of various research projects which have influenced the writing of the book: the Economic and Social Research Council for funding the project 'Ethnography and Religious Education' (project reference number R000232489); the Leverhulme Trust for its support of three projects on young British Hindus' perceptions of their religious tradition; the Arts and Humanities Research Board for funding two projects on Hindu related religious movements and spiritual and values education; the All Saints Educational Trust and the Westhill Endowment Trust for funding projects on dialogue and religious education; the St Peter's Saltley Trust for its support for a project on the contribution of religious education to intercultural education; and the British Academy for its sponsorship of an international seminar at Warwick on religious education and citizenship.

Thanks are also due to various publishers and editors for permission to use revised extracts from several chapters and articles. A revised extract from 'The misrepresentation of religious education', in M. Leicester and M. Taylor (eds) (1992) *Ethics, Ethnicity and Education*, London, Kogan Page, is included in Chapter 2. Chapter 3 is a much expanded version of 'Should the state fund faith based schools? A review of the arguments', which appeared in the *British Journal of Religious Education* (2003) 25(2). Revised extracts from 'Creative pedagogy in religious education: case studies in interpretation', in H.-G. Heimbrock, P. Schreiner and C. Scheilke (eds) (2001) *Towards Religious Competence: Diversity as a Challenge for Education in Europe*, Münster: Lit Verlag, appear in Chapter 6. Edited extracts from Chapters 1 and 4 of R. Jackson (ed.) (2003) *International Perspectives on Citizenship, Education and Religious Diversity*, London, RoutledgeFalmer, appear in Chapters 1 and 8. Chapter 9 is an expanded and revised version of 'Reflections on research in religious education', in T. Dodd (ed.) (2001) *Aspects of Education: Developments in Religious Education*, published by the University of Hull.

Introduction

In Britain, at least until the late 1950s, religious education was a form of Christian instruction that had moral and civic as well as spiritual goals. In the early twenty-first century, Western democracies are increasingly plural societies. British society is now more secular than half a century ago yet, partly through the migration and settlement of peoples, it is observably religiously and culturally diverse. This form of diversity has been called 'traditional' plurality. Plurality has also increased through developments in information technology and media, resulting in easy communication across continents and the exposure of individuals to a flow of competing ideas and values. This diversity of late or post modernity, which affects all religions and ideologies, has been called 'modern' plurality (Skeie 1995).

Since the early 1970s, religious education in Britain has responded positively to religious diversity, providing approaches to the subject that took account of 'traditional' religious plurality at national and global levels. Now, pedagogies are emerging which, in various ways, acknowledge plurality with both its 'traditional' and 'modern' dimensions as the context for religious education. In contrast, there are also responses which attempt to insulate young people from plurality and religious diversity, by advocating the teaching of Christianity as the religion of British national culture, by separating children by religion for teaching in separate faith-based schools, or by arguing for the removal of any study of religion from state-funded community schools.

This book discusses different reactions and responses to plurality. Chapter 1 sets the scene, reviewing changing trends in religious, moral and civic education since the 1950s, as well as debates about plurality and pluralism, modernism and postmodernism. There is also a discussion about the nature of plural societies, with particular reference to the nation state and nationality, ethnicity and culture. This leads into a discussion of religious education in relation to plurality, with particular reference to issues of identity. Subsequent chapters discuss some reactions to plurality from different educational stances.

The most defensive (discussed in Chapter 2) lies in various nostalgic attempts to return to earlier and more secure positions, and to deny the impact of plurality on social and personal identity. This can take the form of continuing to wish to promote the association of morality, religion and citizenship by nurturing a British cultural and national identity or by arguing that Christian indoctrination is an educationally valid approach to religious education in the common school.

Another response (discussed in Chapter 3) recognizes the reality of plurality, but takes religion and education into private or semi-private space in the form of schools with a particular religious character. Thus, for children who attend such schools, particular religious values can be allowed to permeate the whole of their education. Here, in general terms, the aim of religious education is to nurture children into a particular religious world view. This view is sometimes coupled with the argument that religious education should only take place in such schools and is an anachronism in the secular, common school.

A third approach (considered in Chapter 4) takes a radically different view, adopting a normative postmodernist pluralism, rejecting the study of religions as the imposition of oppressive constructions, and promoting 'faith' and value through the exploration of personal narratives. In this case, the distinction between religious education and other forms of related education – spiritual education, education in the emotions and values education, for example – is collapsed, and the aim is to help pupils to develop their own sets of individually constructed beliefs and values that are personally satisfying.

A fourth position also recognizes plurality, but attempts to retain the integrity of different religions as discrete systems of belief, distinct sources of spirituality, and as ideologies with universal claims to truth. This stance seeks to promote religious literacy and to help each pupil to identify with and argue for a particular religious or non-religious position. The aim here is to turn out young people able to handle religious language and claims with intelligence and informed judgement. This view is discussed in Chapter 5.

A fifth position acknowledges plurality but attempts to keep the various debates associated with it open. Pupils are encouraged to participate in those debates at their own level, through a reflexive study of source materials in relation to personal concerns (Chapter 6) and through dialogue and interaction with each other (Chapter 7). The aims here are to help young people to develop and practise appropriate skills for interpreting religious and cultural material – some of it drawn from ethnographic or local sources

– and for working together, to increase their understanding of plurality, to gain insight from their learning and to discuss, clarify and formulate their own views.

In Chapter 8, issues in the relationship between religious education, multicultural (or intercultural) education, citizenship education and values education are discussed, as is a sixth response to plurality, namely that religious education should be removed from the curriculum of the common school, on the grounds that society is now deeply secular. A variant on this argument – that the retention of religious education as a separate subject is unjustified because studies of a variety of religions are irrelevant to the experience of most pupils – is also considered.

Chapter 9 adds some reflections on the relevance and contribution of different types of theoretical and empirical research to the debates about religious education and its practice in schools. Examples of British and international research in religious education are considered, as are issues such as the involvement of practitioners in RE research, training for research, the quality of research, the provision of research funding and the dissemination of research. The internationalization of religious education research through the establishment of research networks within and beyond Europe is also considered.

Chapter 10 summarizes the argument of the book as a whole, suggesting that the most appropriate pedagogical responses to plurality in the common school provide a framework of democratic values which respect diversity within the law and allow pupils to clarify and refine their own positions on religion. Epistemological, political and ethical foundations for such a pluralistic religious education are considered, as is the broader issue of whole school policy towards plurality. Some primary and secondary aims for the subject are discussed in relation to RE's potential role in dealing with issues of social cohesion. This leads to an account of the contribution of religious education to international projects on intercultural education and education for freedom of religion or belief. A discussion about the relationship between patterns of civil religion and education in religion, with reference to France and England, leads to a final consideration of possible ways in which current policy towards religious education in England and Wales might evolve.

Chapter 1

Religious education in the context of plurality

The early years of the twenty-first century find the debate about religion in education reflecting wider controversies about national and transnational identity, ethnic identity, the perpetuation of culture and values and the nature of knowledge. The events of September 11, 2001 in New York and their various on-going consequences give a sharp focus to issues such as the relationship between religious, national and cultural identity, the nature of multicultural societies and the widespread public ignorance about religions such as Islam. In terms of education, the importance of the following questions is clear. Should there be some form of education in religions in schools and, if so, what should be its aims and methods? Should religious education in state-funded schools promote some kind of generic religiosity associated with a national cultural identity, or even the acceptance of a particular faith position? Should it, rather, concentrate on imparting information and increasing understanding of different religious views, or should it primarily be concerned to help young people to develop their own beliefs and values? Alternatively, would it be better to take religion out of the curriculum of state schools altogether? Ought children from different religious and non-religious backgrounds be taught together in the same schools, or should children from families with a particular religious background be taught in separate faith-based schools? Have studies of religions any contribution to make beyond religious education, in citizenship education, multicultural education or moral education, for example? These issues are of importance to all Western democracies, and there are important contributions to the debates from different European perspectives (e.g. Heimbrock *et al.* 2001; Østberg 1997; Weisse and Knauth 1997) and from countries such as Australia (Hobson and Edwards 1999; Mavor 1989; Rossiter 1981), Canada (Johns 1985; Milot and Ouellet 1997; Watson 1990), South Africa (Chidester *et al.* 1992, Chidester 2003a and b; Steyn 2003; Stonier 1997) and Namibia (Kotzé 1997; Lombard 1997). This book will concentrate on debates in England and Wales, but the generic issues covered are of relevance to European discussions about education and to the discussions in all Western democracies, especially since they are set against the background of an increasing globalization, the erosion of autonomy of the nation state and the wider debates about modernity and postmodernity. The internationalization of research in religious education is discussed in Chapter 9 and details of some international development projects are given in Chapter 10.

Changing trends in religious, moral and civic education

In England and Wales, at least until the late 1950s, religious, moral and civic education were seen as closely related. Religious education was equated with Christian education, a form of instruction that had moral and civic goals. In the atmosphere of moral and social renewal following the Second World War, the British Government saw religious – interpreted as 'non-denominational' Christian – instruction as the basis of morality and citizenship, and as an integrating principle for all education (see, for example, ICE 1954: 8).

By the 1960s, this virtual equation of religious education, moral education and good citizenship was being challenged by an increasingly evident secularization. This process was reflected in social trends, but pervaded academic discourse, including contemporary theology (e.g. Altizer and Hamilton 1968; Cox 1965) and the philosophy of religion (e.g. Flew and MacIntyre 1955). The loss of Christianity's authority could be detected among pupils. For example, Harold Loukes' empirical work showed young people who were disenchanted with a 'top-down' approach that provided set answers to religious and moral questions. Loukes, in an early piece of qualitative educational research, audio-taped and then analyzed discussions between 14-year-olds during ordinary RE lessons (Loukes 1961; see also Chapter 9 below). He then transcribed some typical quotations from the young people who had been recorded, and distributed them to just over 500 pupils from eight schools, requesting written comments. From his analysis of the discussions and responses, Loukes noted the ambivalence of students towards RE; they found the content too distant from their own experience and the mode of teaching boring. Loukes recommended a form of RE that concentrated on human questions such as relationships, responsibilities and the problems of evil and death. For Loukes, the key role of the subject was to explore students' questions and concerns in the context of a liberal and secularized Christianity.

By 1966, Edwin Cox could publish a book entitled *Changing Aims in Religious Education*, reflecting the impact of secularization, rather than religious plurality, on the theory and practice of the subject (Cox 1966). Religious education could no longer find its rationale in promoting a Christian national religious and moral identity, and needed to draw back from making assumptions about the beliefs and values of students. Cox's research on sixth formers affirmed their interest in discussing religious and moral issues, but also highlighted their distaste for any form of education that told them what to believe (Cox 1967).

A pluralistic perspective was added through the influence of Professor Ninian Smart, who set up the first Department of Religious Studies in a British university in the mid-1960s (Smart 1967). Smart took a strong interest in religious education in schools, writing an influential text arguing for the secularization of religious education and shifting its focus to the analysis of religion seen in a global context, yet still attempting to relate it to pupils' personal and epistemological questions (Smart 1968). Smart also had the vision to set up a research and development project, which gained funding from the Schools Council. The project team produced an influential Working Paper summing up its philosophy and pedagogy. This advocated a phenomenological approach, adapted from religious studies in higher education, and having the aim of understanding rather than evangelism or nurture, but also retaining an existential dimension, concerned with pupils' development of their own ideas (Schools Council 1971). Smart also became a major figure in the Shap Working Party on World Religions in Education, an influential body bringing together teachers and scholars working in different parts of the education system.

In the 1970s and 1980s, reactions to Smart's phenomenological approach (or to cruder versions of world religions approaches) attempted (like Loukes) to put the pupil at the centre, rather than the subject matter of religion, and included spiritual (e.g. Priestley 1985), aesthetic (Robinson and Lealman 1980) and other experiential approaches, notably in the work of David Hay and John Hammond, which drew on Hay's research on religious experience (Hammond *et al.* 1990). Sometimes experiential elements and phenomenological elements were combined, as in Michael Grimmitt's approach to religious education and human development (Grimmitt 1987).

Turning to moral education, the 1960s saw some significant developments. Loukes' 'life exploration' approach to religious education, taken up in many agreed syllabuses and school books of the day, provided opportunities for pupils to raise and discuss moral issues in an open way. Nevertheless, the context of a liberal Christian theology of human experience still underpinned the approach. Smart's view was quite different. Here, religious education could *contribute* to moral education, but only through the exploration of the moral dimension of religion – examining how a religious way of life affected an insider's moral beliefs and actions (see Chapter 8 below).

It was in the 1960s that moral education appeared as an independent field, with many contributors emphasizing the logical independence of religion and morality. Starting with the pioneering, but over-elaborate, work of John Wilson and his collaborators in the 1960s (Wilson *et al.* 1967), much writing on moral education has also taken account of a secular and pluralistic climate, as indicated over the years in various educational books (e.g. Downey and Kelly 1978; Hirst 1974; McPhail *et al.* 1972) and numerous contributions to the *Journal of Moral Education* which first appeared in 1971. Moral education has never had its own slot on the timetable in English and Welsh schools, and its influence still comes through its impact on particular curriculum subjects (e.g. Winston 1998, 1999) or, since 1988, in meeting the requirement that the curriculum should contribute to pupils' moral development (QCA 1998). Recent discussions take us into the modernity/postmodernity debate, and include radical ideas, such as the conflation of moral, religious, citizenship and emotional education through the articulation and study of pupils' personal narratives (Erricker and Erricker 2000a; see also Chapter 4 below).

Civic education also went its own way in the 1960s, especially through developments in political education. By the late 1960s, Bernard Crick was arguing for education for political literacy in the secondary school (Crick 1969: 3–4), and later set up a curriculum project on political education that produced the report *Political Education and Political Literacy* (Crick and Porter 1978). The advent of the Thatcher government in 1979 retarded any further developments in political education and, not surprisingly, the national curriculum that was introduced via the 1988 Education Reform Act was made up of traditional subjects, marginalizing fields held to be controversial, such as political, multicultural and antiracist education (Tomlinson and Craft 1995). Citizenship was included as a non-statutory cross-curricular theme (NCC 1990), but with an overloaded compulsory curriculum there was little chance of its development. It was only with the election of a Labour government in 1997 that developments in citizenship education were encouraged. In 2002 Citizenship Education appeared as a new and broadly based national curriculum subject for secondary schools, incorporating moral, political and community action elements, and dealing with issues of religious and cultural diversity (DfEE/QCA 1999). The study of religions can once again contribute to citizenship education, not through providing a single metaphysical and moral basis for citizenship, but through helping to clarify the debates on religion, ethnicity, nationality and culture, and through informing pupils about religious diversity (Jackson 2003a; Chapter 8 below).

Plurality

The background to the above developments was both the secularization debate, and the direct experience of an increasing religious and cultural diversity. In recent times, the complexity of the issues concerning plurality has become more evident, and recent debates about religious and values education have taken account of this wider understanding of plurality. In his discussion of plurality as a descriptive concept, the Norwegian scholar Geir Skeie[1] distinguishes between two types, 'traditional' and 'modern' (Skeie 1995, 2002). Skeie also distinguishes plurality – an essentially descriptive concept – from the normative concept of pluralism. Plurality, within limits, can be described impartially, but there are different ideological stances on pluralism.

Traditional plurality corresponds to the observable cultural diversity present in many Western societies. In the case of Britain, especially since the early 1950s, migrants moved from South Asia, East Africa and the Caribbean, bringing significant numbers with, for example, Muslim, Hindu and Sikh family backgrounds and minorities of other backgrounds such as Pentecostal Christian and Rastafarian. In some countries such as South Africa, Norway, Canada, the USA or Australia, that religious plurality also includes the religious ways of life of indigenous peoples. These might have been marginalized for a variety of reasons, but are once again a focus of attention. The emergence of new religious movements and various new age phenomena can also be seen as part of the religious and ideological plurality of Western societies (Beckford 1985, 1986; Heelas 1996). One also needs to take account of plurality at 'local' levels in societies which have appeared on the surface to be culturally homogeneous. Research conducted by Anthony Cohen and his colleagues shows, for example, how people from local communities can re-process symbols, sharing some common features with the rest of the nation, but overlaying them with 'local meaning' (Cohen 1982b; see also Chapter 8 below).

Modern plurality relates to the variegated intellectual climate of late modernity or postmodernity. In Skeie's analysis, modern plurality points to the diversity of modern societies in the sense of being fragmented, with various groups having competing and often contradictory rationalities, and the growth of individualism and the privatization of religion. Such trends are exemplified in debates about truth and meaning, knowledge and power and personal and social identity. Critiques of assumptions, ideas and values that characterized the European Enlightenment have led to a plurality in contemporary thought that is often pictured as a move from modernity to late modernity or 'high modernity' (Giddens 1990) or from modernity to postmodernity (e.g. Lyotard 1984). The very mention of these concepts opens up a huge debate, full of terminological confusion and disagreement. Nevertheless, it is worth attempting a brief, general account of the processes involved.

Modernism

For our purposes, 'modernism' (and some of its new variants) is the ideological response that embraces 'modernity' while 'postmodernism' is the range of ideological responses that embrace 'postmodernity'. This distinction between the normative and descriptive needs to be made, since there are those who accept the idea of postmodernity without adopting a full blooded postmodernism. These include writers who would argue that pupils in our schools are living in a postmodern environment, but ought not to be educated in a way that forecloses debates about postmodernism.

The story is shortened and simplified, but it goes something like this. The formation of modern societies can be traced back to the rapid social and economic development following the decline of feudalism in Western Europe. The formation of modernity is characterized by complex political, economic, social and cultural processes – especially the forces of Western Europe's political and industrial revolutions. The seventeenth and especially eighteenth centuries saw an intellectual response to rising modernity in Europe with the rise of rationalism. Modernity spawned the rationalistic philosophy of writers such as Descartes, who believed that knowledge had sure and certain foundations, and the empiricism of philosophers such as David Hume. Trends in philosophy matched the rise of science in being confident in the authority of empirical knowledge based on observation, and on reason as the source of truth. This 'modernist' view saw knowledge as something to be acquired and is consistent with the predominantly cognitive view of education and learning that dominates the current national curriculum in England and Wales.

The Romantic Movement of the nineteenth century reacted against this rationalistic view, bringing emotion, intuition and individual creativity back into the arts and the educational equation, emphasizing (as in the work of Rousseau) the idea of drawing knowledge out of children, rather than filling them up with it. So-called 'progressive' and 'child centred' views of education were influenced by ideas from the Romantic Movement.

In the twentieth century, the rationalism of modernism prevailed and appeared both in capitalist and Marxist economic guises. Some writers have defended the notion of modernity, but have tried to humanize it by criticizing the manipulation of knowledge by those with power for their own ideological purposes. I am thinking of writers from the Frankfurt school of critical theory, especially Jürgen Habermas (1972). Others (often influenced by Habermas) argue that we have not moved beyond modernity but are living through a transitional process of coming to terms with its limits and contradictions. Anthony Giddens calls this 'reflexive modernization' or 'high modernity'. Here society is subjected to the technological forces it has created. The constant flow of new information that society generates provides a running critique of society's sense of modernity. This process is heightened, according to Anthony Giddens and Ulrich Beck, by factors such as globalization and the emergence of the 'risk society'. Globalization is the process through which local happenings are influenced by distant events which, in turn, are shaped by local events. In the 'risk society', traditional authority (such as religion) has declined and people have to cope with new uncertainties related to the advance of science, such as global warming and pollution (e.g. Beck 1992; Giddens 1990; Giddens *et al.* 1994).

Postmodernism

Postmodernists (sometimes labelled post-structuralists if their pedigree involved developing ideas from structuralism) have gone much further, usually adopting an anti-realist epistemological stance and rejecting modernist ways of thinking. The term 'postmodernism' gets used in a bewildering variety of ways (both in the arts and in social studies), but for our purposes, there are some general trends to which we can draw attention. Postmodernist ideas tend to involve the rejection of 'total' explanations of reality, such as Marxism, capitalism, liberalism, the religions, Freudianism etc. These, or the ideological positions associated with them, are often called 'grand narratives' or 'meta-narratives', following the nomenclature of Jean-François Lyotard (1984). 'Knowledge' within these meta-narratives is 'legitimated' not objectively but by rules that are internal to its 'language game'. So-called knowledge is associated with power and is used to oppress and control rather than to liberate. Lyotard prefers 'small narratives' in which individuals can participate actively and effectively. Michel Foucault's concern with power in relation to knowledge is also a significant influence on postmodernist thinking (e.g. 1971).

Instead of seeing much language as corresponding to empirical reality, postmodernism emphasizes the slipperiness of language. Words and concepts have no necessary connection with each other, and the relationship between the signifier (the word) and the signified (the concept) shifts over time. Meaning is tied to the *use* of language within particular ways of life, and reality is socially and linguistically constructed. Hence there is a radical questioning of the nature of knowledge itself. Whereas 'modernists' regard 'knowledge' as 'objective', supported by reason and scientific observation, postmodernists see knowledge as relative to different ways of life (forms of life and language games [from Wittgenstein]; paradigms [from Thomas Kuhn]; epistemes [from Foucault]). Postmodernism is thus radically relativistic with regard to knowledge and truth. Postmodernists have a broad view of knowledge, sometimes speaking of 'knowledges'. For example, skills are regarded as a type of knowledge (e.g. Lyotard 1984: 18), and are often considered to be more important than other forms of knowledge: knowing how is liberating and enabling; knowledge in the sense of 'information', however, is only relevant if it meets one's needs. The term 'knowledge' can be used in this rather loose way since, in postmodernist terms, all knowledge is constructed. Nothing can be known in an absolute and objective sense.

This view of knowledge has important consequences for the idea of truth. There can be no absolute truth beyond each way of life ('form of life', 'paradigm' etc.). The use of language is governed by the unwritten rules of the 'language game' used in each paradigm, which determine the truth or falsity of what is said. Claims to truth are usually seen in pragmatist terms. Truth is what 'works'. Thus, the postmodernist philosopher Richard Rorty can write that true beliefs are 'those beliefs which are successful in helping us to do what we want to do' (Rorty 1980: 10), and (following Quine) that '… a necessary truth is just a statement such that nobody has given us any interesting alternative that would lead us to question it' (Rorty 1980: 175).

Just as reality is seen as fragmented, so modernist views of individual identity are challenged. Identities are socially constructed in relation to others. The idea of individual genius is abandoned. For example, for Derrida and others (including Foucault) there is no such person as an author, in the sense of originating a text from nothing. Texts are the product of inter-textuality, a complex of allusions to and citations of other texts.

As with Giddens' and Beck's neo-modernist views, there is an acknowledgement of the impact of elements of globalization – the massive improvement in communications and the dominance of computerized technology, for example – and the ways in which globalization can influence 'local' matters. Globalization, in this sense, facilitates the development of 'small narratives' as opposed to 'grand narratives', that stand a better chance of giving people a sense of meaning and purpose. Email can link environmentalists or human rights activists from many countries, just as it can enable children from different national, cultural and religious backgrounds to share concerns and to converse with one another.

In postmodernist thinking, there is also a tendency to be eclectic and to gather beliefs from a variety of sources, often combining symbols from very different frameworks of meaning. Resulting compilations will be seen as tentative and open to modification. Some postmodernists, rather than being depressed by uncertainty, emphasize playfulness, celebrating diversity, spontaneity, eclecticism and creativity. Ursula King gives a flavour of this view in relation to the study of spirituality when she remarks:

> ... if postmodernism is not taken to nihilistic extremes, is not seen as a fixed position that denies all others, then its penchant for experimentation, questioning and diversity, its resistance to closure and definite meanings, open up new transcendent trails and divine disclosure in the midst of all our searching for a wisdom to live by – leading us back to the roots of spirituality.
>
> (King 2002: 6)

Plural societies

Skeie's concept of 'modern plurality' covers the terrain on which neo-modernist and postmodernist positions are situated. His key point is about the relationship between the plurality of different groups and systems and the individual in society. The effectiveness of modern communications ensures that individuals are exposed to a more or less constant flow of ideas, values and ideals, each offering a different choice for action. Thus, the competing rationalities of different groups, systems and structures influence individuals and appear as contradictions within each person. As Skeie remarks, 'We are impelled to question our identity and self-understanding over and over again' (Skeie 1995: 87).

He makes two further points. The first is to emphasize the intertwined relationship between traditional and modern plurality. Thus, changes and developments within a religious tradition have to be seen not just in terms of traditional plurality, but under influences from modern plurality. Attention to modern plurality accentuates the inner diversity of religions and shows, for example, the complexity of the idea of the 'transmission' of a religion from one generation to the next. The second (a point already made above) is to distinguish between plurality as a descriptive concept and pluralism as a normative one. Perhaps we can all agree that there is plurality; the stance we take on delimiting and interpreting that plurality – that is, our stance on pluralism – is a matter of judgement.

This way of looking at plurality helps in the analysis of key concepts that relate to religion in society, such as ethnicity, nationality and culture. The debates show a range of positions from, at one extreme, 'closed' views that reify the concepts to postmodern views, at the other, offering complete deconstructions. The key educational task is to engage learners in a critical analysis of how such terminology is used, both in relation to their own experience and with regard to examples from a variety of other sources. By participating in such discussions, students should also be helped to examine their own and their peers' assumptions and reflect upon their own identities. Different positions within the debates (rather than their technical detail) can be used to clarify, challenge or illuminate positions advanced by students. It would be helpful to attempt a brief overview of the main debates about the nation state, ethnicity and culture (for the debate about religion see Jackson 1997: Chapter 3).

The nation state and nationality

The modern nation state has a relatively short history of around 500 years, with most states being formed within the last century or so. A 'state' is usually regarded as a governed society, supported by a civil service, ruling over a specific area, and whose authority is supported by law and the ability to use force. Thus a 'nation state' is a variety of modern state, in which 'the mass of the population are citizens who know themselves to be part of that nation' (Giddens 1993: 743). Perhaps Giddens' definition should be broadened, for a state can include groups who regard themselves as nations (comprising one or more ethnic groups) and might aspire to their own statehood, as with Scottish and Welsh nationalism in Britain. Nationality is recognized or denied by each nation state on its own rules, and usually gives entitlement to citizenship.

Nationalism, the ideology of one or more privileged ethnic categories, regards an essentialized and romanticized culture as the 'heritage' of the national group. Inflexible and narrow views of national, ethnic and religious identity tend to emerge when fixed and bounded views of the nature of cultures are combined with reified views of nationality, ethnicity and religion (see Chapter 2 below). Nationalism leads both to 'biological racism' and to 'cultural racism', the association of cultural (including religious) factors with biological racism in order to denigrate cultural difference (Modood 1997).

However, some nation states attempt to find ways of incorporating more than one ethnic group through abstracting a romantic idea of 'super-ethnicity', with ideas such as 'the American people' or the idea of assimilation through a melting pot of cultures. However, this notion is in tension with any idea of retaining the distinctive but shifting cultural traditions of minorities. Another way of accommodating ethnic or religious difference is through finding ways to incorporate different groups through the modification of civil religion or national custom. In Britain, for example, there is a gradual incorporation of the main faiths represented in the country into national and local civic religious life – whether a royal wedding or funeral, a mayoral investiture or hospital or prison chaplaincy (Beckford and Gilliat 1998). The current heir to the throne's declaration that he does not see himself as the future 'Defender of the Faith', but as a 'defender of faith' is another example. What is clear from reflections on civil religion is that each nation state has its own variety, conditioned by its own particular history. In this sense the nation state cannot be entirely neutral when dealing with issues of religious and cultural diversity (see Chapter 10 below for a comparison of the different ways in which religion has been handled in English and French education).

Whatever the difficulties, it is crucial that members of different minorities need to be involved directly in the democratic processes of society. Different views as to how this goal might be achieved vary according to the degree to which religions, ethnic groups and cultures are regarded as internally homogeneous. Those taking a 'closed' view (and they might be insiders as well as outsiders) tend to take the line that 'representatives' can speak authoritatively on behalf of their constituencies, while those emphasizing the varied and contested nature of groups look for a much wider range of activities through which many different individuals (including women and children) can participate in dialogue and negotiation with others (see Chapters 7, 8 and 10 below for a view of 'differentiated citizenship' that supports this view in relation to religious education).

Ethnicity

Ethnic groups are popularly thought of as having a common ancestry and descent, marked by some form of cultural continuity which distinguishes them from other groups around them. There is also the common equation of supposedly overt 'racial' difference and ethnic difference. Ethnic differences can also be highlighted by legal definition, as in a judgement made in England by Lord Fraser in 1983, in which he ruled Sikhs to be an ethnic group (Bailey *et al.* 1991; Jones and Welengama 2000: 40).

If a person is labelled as being from a certain ethnic group, then that person can be stereotyped by certain 'outsiders' or members of the majority culture, 'locked' into a particular identity and expected to behave in certain preconceived ways. 'Insiders' might also sometimes have an interest in presenting a closed view of their own ethnic group. This static view has been criticized especially by those who have recognized the situational character of ethnicity through their field research. Thus, Fredrik Barth draws attention to changes that take place across socially constructed ethnic boundaries, where one group influences another, either positively or negatively (Barth 1969, 1981, 2000). Such ethnic re-formation takes place, for example, among groups which have rediscovered religious or ethnic symbols as a result of being marginalized by more powerful groups around them, or groups that have attempted to redefine themselves in response to influences or pressures from other social groups or institutions. Barth's analysis of ethnicity focuses attention on the maintenance of ethnic boundaries. Ethnic identity depends on ascription by both insiders and outsiders; ethnicity is not fixed, but is defined situationally.

In her research on Pakistani Muslim young people in Britain, Jessica Jacobson highlights this shifting nature of ethnic identity. Jacobson observed that a sense of ethnic identity can vary according to context. It could be more related to a Pakistani ancestry or be 'British Pakistani' in certain contexts (in the family, for example), and be 'Asian' or 'British Asian' in another (with members of the peer group, for example). Jacobson's research suggests that, in the case of young British Pakistani Muslims, there is evidence that ethnicity is in a state of flux and rapid change, while religion is perceived as stable and having universal applicability (Jacobson 1997).

Some writers also speak of 'hyphenated' ethnic identities. For example, Michael Fischer's analysis of 'Chinese-American' ethnic identity finds a group with an ancestry that goes ultimately to China (so there is still *some* sense of ancestry). However, he also asserts that ethnicity is dynamic, not taught and learned, and not simply transmitted from generation to generation. To be Chinese-American '… is a matter of finding a voice or style that does not violate one's several components of identity' (Fischer 1986: 196). Shared ancestry is still an element of ethnicity, but the internal variety within an ethnic group is acknowledged, as well as the possibility of utilizing cultural elements from other sources.

The most radical positions in the debate reject the very idea of ethnicity. These range from the Marxist critique, claiming the only significant category to be social class (Castles and Kosack 1973: 5), to forms of 'super-ethnic' nationalism in which ethnic distinctions are assimilated (the 'melting pot' view, for example), to postmodernist views, seeing ethnicity as an oppressive social construction. On this last view, even the situationist analysis of ethnicity, with its use of terms such as 'group', 'boundary' and 'maintenance', is regarded as potentially enclosing individuals within artificial identities.

Many ethnographic field studies find that 'ethnicity' implies *some* degree of identification with an ancestral tradition or a sense of 'shared peoplehood' (Dashefsky 1972), but it also changes situationally, includes an element of cultural choice and can never be fixed or static (Jackson and Nesbitt 1993). As Gerd Baumann puts it, 'Both wine and ethnicity are ... creations of human minds, skills and plans – based on some natural ingredients it is true, but far beyond anything that nature could do by itself' (Baumann 1999: 64).

The culture debate

If we look historically at the term 'culture', then, in the fifteenth century, we find it referring to the tending of crops or animal husbandry. During the next two centuries it is used analogically to refer to the human mind (Hobbes, for example, wrote of the culture of minds). During the eighteenth century, 'culture' became associated with the arts and scholarship – in philosophy and history, for example – and was considered to be for the wealthy.[2] At about the same time, under the influence of the German philosopher Herder, we get an alternative view, namely the idea of distinct and variable cultures, a view developed in the Romantic Movement. An essentialized culture was regarded as the collective 'heritage' of the national group, itself equated with a particular ethnic group.

This closed view of cultures came into early social or cultural anthropology, though not so much with strongly nationalistic overtones. For example, Herder's work influenced Franz Boas and other cultural relativists in the USA. For Ruth Benedict, one of Boas' students, each culture was thought of as distinct, by analogy with types of living organism. For Benedict, cultures either survived or died out, with no possibility of the formation of new cultural expressions through cultural interaction (Benedict 1935). The idea of uniform, bounded cultures was perpetuated in early work in multicultural education in Britain (see Chapter 8 below) and is still to be found in the rhetoric of the political right, in popular newspapers and in the writings of some educators (see Chapter 2 below).

At the opposite extreme there are postmodern deconstructions of the idea of 'a culture', with any idea of continuous tradition being regarded as an imposed and manipulative 'meta-narrative'. On this view, the way of life someone adopts is a matter of personal, individual choice with, in one version, the role of education being to filter out any influences of meta-narratives on the young, whether they be traditional forms of authority or from pre-prepared educational materials, in order to allow children to construct their own personal narratives and faith positions (see Chapter 4 below). In between the two poles are intermediary positions, emphasizing the changing and contested nature of cultures over time. These range from Clifford Geertz's view of cultures as internally diverse, but with cultural continuity maintained through inherited conceptions, expressed through symbols (Geertz 1973: 89) to views emphasizing internal (sometimes inter-generational) conflict or negotiation in creating cultural change (e.g. Said 1978; Clifford 1986). These latter authors also point to the role of the *observer* (whether anthropologist, historian, journalist or student) in constructing 'cultures'. On this view, as with biographies, single definitive accounts are not possible.

There are also those who emphasize process rather than content in making and describing culture. Culture is seen, not so much as an 'entity' (albeit one that is in a constant state of flux), but as an active process through which humans produce change. Instead of having a distinct and fixed cultural identity, individuals and groups identify with elements of culture, or synthesize new culture through bringing different elements together. The emphasis is on people *engaging with* culture, drawing on different cultural resources (e.g. Barth 1994, 1996; Østberg 2003a). The emphasis in identity formation is less on descent and inheritance, and more on a series of identifications through dialogue and communication with others.

Qualitative research studies show that there are *both* inflexible and highly flexible approaches to nationality, ethnicity, religion and their relationship in cultural discourse (Baumann 1996, 1999). In various situations, there are those whose interests might be to present a particular relationship between a fixed view of culture (or cultures) and reified views of nationality, ethnicity and religion. Issues relating to this point will be picked up in Chapters 2 and 8.

Religious education and plurality

An important concern of this book is the argument that religious education in the common school, together with studies of religion in other subjects and streams such as citizenship education or intercultural education, should take close account of the plural situations in which we all live, whilst avoiding the imposition of a particular ideology of pluralism onto children and young people. Such ideologies include particular religious or atheistic viewpoints or closed views of the nature of knowledge. The exploration of plurality involves examining the relationship between individuals' accounts of and questions about personal identity and wider issues of social identity and plurality. Such an integration of the personal and the social sees religious education, not as *defined* by a fixed body of knowledge (although the development of knowledge and understanding is a crucial ingredient), but as a series of existential and social debates in which pupils are encouraged to participate, with a personal stake related to their own developing sense of identity. Religious education's fundamental concerns in relation to existential and social questions and the data of religious traditions distinguish the field from others, though the precise boundaries are open to on-going public debate, including discussion by children in schools. Religious education thus preserves its identity as a field of study, but relates to and can make distinctive contributions to a range of other fields. Some of these relationships will be discussed in Chapters 8 and 10.

The Dutch scholar Wilna Meijer echoes Skeie in her discussion of identity in relation to religious education, drawing especially on Paul Ricoeur's hermeneutics of the self in order to develop a dynamic model of self-awareness. In this, the self is not a fixed point to discover, but is evolving and historical. Self-awareness is a matter of interpretation, of telling a coherent life-story. Since self-aware people inevitably live with ambiguity, each individual's identity is always open to revision. Religious education is thus a conversational process in which students, whether from 'secular' or 'religious' backgrounds, continuously interpret and reinterpret their own views in the light of their studies (Meijer 1995).[3]

Religious education thus requires skills of interpretation, criticism and dialogue as well as access to sources of information. Participation in the relevant debates links the social world and the individual, and is a condition for the kind of inter-religious and intercultural communication that is necessary for the health of plural democracies. The common school is a highly appropriate setting for such explorations, embracing plurality and pluralism in an epistemologically open way (Jackson 1997: 126).[4] The extent to which certain kinds of faith-based schools might allow young people to develop their ideas within the setting of a particular religious outlook is itself an important discussion in a situation where government policy in relation to England and Wales advocates the expansion of state-funded religious schooling (see Chapter 3 below).

Identity formation

Of course, the school and the RE classroom in particular are not the only situations in which children and young people face multiple influences. This especially needs to be remembered by those who tend to over-emphasize the role of teachers in the socialization of young people (see Chapter 2 below). For example, research with young people within particular religio-ethnic groups and families provides insights into the processes of identity formation. The research with a group of 'British Asian' young people from various Hindu backgrounds conducted by Eleanor Nesbitt and myself (Jackson and Nesbitt 1993) portrays young people whose religio-cultural identities are partly shaped by ancestry and partly by exposure to a range of other influences in relation to their own agency. The 1993 report shows that, rather than being individuals with a fixed sense of belonging to this group or that, or feeling comfortable in only one type of cultural situation, many of the children we were studying could move unselfconsciously from one milieu to another. Different children formed particular complexes of partial identifications with members of their own religious and ethnic groups and other groups, but this was not threatening to their integrity as persons. Nesbitt's subsequent work with the same young people seven or eight years on reinforces these findings, showing that 'being Hindu' is still a central aspect of identity, but that a range of other influences combined with this to form new syntheses (Nesbitt 1998a).

Sissel Østberg's work on Pakistani Muslim children and young people in Oslo runs parallel to this, and she develops the concept of 'integrated plural identity' in relation to the young people she studied. As interpreters of multiple narratives they (children whose family is of Pakistani origin) revealed a diversified set of cultural and social identities, but on a personal level this diversity or plurality did not threaten their personal integrity. They were the narrators or the interpreters of their own lives. As long as the children communicated a diversified set of identities (Pakistani, Muslim, Norwegian, Norwegian-Pakistani, Punjabi, Asian etc.) to diversified sets of 'others', they 'narrated' themselves through an interpretation process and in this way developed their selfhood (Østberg 2000a, 2003a, b and c).

These examples happen to be from minority groups for whom identity issues are particularly evident. However, whatever their backgrounds, the worldviews of individual children are being worked and reworked through the interaction of a range of influences in relation to their own volition. All are subject to the influences of traditional and modern plurality. Various researchers, from Harold Loukes onwards, have provided evidence that children and young people are interested in exploring their own sense of identity as persons in relation to the range of influences that affect them and others, as well as wider existential questions. Such influences may include family, community, local environment, peer group and the media (through advertising, music, television, film etc.). For example, Keijo Eriksson's research with a mainly 'white' group of Swedish adolescents shows them especially concerned with matters such as family, education, social concerns, leisure, sympathy and understanding, the environment, health, religion, death, peace, and security in their social environment (Eriksson 2000). Eriksson draws on such concerns in linking the personal experience of students to wider debates about value, including social and religious issues, in their religious education.[5] Research on children and young people's existential questions (Hartman 1986, 1994),[6] on their spirituality as expressed through personal narratives (e.g. Erricker and Erricker 1996) and on their sense of the sacred (Heimbrock 2004) also confirms an interest in exploring elements of human experience and response.

Examples such as these show that influences encountered help to shape the emerging beliefs and values that children bring to the RE classroom. Each child may find that some of these experiences, attitudes and beliefs are shared by some of their classmates while others are not. In interpreting material from religions, in participating in debates about broad issues – about truth and meaning, the pervasive influence of the money culture or human rights issues, for example – and in engaging in dialogue with their peers, pupils will find agreement and disagreement, affirmation and challenge. Such studies should help children to clarify and sharpen their own ideas and commitments. Influences on children are not only from family, community and the media. Various studies show their influence upon one another. For example, Julia Ipgrave's research focuses on the religio-cultural influence of children upon one another, and their formation of new ideas through encounter (Ipgrave 2002; Chapter 7 below). The key element in her work is the direct involvement of children themselves – in having an active role in selecting topics for discussion, in taking discussion in new directions, in drawing on their own personal knowledge and experience, in negotiating meanings with one another and even in being co-researchers.

Conclusion

In the context of education, I have argued that changes in religious, moral and citizenship education from the late 1960s to the end of the 1980s can be seen very much against a backdrop of secularization and an increasing religious plurality. However, since the 1990s there has been a growing awareness of modern plurality – including more direct experience of the various effects of globalization and more awareness of the contested nature of concepts such as religion, ethnicity and culture. Thus, the context for religious education in the twenty-first century is plurality – an interaction between 'traditional' and 'modern' plurality. The nature of the interaction will vary from place to place, but every school in some respects is a plural school and every locality, whether urban or rural, is plural in some of the senses described above. In the Britain of the 1950s, religious education was seen as a binding force, integrating spiritual, religious, moral and civic elements through forms of 'cultural Christianity'. From the 1960s and 1970s, this view of the relationship between religion and education was largely abandoned, and RE, moral education, and different elements of what we now call citizenship education (political education, development education and multicultural or intercultural education) went their separate ways and had their different fortunes. Plurality was seen in terms of the overt ethnic and religious plurality of society, with some attention to global diversity. Now religious education has the opportunity to explore plurality in the complex ways in which it affects everyone. Material from religious and secular sources can be explored in relation to existential, moral and social debates that affect and concern pupils. Moreover, views of childhood that recognize young people's agency have spawned various approaches to pedagogy that engage them and treat them as participants in the subject – as contributors of knowledge and experience, as critics and co-researchers – rather than simply as recipients of information. In this sense, religious education contributes to the child's awareness of and participation in identity issues. Religious education's fundamental concerns in relation to existential questions and the data of religious traditions distinguish the field from others, though not in any publicly agreed way. Indeed the debates about the relationship between religious education and fields such as spiritual, citizenship, intercultural and values education should be part of the discussion for young people as well as for educators.

There have been different reactions and responses to plurality by writers and researchers on religious education. Some of these are discussed in Chapters 2–8.

Chapter 2

Religious and cultural heritage

As noted in Chapter 1, the most defensive response to the fact of plurality lies in attempts to return to earlier and more secure positions of the 1950s, and to resist or even deny the impact of plurality on the social and personal identity of young people. Part of the agenda for some who advocate education for children from particular family backgrounds in separate religious schools has been to insulate them from the influence of plurality. Issues connected with this form of faith-based education are discussed below in Chapter 3. However, some defenders of traditionalism wish to return to a Christian form of religious education in publicly funded community schools, in which children are educated or instructed in Christianity with the aim of nurturing faith. Such approaches usually seek to identify Christianity with particular views of culture, nationality and sometimes ethnicity, especially when combining a right wing political outlook with traditional forms of Christianity such as Evangelicalism. By way of illustration, I will discuss the stance of critics of 'multifaith' RE in the late 1980s, and a recent apologia for a 'confessional' Christian approach to religious education in state-funded community schools.

Religious education and the 1988 Education Reform Act

In the late 1980s, during the debates about religious education surrounding the publication of the Education Reform Bill, there emerged a point of view combining the interests of the radical right in politics and some forms of conservative Christian theology. This lobby argued for a stronger place for RE in schools but against a religious education reflecting the religious plurality of Britain. The argument was for 'predominantly Christian' RE rather than 'multifaith' RE, which was regarded as the norm among many Local Education Authority syllabuses. 'Multifaith' religious education was, for example, associated by this lobby with secularism, was regarded as inherently relativistic and not concerned with issues of truth. It was considered to have a confusing 'mishmash' of subject matter and to betray Britain's cultural heritage. 'Predominantly Christian' RE, on the other hand, would offer close attention to the Christian faith and its role in shaping 'British culture', and would also provide a particular brand of moral instruction with the aim of reducing social problems among the young.

Through publications and the activities of individuals, this traditionalist lobby succeeded in influencing parliamentary debates about religious education. The legislation on RE and collective worship embodied in the Education Reform Act (ERA) can be seen as a compromise between the views of liberal educators and those of the radical right of education in alliance with some theologically conservative Christians. The latter have continued to campaign against 'liberal' interpretations of the 1988 Act's clauses on religious education and have encouraged parents to make use of complaints procedures established under the terms of the Education Reform Act.[1]

This chapter argues that the characterization of religious education by those arguing for a 'predominantly Christian' form of RE is largely mistaken and that their association of Christianity with a particular view of the nature of the national culture is open to criticism. An ethical and political issue is their proposed use of particular interpretations of Christian teaching, in deliberate isolation from alternative views, in order to achieve certain social goals. Their views on authority in relation to personal autonomy also raise moral issues about the agency of the person – especially in relation to childhood – and education (see Chapter 10 below). With regard to plurality, their association of morality with one religious tradition ignores the moral concerns and contributions of other religious and humanistic traditions within British society. Penny Thompson's recent contribution reiterates the issue of the relationship between Christianity and 'British culture', but raises further questions relating to the meaning of 'confessionalism' and to the religious commitments of teachers in relation to their own intentions and their view of the aims and content of religious education (Thompson 2004).

In 1988, following the publication of the Education Reform Bill, a pamphlet was published called *The Crisis in Religious Education* (Burn and Hart 1988). The document was not written by professional religious educators but by members of an Evangelical Christian education pressure group (Christians and Tyneside Schools, CATS) and published by the politically right wing Educational Research Trust.[2] The paper was sent to all MPs and members of the House of Lords before the key debates on the Education Reform Bill's clauses on religious education.

The authors polarized two forms of religious education which are labelled 'multifaith' and 'predominantly Christian', vigorously attacking the former and calling for the restoration of the latter. The document influenced the parliamentary debates about religious education and collective worship which took place in 1988 and the writings and utterances of politicians who supported its case. Some aspects of the story of the debates and their outcome in law are documented elsewhere (e.g. Alves 1991; Brown 1989; Hull 1991). With regard to religious education, the essence of the compromise is contained in Section 8.3 of the 1988 Education Reform Act which states that new Agreed Syllabuses for religious education must: 'reflect the fact that the religious traditions in Great Britain are in the main Christian whilst taking account of the teaching and practices of the other principal religions represented in Great Britain'.

Secularization and secularism

Baroness Cox in her foreword to *The Crisis in Religious Education* juxtaposes points about 'multifaith' religious education and secularization:

> Many of our children are in schools ... where teaching about Christianity has either been diluted to a multifaith relativism or has become little more than a secularised discussion of social and political issues.
>
> (Cox 1988: 4)

That its opponents see 'multifaith' RE as a step in the direction of secularism is confirmed by Anthony Coombs, then a Member of Parliament. Coombs writes of his wish 'to ensure that religious education reflected a Christian view and that ... relative comparative religion shading into blatant secularism was banished from the classroom' (Coombs 1991).

This interpretation ignores the fact that secularization had made an impact on religious education well before 'multifaith' RE had become a widely discussed issue. Harold Loukes' work with teenagers, for example, confirmed that young people were disenchanted with a Bible-based RE that assumed the truth of Christianity (Loukes 1961, 1965). What they wanted was for the controversial nature of religion to be recognized and the opportunity to discuss openly issues of deep concern. Similarly, in the early 1960s, Edwin Cox's research with sixth formers revealed an antipathy towards an RE which made assumptions about the truth of Christianity (reported in Cox 1967). Cox's book *Changing Aims in Religious Education* (Cox 1966) was not a radical attack on religious education as a medium for instruction or nurture in the Christian faith. Rather, it put into words not only Cox's changing views influenced by his research, but also the direct experience of many teachers and pupils; namely, that if the subject was to retain any credibility, it had to acknowledge that religious claims were a matter of intellectual dispute. As noted in the previous chapter, RE was shifting away from Christian instruction or nurture before the overt religious plurality of Britain had become a major issue and before movements to give education a more global perspective were showing any significant influence. To associate a 'multifaith' approach to religious education with secularism, especially by suggesting that the former has a causal relationship with the latter, distorts the history of religious education in England and Wales and is misleading.

Christianity and public morality

It is in the domain of values that the real intentions of this group of critics become clear. With some justification, they draw attention to the marginalization of Christian perspectives in many school personal and social education courses of the 1980s. But then they go further, relating social and moral problems to the decline of a particular form of Christian morality.

> Many of the guidance and personal and social development courses in schools have been so secularised that Christian values are not considered at all. This is a tragic situation and one that goes a long way towards explaining the increasing violence in our society …
>
> (Burn and Hart 1988: 9)

The writers go on to assert their commitment to a particular form of Christian ethics and then imply that exposure of young people to alternative views of morality is undesirable.

> The Christian faith provides God-given moral absolutes for personal and social conduct. It also emphasises human responsibility and rejects determinism. We believe that explanations of conduct as being determined by the environment alone are now seen to be bankrupt … We are concerned that some of the new Locally Agreed Syllabuses with their emphasis on non-theistic life stances have already opened the door to the possibility of exposing the young to political ideologies which deny human freedom, human responsibility and the reality of sin.
>
> (Burn and Hart 1988: 31)

The authors appear to wish to deny the controversial nature of Christian claims by ruling out any consideration of alternative views in religious education. Their concurrence with this view is confirmed by their quotation of a passage from a book called *Education and Indoctrination* which includes the sentences:

> The exposure to alternatives may defeat the purpose of religious education as much as it defeats the purpose of morality: it offers to place idle curiosity where there should be certainty and truth. The crucial feature of religious belief is that, unlike political belief, it is essentially addressed to the individual, his conscience and his salvation. It is a guide to life and a source of confidence.
>
> (Scruton *et al.* 1985: 27)

These passages reveal a number of assumptions. First, there is a complete disregard for the home and community background of children and young people. There seems to be an assumption that children are not nurtured in faith and morality in the home and community. For many children from a variety of religious backgrounds this is simply not the case. Research evidence shows something of the range of variety of formal and informal religious nurture, not only among the different traditions in Britain, but within each one (e.g. Bauer 1997; Jackson and Nesbitt 1993; Nesbitt 2000a; Valins 2003). Second, there is the assumption that a secure framework of values is necessarily tied to religion. Third, there is a mistaken assumption about the unity of Christianity with regard to its approach to human conduct. There are on-going variations of interpretation within the Christian tradition which reflect different theological views of scripture and doctrine (e.g. Outka and Ramsey 1968). Many committed Christians would, for example, reject the view of authority implicit in the above passages. The plurality of Christian ethics and theology is reflected in the variegated character of informal and formal nurture in homes and churches (Jackson and Nesbitt 1992; Nesbitt 1993a). Fourth, there is the ethically dubious assumption that it is proper to deny students access to information on the grounds of achieving an instrumental goal. At the very least this assumption raises serious moral and theological questions about civil liberties and human rights as well as about the nature and aims of education.

There is an interesting difference in the two passages concerning the effects of exposing young people to more than one view. For Scruton *et al.*, exposure to more than one view engenders 'idle curiosity', while exposure to one view can bring about 'certainty and trust'. No evidence is offered to support this assertion. On the other hand, for Burn and Hart, exposure to different views (namely views they do not hold) is dangerous for the contrary reason that young people might adopt them. Again, no evidence is offered in support of this claim. What they both agree on is the exposure of children only to one view of one tradition with the intention that they should adopt it. One obvious objection to this approach is that there are plenty of examples of its failure. Many people who have had a highly specific form of religious schooling have not continued to believe what they were brought up to believe by teachers or indeed by parents.

More importantly, the view that the writers adopt reveals a view of education that rejects the principle that, in areas of experience that are legitimately a matter of public dispute, individuals should be encouraged to make decisions for themselves on the basis of the available evidence. Their view is inconsistent with the argument, also advanced forcefully by these writers, that religious education should not be relativistic and should take seriously the issue of truth claims in religion (e.g. Burn and Hart 1988: 15). If young people are to be taught the skills necessary to make judgements about the claims of religions they can hardly be insulated from these claims or be expected to accept, on someone else's authority, that certain claims are true and others false.

One can understand the psychological force of an argument that seeks to leave young people cocooned within a particular worldview. However, not only do the authors of the quoted passages ignore the religious and secular plurality of British society, they also fail to recognize that young people grow up in a world where such cushioning is not possible. The young are exposed to the influences of their peers at school, the media and the internet. Further, in their lessons they ask critical questions, give voice to prejudices, deliberate, make judgements and express opinions. Is it not better to provide an educational environment in which the skills of debate, dialogue, deliberation and evaluation are well taught and where high standards of argument and discussion are expected rather than to leave young people to learn by default?

This question raises a general issue about the relationship between religious education and religious upbringing or nurture. There are some situations in which certain forms of religious upbringing appear not to be compatible with the educational goal of encouraging young people to make decisions autonomously. Some of the clashes between more narrow forms of religious nurture and the educational processes of critical discussion and analysis are less problematic than they seem to be at first sight. It is not only those children who are brought up narrowly in certain religious contexts who are socialized into having particular beliefs, values and judgements. All children are socialized within the family in an informal and often unconscious way. Many arrive at school with strongly held beliefs and prejudices which have been acquired in the context of the family, peer group and local community. Most children – not just those from particular religious backgrounds – will be challenged through the introduction of a broader range of knowledge and through the development and transfer of critical skills.

The fears of some religious groups about the pursuit of autonomy are often groundless. The perception of members of certain religious groups is that schools encourage children to be a 'law unto themselves' in matters of religion and values. Children, it is alleged, are encouraged to choose beliefs and values rather in the manner of selecting cans of beans or fruit from the shelves of a supermarket. This, of course, is a distortion of what educators mean by autonomy. In the educational context autonomy usually means the capacity to make decisions on the basis of a reasonable scrutiny of available evidence (Gardner 1991). There is no contradiction, then, in deciding autonomously to adopt a position that one has hitherto accepted on authority. Moreover, autonomy does not imply complete individualism, for a consideration of others in relation to oneself is an important factor in autonomous decision making. In this sense all autonomy is 'relative'. Many apparent clashes between autonomy and religious nurture might be resolved by good conversation between parents, pupils and staff at the school. The educational environment in which these skills of dialogue and conversation are learned needs to be one in which religious positions are treated in an informed and serious way, and where other areas of the curriculum – science, for example – are discussed with the same critical rigour. There will, however, from time to time, be disputes where no reconciliation is possible and in these cases parents have the right under the law to withdraw their children from religious education.

Relativism and phenomenology

The quotations above, from Baroness Cox and Anthony Coombs, both refer to relativism – 'multifaith relativism' and 'relative comparative religion'. I take both examples to mean that 'multifaith' religious education is assumed to be approached in such a way that questions of the truth or falsity of religious claims are avoided or that all religions are regarded as being equally true. Burn and Hart relate this to phenomenology, an approach which they claim: 'denies children the opportunity of examining counter claims to truth in religion' (Burn and Hart 1988: 15). This is a misrepresentation of the phenomenology of religion. The approach encourages students to suspend their own judgements temporarily in order to understand the faith, beliefs and practices of people of different religions, but does not rule out critical evaluation as a distinct process (Jackson 1997: Chapter 1; Smart 1968).

Phenomenology is not only characterized by the traditionalist lobby in terms of its supposedly inherent relativism. The phenomenological approach to religious education also, it is claimed:

> ... is to study religion through its observable expressions. It is argued that as children learn about sacred places, festivals, rites of passage and customs, they are led to a more authentic understanding of faith. But such an approach devalues the vital ingredients of faith, belief and practice and so leads to the trivialisation of all faiths.
>
> (Burn and Hart 1988: 15)

Once again no evidence is offered to support the assertion. It should be clear already that phenomenology involves much more than studying the 'observable expressions' of religion. The Dutch scholar Pierre Chantepie de la Saussaye, the probable originator of the term 'phenomenology of religion', points out that the method is not only concerned with religious practices and arts, but also with 'religious impressions, sentiments and states' and he comments on the dialectical relationship between the mental activity in religion and its outward expression (Chantepie de la Saussaye 1891 in Waardenburg 1973: 110). For Gerardus van der Leeuw, probably the most influential twentieth-century phenomenologist of religion, a 'phenomenon' is not a religious object, ritual or custom, nor is it the faith or spirituality of a religious person. It is the relationship between the two (van der Leeuw 1938 in Waardenburg 1973: 412). Many more examples from the literature could be given. Rather than trivializing faiths, phenomenology sets out to grasp the power and meaning of faith within its appropriate religious and cultural context. If any teachers or syllabuses simply require their students to describe the externals of religion then they are not using a phenomenological approach.

I have criticized other aspects of phenomenological approaches in detail elsewhere (Jackson 1997: Chapter 1), and it should be noted that several approaches to religious education that deal with religious plurality are not grounded methodologically in the phenomenology of religion. The 'religious literacy' approach is discussed in Chapter 5 below, for example, whilst interpretive and dialogical approaches are discussed respectively in Chapters 6 and 7.

Thematic teaching

A further criticism is focused on thematic teaching. It is asserted that material drawn together from a number of different traditions and centred on a theme or topic produces a mishmash or a hotchpotch, a confusing mixture of material which is dangerous in its syncretism and confusing to children. There is some validity in this criticism in that there are still some published textbooks which include far too much material from a wide range of religious traditions. This is not a criticism of a thematic approach in principle, however. Themes need to be chosen carefully so that illustrative material from religious traditions does not distort those traditions. Further, it is sensible not to draw on more than, say, three traditions in illustrating a theme. This is a practical way of ensuring that children are not overloaded with material.[3] Also thematic work, like any other work in religious education, needs to be carefully assessed and teachers need to be sure that children have understood the material before moving on to new work. Similar principles apply in considering the integration or combination of religious education with other subjects. As John Hull points out, however, the attack on thematic teaching from opponents of 'multifaith' RE goes further than pointing out the dangers of confusing children. His analysis of the use of food metaphors, particularly their association with disgust and purity, shows the intention to vilify a thematic approach to religious education (Hull 1991).

Cultural arguments

A recurring theme in the rhetoric opposing 'multifaith' RE is the idea that children are deprived of their cultural heritage if Christianity is not emphasized in religious education (e.g. Tate 1995, with a response in Jackson 1997: 78–9; Thompson 2004). Some take the argument further, wanting to exclude all alternatives, denying that Britain is a multifaith society (Burn and Hart 1988: 25) and/or using the cultural argument to justify teaching Christianity as true (e.g. McIntyre 1978). Burn and Hart in *The Crisis in Religious Education* state that 'All citizens irrespective of creed or culture need an understanding of the influence of Christianity upon our literature, laws, customs, architecture and art forms' (Burn and Hart 1988: 26). Anthony Coombs states the argument in this form: 'Unless RE is set in a Christian context it cannot fulfil its academic role of ensuring pupils have a sufficient understanding of the British way of life' (Coombs 1988).

In one sense it is right to agree with these writers. As the tradition which has interacted with the personal and social lives of people in Britain for well over a millennium, it would be unthinkable not to give the study of Christianity an important place in religious education. Moreover, as noted in Chapter 1, Britain, in parallel with other nation states, has its own variety of civil religion, conditioned by its own particular history, although this is gradually changing in character. At another level, however, there is a need for caution. The relationships between individual and group faith and broader religious traditions and between religions and their cultural settings are dynamic and not static. Christianity indeed has helped to shape 'the British way of life', but a Christianity already deeply influenced by Hellenic thought, and open to the influences of social and cultural movements within 'British' culture and within the many cultures in which it now flourishes. Christianity should have an important place in religious education, but not on the grounds that there exists a fixed and unchanging culture or 'way of life' that requires a study of an equally static Christianity for its preservation. Christianity and the other religions need to be seen as living and internally diverse traditions, relating, responding and reacting to one another and to the secularism they all encounter. Christianity also needs to be presented as theologically and ethnically pluralistic (Jackson and Nesbitt 1992; Nesbitt 1993a). Christianity will generally warrant more space on the timetable than the other traditions, not to preserve a particular way of life but because of its historical and contemporary presence in British society together with its significance as a global religion. It must be open to academic discussion and criticism, however, on the same terms as any other religion or philosophy.

Christian confessionalism and the publicly funded school

Penny Thompson has recently revived some of the arguments discussed above, but has introduced some further points that are worthy of consideration (Thompson 2004). She takes us back to 1971, to the influential Schools Council Working Paper on religious education in secondary schools, in order to re-examine its assumptions about 'confessional' religious education. The working paper rejected the 'confessional' approach (the inverted commas are used in the text), described as making 'the assumption that the aim of religious education is intellectual and cultic indoctrination' (Schools Council 1971: 21). It also rejected what it called the 'neo-confessional' approach which it saw as attempting:

> to make 'confessional' or dogmatic religious education more acceptable and effective by improving methods and techniques in accordance with

the findings of educational research, and especially by constructing syllabuses based on the capacities, needs and interests of the pupils.

(Schools Council 1971: 30)

Ronald Goldman's work, influenced by research in developmental psychology, is given as one example of 'neo-confessionalism' (Goldman 1964, 1965, 1966–8). The working paper argued that both types of confessional approach to religious education, together with the totally descriptive 'anti-dogmatic' approach, were unacceptable on educational grounds, favouring a phenomenological approach for the subject in publicly funded schools.

Thompson suggests that the on-going resistance in publicly funded schools to confessional forms of education 'which assumed the truth and worth of the Christian religion' (Thompson 2004: 61) has been in the form of educational and political arguments. The educational arguments are that confessional approaches restrict academic enquiry by confining religious education to particular subject matter and that it is wrong to teach as true a position held publicly to be highly controversial. The political argument is that, in a secular, pluralistic society, no one religion or religious view should dominate. Thompson rejects these arguments.

There are two main strands to Thompson's case. First, in Thompson's view, the working paper did not establish that confessionalism was non-educational, and she argues for an educational form of Christian confessionalism. Second, she claims that any approach to teaching anything is confessional in the sense that assumptions about the subject matter being taught (presumably epistemological ones) are embedded in it. Thus, in her view, approaches to religious education often regarded as non-confessional are really confessional.

In developing the first strand in the argument, she argues that the working paper's view of confessionalism was coercive. Drawing on Philip Barnes' work, she claims that genuine Christian confessionalism cannot have this character, since genuine Christian faith cannot be coerced. She argues for a view of religious education that allows Christian teachers in community schools to present Christian beliefs to children with passion and persuasion, yet working with commonly accepted aims, such as thinking critically about religion or reflecting on ultimate questions. She remarks that 'It is possible to introduce children to religion via the truth of the Christian faith. And it is possible to do this in a way that welcomes debate and takes full account of the fact that others believe differently' (Ibid.: 67).

It is at this point that we slip from the initial issue – the role and intentions of the teacher – to the content of the subject. The content should be mainly 'Those beliefs and practices which have stood the test of time' (Ibid.: 67), taught by Christian teachers who 'should not feel inhibited in presenting their faith with conviction and (humble) devotion' (Ibid.: 68), and as worthy of respect and exploration by non-Christian teachers. Material on other religions would perhaps be introduced in the secondary school, but built upon a secure foundation of teaching within a Christian framework.

At some point in the teaching, perhaps at secondary school, children who are learning by means of the Christian traditions should be introduced to other religious traditions and helped to engage with the fact that not everything in every religion has equal truth status.

(Ibid.: 68)

But why should the content be predominantly Christian? Once again we are given a version of the cultural argument: ' ... the state has a duty to instruct its citizens in those structures, institutions and virtues that both constitute and legitimate it' (Ibid.: 69) and 'To the extent ... that our institutions, customs and mores derive from the Christian faith, it is perfectly legitimate and even necessary for the state to preserve, in its educational system, an important place for the teaching of this faith' (Ibid.: 69). She even goes so far as to claim that 'To give a committed presentation of Christianity is to aid the preservation of society itself' (Ibid.: 70).

The second strand of her argument is that 'non-confessionalism' is an impossible position, since assumptions about the subject matter being taught are inherent to any approach. In the case of RE, she suggests that any approach has an implicit position about the truth of religious claims. Thus:

... non-confessionalism is built on a contradiction: that it is impossible to teach without having a view on what is being 'taught'. Despite official claims to be non-confessional, RE as presently configured either proceeds on the basis of disguised confessions or is based on a radical pluralism which (by definition) can offer no means of resolution.

(Ibid.: 66)

In the former category she places writers such as Clive and Jane Erricker, David Hay, John Hull and Michael Grimmitt. She points out that the positions of such writers on religious education are based on particular epistemological or theological assumptions, and therefore their stances are confessional. She does not discuss the relationship between these writers' personal beliefs about religion and the mode of religious education that they recommend, but assumes that the two are identical. For example, she says: 'At one end of the spectrum there are those who believe (and therefore teach) that religions are the creations of human beings ...' (Ibid.: 64).

In the latter category, she includes Philip Barnes, Trevor Cooling, Brenda Watson, Andrew Wright and myself. These writers, she suggests, want 'religions to speak for themselves' (Ibid.: 65); part of the purpose of religious education is to help children and young people to come to their own decisions about the truth or falsity of religious claims. However, her view is that such approaches are likely to lead to 'a certain indifferentism', remarking that 'Pupils will learn that there is no convincing reason for believing one religion rather than another, for if there were, their teacher would have told them' (Ibid.: 65). Elsewhere in the article she makes a similar point about agnosticism. In not giving children reasons to adopt a particular set of beliefs, religious educators are in danger of 'religiously educating the children into agnosticism' (Ibid.: 64).

Discussion

Thompson is concerned that teachers with conservative religious views feel inhibited about sharing their commitments with children in class. She refers to Schools Council Working Paper 36's discussion of the role of the teacher, which recommends a stance of 'procedural neutrality', but she does not discuss this concept. She simply regards it as the only alternative to taking a confessional stance. By way of clarification, we can recall that the idea of procedural neutrality was advanced by Lawrence Stenhouse as a strategy for handling controversial issues in the classroom, protecting pupils from the bias of the teacher whilst advancing their understanding (Stenhouse 1970: 106), and is looked on favourably by the authors of Working Paper 36. Stenhouse argues that when children are discussing controversial value questions, they should be allowed to do their own thinking. The teacher should act in the role of impartial chair, ensuring that all relevant viewpoints are considered, including her own. However, the teacher's view should be presented indirectly, by means of a book or newspaper cutting, for example. This view recognizes the potential power of the teacher in influencing children's thinking on controversial issues and encourages independent thinking and the weighing of evidence on their part. However, the approach is extremely difficult to apply in practice, and suppresses children's genuine questions to teachers about what they think and believe. Children and young people are very interested in the views of their teachers, just as they are interested in one another's views. The issue is not the revelation of the teacher's views, but the teacher's intentions in sharing them and the methods used when sharing them. If the teacher's intention is to persuade others to adopt her particular religious view, then the teacher is behaving immorally. If the intention is to explain her views, acknowledging that others hold different views equally sincerely, then the teacher is providing good education. It is not easy to identify Thompson's position on this issue with clarity. One of the arguments that Thompson rejects, but without offering a clear refutation, is that it is wrong to teach as true a position held publicly to be highly controversial. Her remark that 'It is possible to introduce children to religion via *the truth* of the Christian faith' (Thompson 2004: 67) (my italics) is consistent with this. However, she also claims that 'it is possible to do this in a way that welcomes debate and takes full account of the fact that others believe differently'(Ibid.: 67). Some clarification of her position is needed here. My point is that it is possible for teachers with religious or secular commitments to teach openly and yet to reveal their own beliefs to pupils. In my career I have met many teachers with strong commitments, including conservative religious ones, who have taught a broadly based religious education in a highly professional way and yet have made use of their own beliefs and practices as positive resources for teaching and learning, just as they have utilized pupils' beliefs and experiences when appropriate (see Chapter 7 below on the involvement of pupils' views and commitments in religious education). There are also theologically conservative scholars who have been able to utilize their own commitments in understanding analogous positions within other traditions (Stringer 2002: 10; see also the discussion of Stringer in Chapter 5 below). The view that teaching must either be procedurally neutral or 'evangelistic' is false. Moreover, Thompson's idea that passion for religious education can only be expressed through the expression of religious commitment ignores the fact that many teachers of the subject – whatever their personal commitments – are passionately interested in it, and are capable of communicating their enthusiasm to their pupils. Incidentally, it is a pity that Thompson only refers to Edward Hulmes' work on commitment and not to wider discussions on the role and commitments of the teacher of religious education (e.g. Cooling 1990; Grimmitt 1981; Hammer 1982; Hull 1982; Jackson 1982), wrongly assuming a general acceptance of the Schools Council Working Paper's distinction between confessional and non-confessional teaching. As John Hull has remarked, 'The Working Paper was right in regarding what it called confessionalism as being other than education, but wrong in calling it confessionalism in the first place' (Hull 1982: 106).

Thompson argues that all forms of religious education are 'confessional' in the sense that they are based on particular assumptions which are communicated to students through teaching. The question as to whether there is a necessary relationship between the epistemological basis for a particular approach and the influence of that approach on pupils is an interesting one. I am inclined to agree with her that some forms of religious education are so strongly related to a particular epistemological position as to inhibit certain debates. I suggest this in Chapter 4 (below) in relation to Clive Erricker's work, for example, arguing that the strongly presented anti-realist epistemology underpinning his pedagogy forecloses debates for those pupils who hold realist views of religion. However, the pluralist approaches that Thompson lists (including Andrew Wright's and my own), although related to particular epistemologies and values, make strong efforts to maintain an epistemological openness, encouraging children and young people to express and formulate their own positions. These approaches acknowledge that the truth of religious claims is not publicly demonstrable, and that the answer to the question of ultimate truth cannot be, at present at least, resolved. They therefore avoid the propagation of any religious or secular view. However, they insist that different religious points of view should be understood as far as possible, and that pupils should be equipped to make their own judgements about questions of truth (e.g. Jackson 1997: 123; Wright 2003: 286). Their moral basis can be seen in terms of prizing and promoting democratic and academic values (see Chapter 10 below). Thompson's main objection to pluralist approaches is that they promote 'indifferentism' and agnosticism. She offers no evidence at all for these claims. There is some evidence that teachers using such approaches with pupils do not find most of their pupils indifferent to religion. Susanna Hookway's teaching, employing some of Andrew Wright's ideas, is reported in an article in the *British Journal of Religious Education* (Hookway 2002). Chapter 6 below reports the teaching of Anne Krisman and Kevin O'Grady, both of whom use adapted forms of the Warwick interpretive approach. Three different dialogical approaches in the classroom that are also 'pluralist' in character are reported in Chapter 7. These examples show children and young people of varying ages and abilities, from a range of religious and secular backgrounds, engaging with religious material and issues and articulating their own positions. They are from different religious and secular backgrounds, yet are not indifferent to religion, nor do they all become agnostics, although agnosticism is as reasonable a position to adopt as any other.

Religious education and confessionalism

Part of Thompson's argument is that all education is inevitably confessional, in the sense that it is based on a particular set of epistemological assumptions. One would expect her conclusion to be that approaches to religious education need to be openly confessional with regard to their religious or secular underpinning. Instead, Thompson concludes that a particular form of Christian confessionalism in publicly funded community schools is justified. Her grounds for this are not epistemological, but are cultural – that Christianity has formed the major spiritual and intellectual heritage of the nation. Insofar as Britain has a common cultural tradition, it is as much grounded in the tradition of secular liberalism as it is in 'Christian heritage' (see the discussion on cultural arguments above and also the discussions of culture in Chapters 1 and 8 of this book and in Jackson 1997: Chapter 4). At best, Thompson gives reasons for the adequate coverage of Christianity as part of the content of RE, but her argument completely fails to establish a case for teaching children religious education within a Christian framework in the common school.

If religious education in the community schools of a plural society has a 'confessional' basis, then its epistemological stance acknowledges that the truth of religious claims is not publicly demonstrable, while its ethical position is one that ensures that the practices and claims of religions are considered with sensitivity, intellectual rigour and fairness. This form of religious education acknowledges the inevitable influence of plurality upon young people, and helps them to engage with it. It is not secularist, and can be supported by citizens with different religious and secular viewpoints, and it is consistent with international codes of human rights supporting the principle of freedom of religion or belief, such as the Universal Declaration of Human Rights (Article 18), the International Covenant on Civil and Political Rights (Article 18), and the 1981 United Nations Declaration on the Elimination of All Forms of Intolerance and of Discrimination Based on Religion or Belief.[4]

To place the traditionalist position discussed in this chapter in a wider context of the debate about plurality, Gerd Baumann, on the basis of his empirical research, shows that there are both inflexible and highly flexible approaches to religion, nationality and ethnicity and their relationship within cultural discourse (Baumann 1996, 1999). Baumann illustrates how, in various situations, there are those whose personal or group interests might be to present and promote a particular relationship between a fixed view of culture (or cultures) and reified views of nationality, ethnicity and religion. The view of British culture presented by Burn, Hart, Thompson and others is of this variety. Similarly, both outsiders and insiders might use terminology such as 'the Muslim community' or 'Asian culture', when it suits their purposes. Baumann calls this tendency to reify, whether from extremist groups, politicians, religious groups, the media or cultural communities, 'dominant discourse' (Baumann 1996). He distinguishes this from 'demotic discourse', the real language of culture making, exemplified in his field research, and characteristically used when people from various different backgrounds interact in approaching topics of common concern. Religious education is well placed to explore this debate.[5]

Conclusion

I have argued that the criticisms of religious education by those arguing for a 'predominantly Christian' form of RE in the common school are largely mistaken and that their association of Christianity with a particular view of 'British culture' is open to a number of criticisms. Moreover, their advocacy of particular interpretations of Christian teaching in isolation from alternative views, with the aim of achieving certain social goals, raises serious ethical and political questions. Their views on authority in relation to personal autonomy also raise moral issues about the rights of children and young people, just as their association of morality with Christianity ignores the moral concerns and contributions of other religious and humanistic traditions within Britain.

Thompson's apparent suggestion that Christian RE teachers should share their commitments with pupils in the common school with the intention of persuading them of the truth of the Christian position ignores the fact that it is possible for teachers with a range of religious or secular commitments both to reveal their own beliefs to pupils and to teach openly, with no intention of persuading children to adopt particular beliefs. Also, Thompson's idea that passion for religious education can only be conveyed to pupils through the expression of religious commitment ignores evidence that passion for the subject need not depend on religious belief. Her assertion that pluralistic approaches to religious education promote 'indifferentism' and agnosticism among pupils is unsupported by evidence and is contradicted by some empirical and curriculum studies. Thompson's conclusion that a Christian confessional approach to RE in the common school is justified since all education is inevitably 'confessional' is illogical. Her further justification for Christian confessional teaching on cultural grounds ignores the changing and dynamic relationship between individual and group-based faith and broader religious traditions, between religions and their cultural settings and between individuals from different back-grounds who create new culture through encounter and dialogue; she also sidesteps the issue of public disagreement about the verifiability of religious claims. For historical and cultural reasons, Christianity may warrant more space in the curriculum of British schools than other traditions, but not to teach Christianity as true or to preserve a particular way of life.

Chapter 3

State funding for religious schools?

Another response to the plurality of late modernity is for religious groups to become increasingly focused on preserving their own sense of identity and continuity in the face of secularization and religious diversity. In terms of education, this might result in religious groups, and especially parents of children within them, setting out to increase separate supplementary or independent schooling, or arguing for separate religious schools funded by the state. In England and Wales, government policy has shifted to provide active encouragement for the extension and broadening of state-funded faith-based education. This has coincided with a push by the Church of England to expand its secondary school provision within the state sector very significantly, against a background of falling church attendances. Similarly, in a climate in Britain in which the numbers engaged actively in Jewish religious practice has been declining and an increasing number of Jews have been marrying non-Jews, there has been a significant expansion of the number of Jewish state-funded schools. Lobbying by other minority religious groups has also influenced government policy, and England now has a small number of state-funded Muslim and Sikh schools, together with a Greek Orthodox and a Seventh Day Adventist school.

The history of state-funded religious schools

Close collaboration between Church and state in education in England goes back to the 1870 Education Act which introduced state-funded education.[1] The 1902 Education Act established the 'Dual system' of partnership between the state and the Churches in providing a national system of education. The 1944 Act clarified this system, by distinguishing different types of maintained schools. County schools were entirely publicly funded and had no Church appointed governors. Voluntary schools were originally funded by religious bodies, but went into voluntary partnership with the state. They were of three types: Aided, Controlled and Special Agreement. A key factor was that the Church (or other religious body) owned the buildings, having originally provided them, with the aid of a grant in many cases. Voluntary Aided schools (Church of England, Roman Catholic, some other Christian schools and, significantly, a few Jewish schools) had a majority of governors appointed by the sponsoring religious body and the character of religious instruction was determined by the governors of each school.[2]

Voluntary Controlled schools had fewer Church governors than Aided schools and were controlled by governors who were not appointed by the Churches. The Churches no longer put money into these schools, but they were originally Church foundations. Religious education had to be taught according to the local agreed syllabus unless parents specifically asked for denominational teaching, and admissions were in the hands of the local authorities.

Voluntary Aided schools were aided by the state. The state paid staff salaries and 50 per cent of building and maintenance costs. The balance had to be raised by the religious body. In the 1960s, the proportions changed to 85 per cent paid by the state and 15 per cent by the religious body. At the time of writing, the government has agreed to lower the contribution of the sponsoring body to 10 per cent. Religious education was taught according to the tenets of the particular religious group involved with the school. In 1944 there were Church of England, Roman Catholic and a few non-denominational Christian Voluntary Aided schools, plus a small number of Jewish Voluntary Aided schools. Since 1988, Voluntary Aided schools, like all other maintained schools, have had to follow the national curriculum. However, they have continued to teach RE and to have collective worship according to the religious tradition represented in the school, although some governing bodies of Church of England Aided schools, following advice from their Diocesan Education Authorities, are using the local agreed syllabus.[3]

The fact that some Jewish Voluntary Aided schools were established in 1944 has lent weight to the argument that other non-Christian religious bodies should apply for certain independent schools to be granted Voluntary Aided status. There was an attempt to establish a Hindu Voluntary Aided school in the 1970s. The proposed coeducational comprehensive school (the Vivekananda Hindu High School) was to be situated in London, catering for around 1,000 children from Hindu families. The steering committee failed to get the full support of Hindu communities and Local

Education Authorities in London, and the project was abandoned in 1981 (Kanitkar 1979).[4]

Several Muslim independent schools attempted to obtain Voluntary Aided status during the 1980s and 1990s. For example, the Islamia school in Brent (established in 1982) made several spirited attempts – the first in 1985 – which were turned down by the government on the basis that there were already sufficient primary school places available elsewhere in the area. The continuing official rejections of applications from the Islamia school became increasingly unconvincing, especially when the Conservative government allowed new City Technology Colleges to be set up in areas that had spare school places.

However, a new possible route to state funding for independent religious schools was introduced in the 1993 Education Act. The 1988 Education Reform Act had introduced Grant Maintained schools. Following intense lobbying by a number of pressure groups, including the Christian Schools Campaign – lobbyists from independent Evangelical Christian schools seeking state funding – the 1993 Education Act introduced sponsored Grant Maintained schools. From the implementation of the Act in April 1994, groups of parents, charities, religious bodies etc. could apply directly to the Department for Education to establish their own Grant Maintained schools. Proposals could include a change of status for a private religious school. As with Aided schools, sponsors would have to pay 15 per cent of building and maintenance costs. However, there was no flood of new religious schools by this route. The strict financial and demand-led criteria imposed by the incoming Secretary of State, Gillian Shepherd, kept independent Evangelical Christian schools and Muslim schools out of the state system (Walford 1995, 2000).

Law and policy since 1997

Since 1997, the Labour government has introduced radical changes, enabling a range of independent schools associated with various religious traditions to become Voluntary Aided. This represents a complete about-turn from the party's position in the 1980s, when official Labour policy was opposed to the establishment of Voluntary Aided schools for religious minorities (Anon. 1988). In addition to the government's stated aim of achieving fairness and good community relations, evidence (from Ofsted statistics) of higher attainment and a stronger sense of community in some religious schools, an increased demand from parents and lobbying from pressure groups have all contributed to this more pluralistic view of the state school system. When the Labour government came into office in 1997, they were able to use the 1993 legislation to bring independent schools sponsored by various religious minorities into the state system. One of these was the Islamia school in Brent, one of the first two state-funded Muslim schools in Britain, which became a Grant Maintained school in April 1998.

Parliament soon passed the 1998 School Standards and Framework Act which introduced the concept of 'religious character' and modified the range of types of school receiving state funding (UK Parliament 1998). Thus, from the implementation of the Act in September 1999, there were four categories of school within the state system: Community (formerly County schools); Foundation (formerly Grant Maintained schools); Voluntary Aided; and Voluntary Controlled.[5] All Community schools must use the local agreed syllabus as a basis for religious education and may not have a religious character. Schools within the other categories may have a 'religious character'. This reflects the school's trust deed or, if there is no trust deed, the traditional practice of the school. Most, but not all, Voluntary Aided and Voluntary Controlled schools and some Foundation schools have a religious character. All schools with a religious character can have collective worship that is distinctive of the religious body concerned. Only Voluntary Aided schools can have 'denominational' religious education. Voluntary Controlled and Foundation schools with a religious character have to use the local agreed syllabus, except in the case of children whose parents have specifically requested 'denominational' religious education. In these cases, the school has to make special provision. Under the School Standards and Framework Act, an Order was published in September 1999 listing nearly 7,000 schools with a religious character and also stating its nature, for example, Church of England, Roman Catholic, Jewish, Muslim or Sikh. A school may have a religious character of more than one religion or denomination.[6] All schools with a religious character must have an ethos statement. This statement becomes part of the Instrument of Government for the school, and the governors are responsible for deriving a mission statement or set of aims for the school from it. In effect, a wider range of religious schools has been incorporated into the state system, partly for reasons of fairness and partly because such schools are recognized as potentially having certain qualities that might be more difficult to develop in some Community schools.[7]

With the implementation of the School Standards and Framework Act in September 1999, schools such as the Islamia school became Voluntary Aided, and several other new Voluntary Aided schools for religious minorities were established, including the Guru Nanak primary and secondary schools in Hillingdon, the first state-funded Sikh schools in Europe. There was also an expansion of Jewish schools (which continues), and the Archbishop's Council appointed the Church Schools Review Group, under Lord Dearing's chairmanship, to review the achievements of Church of England schools and to make proposals for their future development. Its report – *The Way Ahead* – includes a recommendation for the establishment of 100 new Church of England secondary schools especially to be located in dioceses where Church secondary schools are thin on the ground and in areas of economic and social hardship (Archbishop's Council 2001). The expansion of state-funded Jewish education (very much at the primary level) should be seen against a background of assimilation (the Chief Rabbi's 1994 book is entitled *Will We Have Jewish Grandchildren?* [Sacks 1994]), while the expansion of Church of England secondary provision should be seen in the context of falling church attendances. Church schools are seen as an important instrument for the Church's mission, and the report recommends the establishment and maintenance of their Christian character, partly through the selection of teachers and a tightening of admissions criteria (Archbishop's Council 2001).

Several schools associated with religious minorities have received state funding in recent years. On 9 January 1998, the government approved the first state funding for Muslim schools. The Islamia school in Brent at last had its application for state funding accepted, along with the Al Furuqan Primary School, Sparkhill, Birmingham. Both schools were given Grant Maintained status with full public funding prior to becoming Voluntary Aided schools in September 1999. Approval was also given for three Jewish schools, including the Mathilda Marks Kennedy Primary School in Barnet, North London. In October 2000 approval was given for the first Muslim Voluntary Aided secondary school. This is Feversham College, Bradford, a former independent Muslim school, finally achieving its goal of state funding at the second attempt. The Guru Nanak Sikh Primary and Secondary school, in the London Borough of Hillingdon, was opened on 30 November 1999 by the then Home Secretary, Jack Straw, and became the first Sikh state-funded school in Europe. It opened as an independent school in 1993 and applied for Voluntary Aided status in April 1999 following a two year campaign by local parents (with the support of the Local Education Authority) who felt that children's religious and cultural needs were not being met by other schools in the area. Voluntary Aided status has also been given to a Seventh Day Adventist school in Haringey, and the first Greek Orthodox Voluntary Aided school – St Cyprian's, Croydon – opened during 2000. Various London communities are drawing up plans for more Jewish schools and a Hindu school, and there are proposals for more Muslim and Sikh schools.

School organization committees

The 1998 School Standards and Framework Act also introduced school organization committees, one of whose roles is to make decisions at the local level about proposals for new faith-based schools. They are composed of groups (with each group having a single vote) representing the Local Education Authority, schools, the Further Education Funding Council, the Church of England and the Roman Catholic Church, with the possibility of a sixth group (at the LEA's discretion) representing some other local interest(s). There is a huge responsibility on the shoulders of committee members who have the power to make very significant decisions.

Estelle Morris, the Secretary of State for Education and Skills at the time, in her speech in the debate in the House of Commons on admissions to faith-based schools (5 February 2002), was at pains to point out that the responsibility for approving or rejecting applications lay with these committees and not with government.

If members of a faith want to start a new school, they will not come to me or to any of my successors. They will go to the local school organisation committee, on which are represented schools, the local authority, parents, governors and churches, which are likely to be Roman Catholic and Church of England churches.

The committee has a statutory obligation to consult. It will consult and make a decision. It will not ask us in the Department, it will not seek our permission and I will not authorise the decision. It will be nothing to do with me. That is what I mean when I say that we are not giving our energy or our time to promoting more faith schools ... [W]e have said to local people, 'You decide whether you want to admit to the family of local schools a new school of a Voluntary Aided nature.' I have emphasised that for two reasons. First, it is important for people to know that the Government do not intend centrally to create, authorise or designate more faith schools. Secondly, and probably more importantly, I know that people feel – I say this in the most sensitive way – that we have given the green light to members of various faiths who are at the more fundamentalist, more extreme end of their faith. Every faith has such members, and people feel that we have given them the green light to open schools. Whether that happens will be up to the local school organisation committee. Every new school must go through the school organisation committee, where the decision will be taken.

(Morris 2002)

The responsibility and power given to these local committees is indeed considerable.

Diversity of state-funded religious schools

Press reports of faith-based education tend to play down the fact that there are different types of school within the English and Welsh state system. We have already noted the distinction between Voluntary Controlled and Voluntary Aided schools. The Church of England has over 2,500 VC schools (all but 17 are primary), over half the total number of C of E schools. Voluntary Controlled schools have full government funding. They have a religious ethos and their own collective worship, but pupils follow the same broadly based religious education syllabus as children from Community schools. The Local Education Authority controls admissions, so there is no religious test for entry. In the debate in the House of Commons (5 February 2002) Geraint Davies MP pointed out some of the advantages of the Controlled model, especially in terms of flexibility in admissions arrangements (Davies 2002). However, Church of England policy as reflected in *The Way Ahead* is to promote Aided schools, with a stronger religious identity and tighter admissions requirements.

Faith-based schools also reflect a theological spectrum from liberal to highly conservative. Various research studies suggest that the most theologically conservative schools are the ones most likely to avoid 'outreach' in terms of collaborative work with schools of other types. There is also a tendency to discourage multicultural education or work on inter-faith dialogue in the most theologically conservative schools.

To take the example of Jewish education, British Jewry includes strictly Orthodox (or ultra-Orthodox – *Haredi*), central or mainstream Orthodox, Conservative (*Masorti*) and Progressive (including Reform and Liberal) groupings. The strictly Orthodox represent about 10 per cent of British Jewry, but 43 per cent of the population of Jewish schools (Valins 2000; Valins *et al.* 2001). It is these schools that construct the tightest educational boundaries in attempting to form and institutionalize identity. For example, strictly Orthodox schools monitor teaching materials and may censor topics such as Zionism or the theory of evolution. They also are likely to have the most exclusive ethos statements and the tightest admissions arrangements (Valins 2003).

Short and Lenga's research on Jewish primary schools also reveals a diversity of practice, with some Orthodox schools 'less than enthusiastic about engaging in multicultural education' (Short and Lenga 2002: 49).

However, their study shows that Orthodox Jewish primary schools should not be seen as a homogeneous group in relation to multicultural education.

> The most positive attitudes were found among spokespersons for the three progressive schools in the survey, and it may be no coincidence that it was one of these schools that published the only prospectus containing a reference to teaching about other faiths. While the schools that were indifferent or hostile to multiculturalism were, in all cases, orthodox, there is no warrant for assuming that such schools are uniformly unsympathetic to multicultural education.
>
> (Short and Lenga 2002: 53)

Some of these were keen to establish links with non-Jewish schools. However, there was no formal provision for teaching about other religions, and respondents simply reported that opportunities were taken to draw pupils' attention to aspects of these faiths.

With regard to admissions policies, stricter entrance criteria tend to be applied in over-subscribed schools and more theologically conservative schools. Schools tend to be more inclusive where there is less demand from parents for places. In the case of Judaism, for example, Jewish schools in Birmingham and Liverpool are much more pluralistic in intake than those in certain parts of London for both reasons.

Arguments for state funding

So far, we have traced the history of state-funded faith-based education in England and Wales, and have noted that there are different categories of school, and also that schools can be placed on a theological spectrum ranging from liberal to highly conservative. The question remains as to why the democratic state should fund overtly religious schools at all. It is worth recalling that in England and Wales, Labour Party policy, during opposition in the 1980s, was unsympathetic to the idea of state-funded religious schools on the basis of their potential for increasing religious, racial and cultural divisiveness. The change of heart came as a result of experiences of racism against children from ethnic minorities in County schools, many of whom happened to be from particular religious backgrounds. The two key reasons for a change of policy were a serious concern on the part of parents or children from South Asian religious minorities that their languages and cultures were not sufficiently respected and fostered in County (now Community) schools and that research (specifically the Commission for Racial Equality's Report *Terror In Our Schools*) revealed a high degree of racism in the County school system (Anon. 1988). In the shift of policy, the Party upheld the right of religious minorities to establish Voluntary Aided schools, on the grounds that they already existed for some religious groups and on condition that they were educationally sound, financially secure and did not operate on the basis of race (Anon. 1988).

Thus, when in power, the Labour government responded to the argument from justice and fairness for extending provision to include religions not currently accommodated within the state system. There were already state-funded Christian and Jewish schools, so why not extend the provision to Muslims, Sikhs and other groups, if there were enough parents with children to fill them? Such an expansion was also consistent with the government's policy to encourage diversity within the secondary school system and to increase autonomy for schools. Welcoming more schools provided by the Churches and other major faith groups where there was clear demand from parents and communities was seen as an important aspect of this policy (DfES 2001: par. 5.30–1).

Moreover, the Human Rights Act (1998) raises the issue of parental rights in relation to faith-based education. Article 1 of the Act states:

> No person shall be denied the right to education. In the exercise of any functions which it assumes in relation to education and to teaching, the State shall respect the right of parents to ensure such education and teaching is in conformity with their own religious and philosophical convictions.
>
> (Human Rights Act 1998)

The Human Rights Act was used to support the parental rights argument, by the then Secretary of State for Education and Skills[8] and by others who support state funding for religious schools (e.g. Felderhof 2000).[9] Thus the argument from justice and fairness has been supported and extended by arguments for diversity within the education system and for parental rights.

The question then arises as to where the line should be drawn in offering support to particular groups. If the major religious traditions are to have funding on the grounds of justice, fairness and parental rights, should not parents from smaller religious or spiritual movements, or non-religious philosophies such as humanism, or philosophies supporting particular forms of education, such as Rudolph Steiner's educational theories, or postmodernist theories of education (see Chapter 4) have an equal opportunity to claim state support for separate schools if there is sufficient parental demand? A further awkward question is whether there might be circumstances in which particular groups might be refused funding on the grounds that their particular ideologies were deemed to be erosive of the democratic process or in other ways potentially harmful to children, to family life or to society. As the law stands, school organization committees could only support applications from religious bodies, but one does not envy them their task of discriminating between different applications.

Another cluster of arguments for separate religious schools hinges on the special qualities that such establishments are alleged to bring to education. These arguments refer to the ethos of schools, the quality of teaching, the attainment of pupils and the views of parents. Because of the large numbers of Church of England and Roman Catholic schools in relation to others, most of the evidence available from Ofsted inspections and from test and examination data refers specifically to Church schools.[10] The ethos of a school is very difficult to quantify or measure. If we take evidence from Ofsted reports of provision for pupils' spiritual, moral, social and cultural development as some kind of indicator, then it is clear that, during the period 1996–9, provision for spiritual development was judged to be very much stronger in Church schools, especially Church secondary schools, than in other schools. High quality provision for spiritual development was also reported in inspections of some Jewish schools. However, the *overall* provision for spiritual, moral, social and cultural development in faith-based schools was not qualitatively much different to that of other schools. There is some evidence for better pupil behaviour in Church schools. In 1999–2000, for example, behaviour in primary schools was judged to be excellent or very good in 49.8 per cent of Church of England schools inspected and 56.4 per cent of Roman Catholic schools as opposed to 39.5 per cent of other schools.

There is also some evidence of slightly better quality teaching in Church schools. For example, in primary school inspections during 1999–2000, 65.7 per cent of lessons in Church of England schools, 66 per cent of lessons in Roman Catholic schools and 60.5 per cent in other schools were judged by inspectors to be well taught. Moreover, Ofsted evidence shows that Church schools have been less likely to require special measures or to have serious weaknesses than other schools.[11]

With regard to pupil performance, at the end of Key Stage 1, attainment in English and Mathematics (virtually the same in CE and RC schools) was higher than in other schools. This was also the case at Key Stage 2, except that performance in Church of England Controlled schools was little different from that in non-Church schools. GCSE attainment in secondary schools was best in Roman Catholic schools while, in Church of England schools, results were only slightly better than those of non-Church schools. The exception was in the sixth forms of Roman Catholic schools, where attainment was lower than that in Church of England and other schools. The national picture of parents' views of Church schools is very positive. For example, applications for places in Church primary and secondary schools, at the time of writing, outstrip availability nationally.

However, the interpretation of these inspection findings is not at all straightforward. For example, Ofsted data show that during 1996–9, the intake in Church of England schools was relatively more economically favoured compared to Community schools. Of Church of England Voluntary Controlled primary schools, for example, proportionally there were half the pupils eligible for free school meals than in all other non-faith-based schools. Also, Church of England Voluntary Aided secondary schools had a more academically advanced intake than any other secondary schools. Thus better results might be expected from these schools.

Research by John Marks on attainment in literacy and numeracy, comparing Church of England, Roman Catholic and Community schools, also shows the complexity and ambiguity of evidence for higher attainment in Church schools over against Community schools. Marks reports that while there is a slightly better average performance in Church schools than Community schools (the gap getting wider as children get older), there is a huge variation in standards between faith-based schools (Marks 2001: 5–36). A literature review and analysis of performance at Key Stage 3 and GCSE in specialist schools and faith schools (Roman Catholic, Church of England, 'other Christian' and Jewish) presented a varied picture in terms of performance of different subjects and at different stages (Schagen *et al.* 2002). The report states that Church schools do consistently achieve better than expected results in English and that the five Jewish schools studied achieved results above the norm at GCSE and in most of Key Stage 3 in 2000. The authors point out that the relationship between faith-based education and performance may not be causal.

With regard to Church schools, the authors conclude that:

> Although C of E and RC schools perform above the norm on some outcomes, there is no clear pattern of enhanced performance. It seems likely therefore that the good 'raw' results achieved by many church schools reflect the nature and quality of their intake. There is no evidence to suggest that an increase in the number of faith schools would improve overall performance, although it could of course have other benefits.
>
> (Schagen *et al.* 2002: 47)

Those who tend towards a communitarian position, emphasizing group responsibilities and commitments rather than individual autonomy, often argue in favour of faith-based education. One example is David Hargreaves, former Chief Executive of the Qualifications and Curriculum Authority, who argues that children from religious backgrounds should be educated in schools run by their communities, so they can be taught the moral values of the group, which they can then take out into wider society. Hargreaves recognizes that, in a secularized and pluralistic society, religion can no longer be the basis for a socially cohesive civic education for all, pointing out that

> the problem of Britain as a pluralistic society is how to find some social cement to ensure that people with different moral, religious, and ethical values as well as social, cultural and linguistic traditions can live together with a degree of harmony.
>
> (Hargreaves 1994: 31)

In order to produce this social cement, Hargreaves proposes an expansion of religious schools within the state system. These should have a distinctive ethos, showing the links between religious faith and morality and expressing a joint commitment by home and school to 'the transmission and living experience of a shared moral and religious culture' (Hargreaves 1994: 35). He couples this with the abolition of religious education in non-religious schools and its replacement with citizenship education. (There is a critical discussion of Hargreaves' views on citizenship education and religious education below in Chapter 8.)

Some arguments for separate state-funded religious schools claim that they can promote social cohesion, through encouraging participation by religious and ethnic minorities in democratic institutions and practices, for example. Philip Lewis makes the point that the integration of Irish Catholics into British society was facilitated through state subsidies given for separate Catholic schools (Lewis 1997). In parallel, Pnina Werbner, in writing about the integration of British Muslims into democratic institutions, argues that Muslim mobilizations 'have been key moments in the development of a Muslim British civic consciousness and capacity for active citizenship' (Werbner 2000: 309). For example, the Salman Rushdie affair, though traumatic, led to 'a new consciousness of citizenship as a legal struggle for rights and as a subjective commitment to permanent settlement' (Werbner 2000: 315), and this included discussions of blasphemy law and the role of faith-based schools.

Arguments against state funding

So far, I have summarized arguments in support of state-funded faith-based schools. These have included a response to racism and arguments from justice and fairness, parental rights, the high quality of education (as reflected in attainment, teaching quality, ethos and pupil behaviour), the promotion of social cohesion and the integration of minority communities into democratic life. The key arguments against centre on the issues of personal autonomy, the promotion of social cohesion through communication and understanding between young people of different religious and non-religious backgrounds, doubts about the representativeness of sponsoring bodies and the internal coherence of 'communities', whether the democratic state should, in effect, fund proselytization, and the accusation that faith-based schools disadvantage other schools through selection procedures that cream off the most able students.

One of the main arguments against state-funded religious schools is that they do not acknowledge the autonomy of the individual child in making judgements about religious claims, and expect children to accept particular teachings and practices on the authority of others. This view is advanced by a group of Humanist philosophers who argue that religious and value commitments should be entered into only subject to all the requirements for valid consent (Humanist Philosophers' Group 2001: 10). These include competence, full information and voluntariness. Thus, it is argued, young children lack cognitive competence and the necessary experience to make judgements about religious claims. Information about religions, they argue, is likely to be biased in religious schools. Finally, tacit assumptions by teachers about the truth of religious claims or the desirability of practices limits the voluntariness of children's responses and judgements. Although schools might not set out to indoctrinate children, the processes referred to above amount to a subtle form of indoctrination. In the authors' view, the individual autonomy argument overrides that of the rights of parents.

A second argument is about social cohesion. There are those (from within the religious traditions as well as others such as many Humanists) who argue against state funding for separate religious schools on the grounds that future citizens should learn together to live in society despite their religious and cultural differences. Will Kymlicka makes this point by arguing that the deliberate separation of children by religion for schooling *by definition* militates against education for good citizenship – in effect, learning citizenship involves learning and interacting with others from different backgrounds (Kymlicka 1999: 88–90). In England, following unrest and conflict between young people from different ethnic backgrounds in Oldham, Bradford and Leeds during the summer of 2001, stirred up by the opportunism of far right political groups, the force of this point is clear. Moreover, the intimidation and violence experienced by parents and children on their way to and from the Holy Cross Catholic primary school in a small Protestant enclave in north Belfast, show how separate schools can be sucked into political and religious disputes, despite the best intentions of teaching staff (Woodward 2001). There are also those who argue that the events on September 11, 2001 in New York and Washington and their consequences have raised religious tensions and reinforced doubts about the wisdom of separate religious schooling (e.g. Beckett 2001).

It will be recalled that one of the reasons the Labour Party changed its policy on state funding for religious schools was to avoid incidents of racial conflict and to create an environment that was conducive to learning for Black and Asian children. A parallel policy in the United States, with regard to race, resulted in the re-introduction of segregated schooling. However, recent American research raises serious concerns about the dangers of segregation (Orfield and Gordon 2001). Segregated schools are failing, not simply because Black schools tend to be in areas of economic deprivation, but because White students are unprepared for future life in an increasingly mixed society. In the words of Gary Orfield, co-director of the Harvard University Civil Rights Project: 'These suburban white kids are vastly unprepared for the future'. In England and Wales, the segregation issue is not confined to the dual system of education. In some areas there are *de facto* segregated schools, because economic conditions, patterns of residence and parental choice taken together result in virtually all-Muslim or all-White schools within parts of a single town or city. Lord Ouseley's report on community fragmentation in the city of Bradford highlights the dangers, speaking of a drift towards self-segregation. The report points out the great desire among young people for better education to overcome a negativity that leaves them ignorant of other cultures and lifestyles, but it also points out a 'fear of confronting all-white and/or all-Muslim schools about their contribution, or rather lack of contribution, to social and racial integration' (Ouseley 2001: 1). Speaking of new initiatives with regard to leadership, the report concludes that 'they must bring people together so that they can learn with and from each other ...' (Ouseley 2001: 1). The same could be said about schooling. As an educational response to the problem, the independent review team into community cohesion chaired by Ted Cantle specifically suggested programmes of cross-cultural contact (Home Office 2001a: par. 5.8.18: 36).

There is a strong case for finding ways for children from different backgrounds to interact with each other at school. It is interesting, in the wake of the terrible acts of genocide in the former Yugoslavia, that educators in Bosnia-Herzegovina are attempting to promote dialogue between young people from groups for which conflict has promoted a perception of identities that equate stereotypical representations of religion and ethnicity (Orthodox

Serbs, Catholic Croats, Bosnian Muslims). The aim is to introduce a new subject 'Culture of Religions' in order to give a critical analysis of such representations and to promote tolerance, reconciliation and mutual understanding between groups (ICCS 2001: 2–3).

A third argument questions the representativeness of sponsoring bodies and the internal coherence of 'communities'. Hargreaves' argument (outlined above) supports separate schools partly on the basis that their existence results from constructive involvement of community leaders and others in national and local democratic processes. Religious schools are seen by Hargreaves as havens for particular moralities, in which home and school are jointly committed to 'the transmission and living experience of a shared moral and religious culture', while key adult members of religious communities are regarded as their spokespersons and negotiators. This view exhibits an over-uniform view of the nature of religious or religio-cultural groups. Treating religious and cultural groups as homogeneous allows the possibility for 'leaders' to invoke traditional authorities and practices in order to impose restrictions on their own members. Rather than being clear partners with families, promoting shared community values, faith-based schools could set out to promote a particular view of orthodoxy or the views of the school's sponsors rather than reflecting the diversity of tradition to be represented by pupils and their families (see Chapter 8 below).

A fourth argument against faith-based schools raises the question as to whether the democratic state should, in effect, fund mission. Whatever sponsoring bodies might say about how their schools might offer something distinctive to the populace, there remains an underlying desire to propagate particular religious views, as is revealed by this statement from *The Way Ahead: Church of England Schools in the New Millennium*:

> The Church has a major problem in attracting young people to its services as a means of discharging its mission, and one that causes much concern. This bears directly on the future of the church.
> (Archbishop's Council 2001: par. 3.3)

It appears that state funding is accepted as a means to support a wish to increase the numbers of young people going to church.[12]

Finally, critics of separate religious schools make the accusation that they disadvantage other schools through selection procedures that cream off the most able students. Church schools are accused of operating selective admissions policies, sometimes, it is claimed, applying criteria beyond that of religious affiliation. Such schools would be in a position to select more able and/or better behaved students, favouring themselves and disadvantaging other schools in the locality.

Discussion

The argument against faith-based education on the grounds that it limits the autonomy of children has to be seen against the wider background of education. The voluntariness of children's responses and judgements can be limited as much by their encountering teachers with anti-religious views and school policies which assume a secularist view of religion or are insensitive to families from religious backgrounds as by encounters with teachers holding religious views. Unlike some commentators (e.g. Burtonwood 1998), I do not see the distinction between personal autonomy and religious nurture as a rigid dichotomy. Autonomy does not imply complete individualism, for a consideration of others in relation to oneself is an important factor in autonomous decision making. In this sense all autonomy is 'relative'. Children absorb values and habits from parents though, of course, later they may question these. Moreover, children and young people face many forms of persuasion in their lives – from advertising, the media, from peers and others, including teachers. Children may well encounter overt anti-religious prejudice in some school settings (Weller *et al.* 2001; White 2003), and in policies which assimilate rather than accommodate plurality. This last distinction is between approaches which impose a secularist view of religion (for example, that religious belief and issues of the truth claims of religions are purely private matters) and approaches which take the religious beliefs of children and parents seriously (Cooling 1997a). Accommodating plurality:

> … accepts the realities of religious truth as of universal significance for religious believers and therefore as public in its implications. Its approach is to encourage debate between people of very different, and often fundamentally opposed views, and to assist in the development of strategies which enable people to work together for the common good despite their deeply held differences. It does not privatise religions, but rather welcomes religions into the public domain and seeks to take seriously people's actual beliefs. It is not afraid of the expression of religious distinctiveness in either cultural or doctrinal realms.
>
> (Cooling 2002)

The key issues for all types of schools are the integrity of teachers and whether pupils are taught and encouraged to use skills of critical enquiry so they can scrutinize and reflect upon beliefs and values they encounter. Both faith-based and Community schools need to value both.

Of the arguments for faith-based schools, the weakest is the one that appeals to their high quality of education. The ambiguity of Ofsted findings has already been noted. Also, as the research from John Marks on attainment in literacy and numeracy reported above shows, there is a huge variation in standards *between* faith-based schools, suggesting that high performance is not intrinsic to faith-based education (Marks 2001: 5–36). Further, the NFER report on the impact of specialist and faith schools on performance concludes that 'there is no evidence to suggest that an increase in the number of faith schools would improve overall performance' (Schagen *et al.* 2002: 47). In any case, the argument from attainment is something of a red herring. However Ofsted and other research findings are interpreted, it is highly questionable that state funding of separate religious schools can be justified for purely instrumental reasons to do with attainment, teaching quality and good behaviour. The key question to ask is why these better standards and qualities have not been reached in many Community schools, and to seek ways of taking action to achieve them.[13]

The most convincing argument against faith-based schools lies in their potential to create barriers between groups, thereby eroding social harmony. Although there is some force in Werbner's argument that the politics of faith-based education has drawn minorities into democratic practices and institutions, any benefit could be outweighed by the fact that faith-based education necessitates the separation of children by religion. There is also a danger, in some cases, that separation by religion could also mean separation by 'ethnicity'. The government has sought to reduce the dangers of separation by religion by encouraging policies of inclusiveness on the part of faith schools. Estelle Morris, when Secretary of State for Education and Skills, stated:

> [W]hat we must ensure is that inclusiveness is placed at the very heart of our faith school policy – that new faith schools, and independent schools wishing to join the maintained sector, work in partnership with non-faith schools and schools of other faiths. I want to see all schools – including faith schools – working with others, sharing facilities and bringing children of different backgrounds together.
>
> (Morris 2001b)

This is a laudable aim but, as we have noted, there is some research evidence indicating resistance from some of the more theologically conservative types of faith schools to making such contacts or to raising pupils' awareness of the religious and cultural diversity of society (Short 2003; Short and Lenga 2002; Valins *et al.* 2001; Valins 2003).

Also, the government's views on inclusiveness do not extend to modifying requirements on Voluntary Aided schools with regard to religious education.

Currently such schools can avoid any study of religions other than that of the school's foundation. In a written reply to an MP's question as to whether the Secretary of State for Education and Skills would 'extend government guidelines on multi-faith education in community schools to all maintained religious schools', the Schools Minister, Stephen Timms, stated:

> Extending the guidelines in the way my honourable friend suggests would undermine the purpose and ethos of faith schools. Religious education in these schools will continue to be taught in accordance with the trust deed or with the tenets of the religion in question.
>
> (Timms 2001)

This response implies that raising awareness about or studying other religions is incompatible with nurture in and the practice of one's own. This is not the case as all work on inter-faith dialogue and inter-faith relations and much theological work in the fields of religious studies and comparative religion have demonstrated. Moreover, many Voluntary Aided schools choose to include some study of other religions in their religious education, and a few are involved in inter-religious dialogue at the child's level (Ipgrave 2001). In these cases, study of other religions is seen as a theological activity entirely consistent with the purposes of the school. It is those Voluntary Aided schools that deliberately avoid such studies and activities that give cause for serious concern. It seems remarkable, especially in the wake of the events of September 11, 2001, that any young people could leave school having had no formal study of any religions other than their own.

The introduction of citizenship education into the national curriculum in England and Wales has placed on *all* state-funded secondary schools (including faith-based schools) a clear requirement to explore with pupils the nature of Britain as a multi-religious and multi-ethnic society. For example, at Key Stage 4, pupils have to study 'the origins and implications of the diverse national, regional, religious and ethnic identities in the United Kingdom and the need for mutual respect and understanding ...' (DfEE/QCA 1999, ks4, 1b). It is vital that all schools give proper attention to this requirement. Future Ofsted reports should reveal whether any schools seek to avoid this obligation.

What is encouraging is that some of those involved in faith-based education are taking steps which respond to some of the critics. For example, Abdullah Trevathan, Head of the Islamia Primary School in Brent, has stated the view that Muslim schools should not be 'ethnic enclaves', but should provide a forum for young British Muslims to engage in a critical quest to make new British and European Islamic culture (Trevathan 2002). Writers from various traditions, including Catholic educators, also seek to promote inclusiveness and critical openness (e.g. Groome 1980; Sullivan 2000, 2001) as well as the faith school's potential role in formulating critiques of various aspects of contemporary society such as materialism (e.g. Grace 2002).

Some faith-based primary schools have been involved in a project on inter-religious dialogue by email (Ipgrave 2001, 2003; see also Chapter 7 below). This initiative gives children their own voice and provides a more 'differentiated' approach to dialogue and citizenship (Jackson 2003b; Young 1990) than more 'top down' approaches.

Conclusion

The realities of British educational history, together with the dilemmas posed by some of the reasons for supporting or rejecting faith-based education, suggest that a pragmatic policy of compromise is the most appropriate. The provision of unfair educational advantages, acts of deliberate proselytization in schools, the disempowerment of children through authoritarian policies, the forcing of identities upon children, the removal of means of communication with children from other backgrounds, the suppression of knowledge and the stereotyping of others are all highly undesirable practices. No doubt cases of each could be found in some faith-based educational settings. However, none of these is intrinsic to a faith-based education. The arguments that *all* schools should promote social justice (including religious tolerance), knowledge about religions, the development of pupils' skills of criticism and independent thinking, and also dialogue and interaction between pupils of different backgrounds are convincing. Policy should support faith-based education that promotes justice and fairness, the provision of information about religions, a critical approach, relative autonomy for children, social cohesion through dialogue and communication, and the opportunity for all children to participate in debates about plurality.[14] Whether the responsibility for discriminating between applications to set up faith schools should be entirely devolved to local school organization committees remains an important question.

Finally it is important to register that, in its enthusiasm to promote the benefits of faith-based education, the government has played down the potential of the Community school as a centre for dialogue between young people of different backgrounds.[15] The Community school should be the 'plural' school and not the kind of secular school envisaged by David Hargreaves (Hargreaves 1994), devoid of both religion and religious education.

Chapter 4

Postmodernist approaches to religious education

In relation to religious education, one possible reaction to the plurality of late modernity is to adopt a postmodernist stance, attempting to deconstruct the subject and to reconceive it in relation to a radicalized view of education. There have been few attempts to do this so far in religious education. There are strongly postmodernist elements in the work of the Dutch scholars Wim Wardekker and Siebren Miedema, for example (Wardekker and Miedema 2001). They reject what they call 'transmissionist' models of RE, choosing to emphasize the life-world related questions of young people rather than the abstract 'grand narratives' of religious systems. Drawing on the work of William James, John Dewey, G.H. Mead and others, Wardekker and Miedema develop a transformative, neo-pragmatist view of education and knowledge in general and of religious education in particular. Humans are seen as signifiers, while religious rites, practices, doctrines and narratives are interpreted as cultural artefacts, available to the learner as instruments for guiding thoughts and actions and for reinterpreting ordinary experience. By *interacting* with religious source material, pupils are offered the possibility of creative personal transformation. Religious rites, practices, doctrines and narratives are seen as potentially transformative resources of the life-world (Wardekker and Miedema 2001: 30). Students thus 'take an active part in the construction of new interpretations and new meanings', developing a capacity to integrate different perspectives into their own personality (Wardekker and Miedema 2001: 32). According to this view, meanings are never objective but always result from 'the instantaneous and creative relation between the human being and its environment'. The theological underpinning of this is a reinterpretation of William James' pragmatist view: 'The function of the enveloping whole, of the concept of God, is to assure the self that its aspirations can be fulfilled, providing that the self works and contributes' (Wardekker and Miedema 2001: 31).

Despite its attractions, the main problem with this transactional approach is in the accommodation of children who hold views about religion and theology that are significantly different from those underpinning the approach itself. For example, children and young people who hold realist views of religious language and who see themselves as part of distinctive religious communities are unlikely to feel comfortable with a general approach that sees no problem in using religious source material eclectically and instrumentally, and sometimes out of context.

Wardekker and Miedema do not relate their work to particular empirical research projects or to practical curriculum development in the classroom. In these respects, Clive and Jane Erricker have gone further in developing a thoroughgoing postmodernist approach to religious education. They give an account of this in their book *Reconstructing Religious, Spiritual and Moral Education* (Erricker and Erricker 2000a) and in a number of related publications (e.g. Erricker and Erricker 2000b).[1] They adopt a non-realist and strongly relativistic stance, embracing postmodernism fulsomely. Their ideas are informed by empirical research conducted as part of the Children and Worldviews Project. This is in the form of interviews with about 200 children aged 6–11 about matters that concern them strongly. Each of these personal narratives consists of an edited interview, with the interviewer's questions and comments taken out (e.g. Erricker *et al.* 1997).

Reconstructing Religious, Spiritual and Moral Education is not just a challenge to religious educators, but to educators in general. It shows a deep concern for children and their spiritual, moral and emotional needs, seeking to centre education round their personal narratives rather than any pre-set curriculum, and arguing for the conflation of religious, spiritual, moral and cultural education. The main theoretical contributions to the book are by Clive Erricker, and it is these that are the focus of discussion here. An exposition of Clive and Jane Erricker's work is offered, followed by a critique of some of Clive Erricker's ideas. His own critique, of aspects of the interpretive approach in particular, is also considered (see Chapter 6 below for a discussion of interpretive approaches to RE).

The personal narrative approach

Clive Erricker laments what he sees as the modernist spell on current education, characterized by rationalism, subject centredness, closed ideas of knowledge and a lack of concern for the nurture of the individual's creativity and imagination (Erricker and Erricker 2000a: 1–11). Modernism, he contends, has given a rough ride to progressive education, and current policies in Britain simply pay lip service to areas such as spiritual and moral education. Religious education in particular is dominated by content and avoids existential engagement. Control of content tends to be (as with the English and Welsh RE model syllabuses) in the hands of religious insiders who construct knowledge according to the rules of their own language games. This knowledge is then 'delivered' to the young who are thus prevented from using their own imaginations to construct their *own* knowledge, and whose existential concerns are left unaddressed. Whether the knowledge is constructed by religious insiders or educationalists (who both would construct curricula in their own interests rather than those of children, claims Erricker), the children on the receiving end are left out of the equation. 'The issue', says Clive Erricker, 'is one of children expressing themselves and being heard' (Erricker and Erricker 2000a: 6).

Turning specifically to religious education (Erricker and Erricker 2000a: Chapter 2), Clive Erricker aims to demonstrate how the various positions adopted by writers in the field (whether conservative or liberal) conceal personal and ideological stances. He also points out that these authors write within a context of ideological struggle between the forces of secularism and theology. Religious education is seen as the battleground with the Churches marshalling their forces with the goal of retaining a place in education. In Erricker's view, the smoke of the battle can conceal the partiality of those defending more educationally open approaches. Erricker's key criticisms of those who support an apparently liberal and non-indoctrinatory religious education are three.

The first is that any form of religious education which provides information for children – any kind of prepared curriculum – is providing children with a pre-packaged construction of knowledge that unavoidably includes the moral and political sentiments of whoever has assembled the material. Here he discusses my book *Religious Education: An Interpretive Approach* (1997) as an example of an attempt to address some of these issues, which turns out to provide an alternative, though less ideologically motivated, construction of the standard presentation of world religions as systems.

The second is that the very focus on religion privileges the religious against the secular. This can only be corrected in Erricker's view, by an approach that deals broadly with values and spirituality, pulling down the barrier between the religious and the secular, and being meaningful to all children including those (the majority) who are not from an overtly religious background.

The third is that RE liberals, in seeking to avoid Christian nurture (and therefore the charge of indoctrination), have ceased to offer children faith. This point perhaps comes as a surprise, but we must wait for the moment to see what Clive Erricker means by 'faith'.

Erricker goes on (Erricker and Erricker 2000a: Chapter 3) to review writing on spiritual education. Whether the writers of documents produced by government agencies (such as the School Curriculum and Assessment Authority and the Office for Standards in Education), theologically inclined academics (such as Adrian Thatcher or Andrew Wright) or liberal scholars (such as Dennis Starkings, David Hay or Jack Priestley), all are judged to operate within the same modernist framework and all are accused of making the same basic error. In varying ways and degrees all are considered to be constructors of knowledge, rather than facilitators of children's construction of their own knowledge.

Erricker's own strongly relativistic stance is radical in the sense that the adoption of an epistemological position on the issue is regarded as irrelevant. 'Relativism posits that we are not engaged in epistemological enquiry at all.' He continues:

> Rather, we are engaged in, and are seeking to engage with as insiders, the processes of world construction for practical and moral purposes. This involves attempting to understand 'faith' and ideological stances of various kinds, and making judgements as to our relationship with each as part of the process of our own world construction.
>
> (Erricker and Erricker 2000a: 62)

This he sees as a spiritual as well as political and social activity; 'it would be distortive to treat the three terms as entirely distinct from one another' (Erricker and Erricker 2000a: 62). Indeed, since realms such as the 'moral', 'cultural', 'social' or 'spiritual' are constructions, there can be no reason, argues Erricker, for treating them as separate categories.

Erricker develops his idea of 'faith' by adapting Kierkegaard's usage of the term (Erricker and Erricker 2000a: 64). He takes Kierkegaard's question written in *Philosophical Fragments*:

> Is an historical point of departure possible for an eternal consciousness; how can such a point of departure have any other than a merely historical interest; is it possible to base an eternal happiness upon historical knowledge?
>
> (Kierkegaard 1962, quoted in Erricker and Erricker 2000a: 64)

Kierkegaard's idea of the 'leap of faith' conveyed the idea that God cannot be known objectively through dogma and doctrine but through faith, subjectively by intuition. Faith for Kierkegaard was an ontological rather than an epistemological category and the spiritual was seen as subjective, unsystematic and opposed to constructions of a formulaic kind. Erricker radicalizes Kierkegaard's view, extending it beyond religion:

> ... Kierkegaard's investigation of faith allows us to see that any attempt to place spirituality within a closed system constructed according to the formulations of doctrine or ideology is false; whatever form or character that system may have and on whatever premises it may be based. ... My contention is that ... Kierkegaard allows us to consider the notion of faith beyond the confines of Christianity or religion, and beyond the idea that faith is that which delivers salvation.
>
> (Erricker and Erricker 2000a: 64, 65)

Faith for Erricker seems to be an intuitive and ontological sense of how the different elements of personal life – emotions, values, motivations etc. – can be discovered inter-subjectively and integrated as a personal 'spiritual' stance that informs and governs one's positions in social relations, and on moral and political matters, for example. Intuited personal spirituality is to be trusted over against external epistemological claims of any kind, which are seen as manipulative constructions. Once one's personal spiritual stance is clarified and established, healthy stances on ethics and citizenship will follow, more or less automatically.

The key elements of Clive Erricker's position might be summarized as follows. Reality is entirely socially/linguistically constructed. There is no objective reality; the position adopted is an anti-realist one. Thus all knowledge is a social or linguistic construction, inherently containing within itself the ideological assumptions of whoever constructed that knowledge. There can be no objective knowledge. There can only be different contestable knowledges. There can be no alternative to relativism.

Therefore any curriculum (which by definition claims to be a body of knowledge) contains within itself the ideological assumptions of whoever constructed that knowledge. No education should be based on a pre-set curriculum. Some constructions of knowledge (meta-narratives or grand narratives), carrying with them the power of political authority or the received wisdom of tradition, are especially ideologically loaded and therefore particularly manipulative. They 'imprison' individuals (including children in school) rather than liberate them. These meta-narratives need to be deconstructed, and shown to be what they are. This deconstruction is an emancipatory process.

In religious education in schools, children are faced with both the meta-narratives of content dominated education which pervades the whole system and with the meta-narratives of the religions, pre-packaged from the point of view of insiders with an ideological interest in perpetuating each religious system's assumptions. *Any* attempt to present children with alternative, more critical, constructions of knowledge is doomed to failure, for *all* knowledge is socially or linguistically constructed. However well intentioned the attempt, some or other construction will be imposed on children.

Traditional divisions of knowledge are constructions, and categories such as moral, spiritual, religious, cultural, social and emotional are constructions. There is no reason why these divisions and classificatory schemes should be imposed in education. Education should be conceived more holistically. The only authentic knowledge is knowledge that children *construct for themselves*. This cannot be done through any kind of pre-designed curriculum. It can only be done by listening to and responding to the 'small narratives' of other individuals, whether these 'texts' be personal stories of other children, works of art or whatever. The point is that no interpretation must be imposed on the material. The children must construct the knowledge for *themselves*. The teacher's role is to facilitate this process. This personal knowledge is constructed through emotional as well as rational responses to narrative. This knowledge is not final. Children may change their minds as a result of reflecting on more narratives. This would simply be a *change* in knowledge; it would not be a *development* in knowledge or understanding, for there is no absolute knowledge to be attained and no external criteria for judging one narrative against another.

The 'truth' of personal narratives is intuited by means of faith. This is a type of inter-subjective intuitive awareness rather than knowledge. It is ontological rather than epistemological in character, transcending the 'religious'-'secular' divide, and determining one's position on and approach to moral, spiritual, cultural, social and emotional matters. Faith in this sense is open to anyone. Thus, spirituality for both Clive and Jane Erricker (seen as encompassing or at least conditional for other elements of affective education) is a *process*, something like constructing an integrated and meaningful view of life, the integrity of which is grasped and trusted intuitively. The construction of personal narratives is an *artistic* process, creatively on-going, drawing on the rational, the emotional and the intuitive, and with no prescribed outcome.

In pedagogical terms these personal narratives are voiced in the classroom and may be affected by the 'knowledges' of others (Erricker and Erricker 2000a: 136). Only children can contribute representations of others (whether as individuals, groups or wider traditions) for consideration (Erricker and Erricker 2000a: 148). Anyone else who does this (teacher or learning resources) is imposing pre-structured knowledge with an implicit agenda to control outcomes.

The classroom

The Errickers' work has been developed partly in primary school classrooms, and their approach reflects this. There would be no lessons specifically devoted to religious education. Ideally, there would be no curriculum and no subjects, in the sense of organized bodies of received knowledge and experience. The 'affective' area would cover what might be traditionally divided up as religious, moral, spiritual, cultural and emotional education. The emphasis would be on skills (especially knowing how to listen and look, and how to speak, to give voice).

Lessons could (and mainly would) start with hearing someone else's (often another child's) personal narrative, and then responding to it. The narrative could be an interview with a child on topics of deep concern to that individual, with the interviewer's or facilitator's questions and prompts edited out. This could be read out by a third party, perhaps the teacher. The response of the listener could be, initially, in the form of a concept map, in effect summarizing the child's response by showing a network of concepts and their relationship, as a personal reaction to the narrative. Children would be likely to respond in different ways as elements in the narrative connected with particular aspects of their experience. This map could be discussed and elaborated and could form the basis of the child's own narrative. In effect, the child would be *constructing* knowledge, in the sense of formulating and clarifying values and beliefs for practical use in living. Knowledge would *be* that which is of practical use in living. It would not need to satisfy any other test of 'truth'. There would be a strong sense of learning by experience and by reflection. A lesson could also start with a poem or story connecting with children's experience or a 'visual narrative', perhaps some form of iconography which pupils interpreted with the help of the teacher as facilitator (not as provider of knowledge about how the work *should* be interpreted). It is not clear what criteria would be used for selecting these stimuli. There would be no presentation of 'information', unless children asked for it in order to meet their perceived learning needs. It is not clear what kind of resources might be used to provide this 'information', given the Errickers' suspicion of any pre-prepared materials.

The role of the teacher would be that of facilitator. The teacher would not aim to be a neutral chairperson and would not conceal his or her personal views but would participate in debates and discussions, without abusing his or her power. All children would be accepted and valued equally, but there is no indication of how any clashes between the ideological backgrounds that some children might have and the assumptions about knowledge and truth which are presupposed by the method might be resolved.

Discussion

Anti-realism and knowledge

The philosophical position adopted by Clive and Jane Erricker entails an anti-realist and strongly relativistic position in which *all* knowledge is socially or linguistically constructed. As they write (quoting John Smith):

> The first principle that underpins a narrative pedagogy is that all 'knowledge' is relative. Relativism posits that there is no absolute or objective knowledge; in effect 'there is no "contrary" to place in opposition to relativism'.
>
> (Erricker and Erricker 2000b: 194)

The only trustworthy 'knowledge' is that which individuals construct for themselves and intuit (by 'faith') to be an integrated and pragmatically useful whole. One consequence is that there can be no public criteria for discriminating between one set of claims and any other. Thus, Clive Erricker can say that if a child changes her or his personal narrative, there is no 'development', simply the expression of a new narrative. On this view, there can be no public criteria for making judgements of value, for example in discriminating between different accounts of an historical event. If a child constructed a narrative that was socially repugnant, including racist ideas for example, there could be no *objective* grounds for rejecting it.

On the Errickers' view, all constructions of knowledge, other than those put together by individuals through their personal narratives, are fictions in the sense that they do not correspond to any external reality. They also embody the political purposes of those who have assembled them. Thus Clive Erricker sees a straight 'either/or' between formulaic constructions presented as indisputable knowledge and individual, personal constructions of worldviews. There are no positions in between. This stance is even more radical than Lyotard's view of knowledge. Although Erricker adopts some key ideas from Lyotard, especially his critique of meta-narratives, his own idea of a 'small narrative' is very different from Lyotard's. For Lyotard, a little narrative is inter-personal and is shared by those who follow the rules of a particular language game (e.g. Lyotard 1984: 60). For Erricker, a small narrative is an *individual's* own personal knowledge constructed in response to another's constructed narrative. Erricker's account is thus radically individualistic, even more so than many postmodernist writers who have a stronger view of social experience.

Thus, in terms of pedagogy, the Errickers cannot accept the possibility of a range of source materials that can be scrutinized critically by students.

Either 'small narratives of learners' or 'grand narratives' have to be at the centre of pedagogy.

> Any attempt to balance these two objectives must fall down on one side or the other because they operate according to opposing epistemological and pedagogical principles. This cannot be rectified by attempting to employ a pedagogical process that apparently hides this radical difference.
>
> (Erricker and Erricker 2000b: 195)

Yet if children can respond to individual children's narratives, why is it not possible for them to move from an individual's personal narrative to the wider social context in which that individual is set and respond to other accounts? The idea that an individual's experience can be connected to wider contexts through curriculum material is rejected by the Errickers as a form of manipulation. If any connections are made, they must be made by the children themselves (though one wonders what resources they would be allowed or encouraged to use in order to do this).

Following Lyotard, the Errickers use the term 'knowledge' broadly and ambiguously. Systems of belief are counted as knowledge, as are provisional accounts of ways of life or other people's interpretations of works of art etc. Since all 'knowledge' is a construction, there is no need to distinguish between knowledge and belief and there are no criteria for judging better or worse constructions. The assumption is made that someone constructing a framework for understanding intends that understanding to be adopted as knowledge rather than an explanatory tool open to criticism or modification. The idea that education can involve the presentation of curricula that are regarded as *provisional* and open to the critical scrutiny of pupils is left aside. There is no room for discrimination between better or worse constructions of knowledge, no space for critical appraisals of different representations of reality.

Non-realism and plural classrooms

Turning to other weaknesses in the personal narrative model, Clive Erricker and Jane Erricker claim that their argument and approach does not intend to undermine religious faith positions that might be held by pupils.

> … it is necessary to present the case for a pedagogy based on relativism. In presenting this argument we are not seeking to undermine religious faith positions but to place them alongside non-religious alternatives

as the appropriate range of enquiry that should be engaged with in an educational system that concerns itself with spirituality and values.

(Erricker and Erricker 2000a: 58)

However, if an axiom for the approach is strong relativism, with its attendant anti-realism, then *any* realist position, presented by children in class, for example, must be called into question. Wardekker and Miedema's work, with its purely instrumental view of religion as source material for the individual's construction of meaning, seems open to the same criticism. Julia Ipgrave's research on pupil to pupil dialogue in the primary religious education classroom shows that a realist view of religious truth is common among her pupils. Their conversations reveal that their views are grounded within communal ways of life, but also that their own understandings and beliefs are not simply accepted on the authority of their parents or teachers in the faith context. Children learn and form their identities in relationship with and response to others, in families and in other kinds of group, including their peers in school. They remain individuals, with their own uniqueness, but they absorb and filter the ideas and values of others, modifying some and rejecting others. Nevertheless, many of them consider their beliefs to be true in a realist sense (Ipgrave 2001, 2002, 2003; see also Chapter 7 below). These children's views would be incompatible with a pedagogy underpinned by anti-realism. The Errickers' approach could only be taken on in full if the participants shared their particular view of reality and knowledge.

Faith and foreclosure

Clive Erricker's justification both for the conflation of religious education with areas such as spiritual, moral, social, cultural and emotional education, and for the ontological character of this domain in terms of an existentialist view of 'faith', are open to the same objections as any other argument from intuition – namely that others might intuit something different. There are no objective criteria for discriminating between one intuition and another.

While the Errickers' conflated 'affective' domain deals with many important personal matters in an integrated way, it omits or marginalizes particular dimensions from each field. For example, unless they specify an interest, children will be given a narrow and partial view of debates about religions and cultures. We should be introducing children to the debates about modernity, plurality, religion, culture, morality etc., rather than constructing an approach that requires the adoption of a particular stance as axiomatic or that forecloses debates because of its own ideology. Though there are elements to admire in the Errickers' work, their total focus on the individual, and their commitment to a very particular deconstructive view of cultures and religions, means that the debates about cultures and cultural formation are foreclosed for children. Rather than being confronted with a particular view on religions or on modernity and postmodernity, children and young people, at their own level, need to be helped to *participate* in the relevant debates as part of their religious education. This is a condition for the kind of intercultural and inter-religious communication that is necessary for the health of plural democracies. Rather than being a refuge from cultural difference, the common school should embrace pluralism in an epistemologically open way, ensuring that children are equipped to deal with data presented to them critically (Jackson 1997: 126).

Tradition and the interpretive approach

Clive Erricker discusses some aspects of the interpretive approach that has been a feature of much of our work on religious education at Warwick. An example of Erricker's insistence that all representations are politically loaded fictions is his discussion of Wilfred Cantwell Smith's use of the term 'tradition' (Smith 1978), and what he sees as my adoption of this concept as a tool in the interpretive approach to religious education (Jackson 1997). Smith had presented the concepts of 'faith' and 'tradition' as a means to avoid religious essentialism and to find a model to place each person's unique, individual faith position within a historical totality. Erricker's critique misinterprets Smith on the concept of tradition and makes the mistake of assuming that I adopt Smith's faith and tradition hermeneutic.

It would be as well to clarify Smith's work and my adaptation of it. Primarily, Smith was interested in theological rather than methodological questions. His theology is liberal Christian, and his view of the relationship of religions is close to John Hick's version of theological pluralism (e.g. Hick 1990: 109–19). For Smith, the different traditions provide symbols which indicate and mediate experience of the transcendent in culturally different circumstances. A common religious experience is articulated into more or less distinct symbol systems because of cultural and historical circumstance. His epistemology is critical realist. Experience rather than language is at the root. The task of theology for Smith is to work towards convergence through a form of communication (Smith prefers the term 'colloquy' to 'dialogue') that reflects what he calls 'corporate, critical self-consciousness' (Smith 1981). This is non group specific, critically open and self aware, and is fostered especially through contact between individual people of faith.

What I do in my own work is to adapt Smith's *methodological* approach (which was of secondary interest to him) and to leave aside his theology. The methodological ideas are developed as an aid to understanding or interpreting religious material and are not used for theological purposes. It was Smith's introduction of the individual/tradition dynamic as an alternative way of representing religions, reflecting individual personal views and avoiding stereotyping individuals as subscribers to monolithic belief systems, that appealed to me. However, I do not adopt Smith's view of either faith or tradition. The way in which I use the term 'tradition' is different from Smith's and I deliberately do not use Smith's term 'faith' at all, explicitly setting it aside as a theologically loaded concept. Whereas Smith uses the idea of the interplay of individual faith and cumulative tradition as a hermeneutical tool to indicate the uniqueness of each person's theological position in relation to the total historical deposit of the tradition, I adopt a three level model (individual, group, tradition) as an interpretive device in which tradition is seen as a contested broad picture.

In arguing against the interpretive approach, Erricker equates Smith's use (and what he sees as my use) of the term 'tradition' with Lyotard's idea of meta-narrative. However, Smith's use of 'tradition' is different from a Lyotardian grand narrative. For Smith a cumulative tradition is:

> ... the entire mass of overt objective data that constitute the historical deposit, as it were, of the past religious life of the community in question: temples, scriptures, theological systems, dance patterns, legal and other social institutions, conventions, moral codes, myths, and so on; anything that can be and is transmitted from one person, one generation, to another, and that an historian can observe.
>
> (Smith 1978: 157)

This would encompass more than one meta-narrative in Lyotard's sense. A meta-narrative would be a particular deeply institutionalized pathway through the tradition, a particular language game with its own internal rules for establishing knowledge and truth. My use of the term 'tradition' is different from both Smith and Lyotard. As I wrote in *Religious Education: An Interpretive Approach*:

> [Smith's] concept of tradition needs some modification. Smith's view of 'tradition' as 'the entire mass of overt objective data that constitute the historical deposit ... of the past religious life of the community in question' avoids the issue of disagreement over the limits of any religious tradition. Not only might there be scholarly disagreement over the

classification of religious material, the tradition also will be perceived differently by individuals according to the way of life in which they are operating and their background knowledge and experience, and one's view of the tradition is likely to be modified as one encounters new material. Moreover, 'insiders' may have different views from one another of the scope of the tradition and of the relative importance of its different aspects. The precise nature of a religious tradition will be a matter of negotiation or even contest … Nevertheless, despite its fuzzy edges, the general idea of 'a tradition' is useful for interpretive purposes.

(Jackson 1997: 62–3).

This view is closer in some respects to Lyotard's idea of meta-narrative than to Smith's view of a tradition. It acknowledges the political and contested nature of tradition, and that there will be different constructions of that tradition, whether made by different insiders or different outsiders. The difference from Lyotard is that the view allows both macro and micro as well as 'orthodox' and dissident versions of a tradition. The tradition can be represented through an individual's eyes as well as through those of institutional orthodoxy or heretical dissidence. The concept is simply part of an interpretive framework for handling religious material. An acknowledgement of the disputed nature of a tradition is crucial, to the extent of contesting or even denying boundaries. Also, my view concentrates on the *interplay* between individuals, various groups to which they might belong and one's sense of the wider tradition.

Clive Erricker continues:

The second shortcoming of Jackson's approach is revealed when he proceeds to incorporate Smith into his own empirical research and subsequent school resources. His aim is to record young people with traditions speaking of their faith and how this is put into practice in the context of tradition and membership group (Jackson 1997: 95ff). The question is whether the children represent themselves or whether they are representatives of the tradition/membership group. This might seem to be a false dichotomy until we take account of the political processes involved in such research and the ethical questions posed. Here the question of representation is highly ambiguous. Who decides which children and from which families representing a particular membership group (say Orthodox Jews or Roman Catholics) will be researched and presented in materials representing that group? Who decides which membership groups will be represented in a faith tradition? Who decides what questions may be asked in interviews and what responses published? In a sense of course these questions are rhetorical. In an area of such political sensitivity, and with the researcher's wish to promote positive images of these groups and the need for these groups to agree to the publication of the findings, the process of representation that needs to be followed becomes clear (Jackson 1997: 107–11)).

(Erricker and Erricker 2000a: 25)

The first thing to reinforce is that I do not attempt to 'incorporate Smith' into our Warwick empirical research and school materials, but use a three level model adapted and developed from Smith's work as a methodological tool. The aim is not to record 'young people with traditions'. The word 'representation' is not used in this sense. A tradition is not something you 'have', like membership of a trade union, but a reference point to be used by oneself or another for situating an individual's religious worldview in relation to others. The individual position is not 'faith' in Smith's sense, but a complex of beliefs, values and practices articulated by the young person over time and interpreted by an ethnographer using techniques such as participant observation and informal and semi-structured interviewing. In this sense each person's story is unique. However, the placing of an individual in one or more groups recognizes the group tied nature of each individual's social experience, as refracted through carefully structured ethnographic study (Jackson 1997; Nesbitt 2000a). Children are not presented as being 'representatives of traditions', and strong emphasis is put on the idea of diversity within traditions, in which different elements of group or individual life are connected by family resemblance rather than essence. Nor do the children only draw on resources relating to their family background (whether ethnic, cultural, religious, spiritual or moral). From the angle of cultural continuity (albeit culture under contest and change), the children can be seen to be part of a shifting and dynamic cultural scene. From the angle of personal identity formation, they can be seen to draw on a range of cultural and other resources, some of them from within the family background, some of them not. Also, the picture provided (its artistic nature is acknowledged) is open to the critical scrutiny of users.

Research with children

A related aspect of Clive Erricker's critique is his discussion of the use and appropriateness of particular research methods when working with children. He criticizes the ethnographic methods used in our various Warwick studies (e.g. Nesbitt 1998a), claiming that any interview that includes a pre-prepared agenda distorts findings and therefore produces corrupted knowledge. The findings match the interviewer's agenda rather than that of the child; the interviewer selects responses to suit her theories or purposes (Erricker and Erricker 2000a: 25). The only authentic interview, in Erricker's view, is a personal narrative in which the interviewer simply acts as a facilitator, enabling the child to tell her or his own story. Yet the researcher still has to elicit personal stories, and Erricker's research team uses various stimuli to draw out responses. For example, Clive Erricker has used Brian Patten's poem 'Looking for Dad' as a stimulus (Erricker 2001: 158), which educed some moving responses about family breakdown and loss. However, there is a clear relationship between the responses and the stimulus. It is difficult to make a clear distinction between well thought out questions, formulated following a sustained period of observation (see, for example, Eleanor Nesbitt's interview schedule used when interviewing children from various Sikh family backgrounds [Nesbitt 2000a: 264–72]), and the use of, say, a poem as a means to stimulate responses. Both methods are likely to draw out a particular range of responses related to the interviewer's or facilitator's purposes. Is not a poem about loss and family breakdown likely to stimulate listeners to recall similar events rather than others that might be of equal importance in a different context? Enabling a child to tell a personal story is most certainly a valuable educational and therapeutic tool. However, that narrative may well omit all sorts of elements of a child's social relationships that might show a range of influences and responses. Without entering the social world of the child, using a variety of methods, one cannot detect the processes of influence, reaction and filtering that are there, whether they be a combination of methods such as participant observation in family and community contexts and semi-structured and informal interviewing with children and other family members (e.g. Nesbitt 2000a; Østberg 2003b) or analysis of children's classroom dialogue over time showing mutual positive and negative influence, filtering of ideas, and the accommodation and reshaping of concepts (Ipgrave 2001, 2002, 2003). My point is that the Children and Worldviews Project Team are simply using a different type of data collection method which aims to capture a particular range of responses. They cannot escape the charge of influencing the construction of a narrative. All interviewing approaches (including facilitation) can only create a partial picture and all interviewing is to a degree distorting (Lewis and Lindsay 2000). This is as true for elicited children's narratives as it is for any other form of data collection. Some approaches are better or worse according to purpose, and some interviewers are technically more adept and/or better informed or self critical than others.

Erricker is right to draw attention to the issues of power and negotiation involved in representing others (whether in ethnography or curriculum development), and these have been central to the debate about representation in social anthropology and other disciplines, and are a feature of our own discussion (Everington 1996a; Jackson 1997, 2000b; Nesbitt 2000b). However, the same issues are there within Erricker's own approach. The important educational point is that children and young people should themselves be encouraged and taught the skills to criticize source materials, whether they be curriculum texts, historical or ethnographic accounts or indeed personal narratives.

Conclusion

We have already noted the principal difficulties with Wardekker and Miedema's transactional approach, namely the difficulty in accommodating children who hold views about religion or have religious commitments that are significantly different from the view of religion and theology that forms its theoretical foundation. Children and young people with conservative religious views are especially likely to feel marginalized by this approach.

The fundamental problem with the Errickers' version of a postmodernist religious education is its requirement of anti-realism as a prerequisite. In terms of its ideological underpinning, the approach has features in common with various forms of faith-based education. The Errickers' non-realist view removes any criteria for evaluating different sources and personal narratives. The total emphasis on the child's personal narrative (or that part of it revealed in the narratives researchers educe) denies children the opportunity to scrutinize wider issues, and is to be differentiated from other postmodernist accounts of 'small narratives' as socially shared. Further, the Errickers' approach to the merger of religious education with other fields results in the omission of important elements. The justification both for the conflation of religious education with other areas and for the ontological character of spirituality in terms of an existentialist view of 'faith' faces the objection that there are no objective criteria for discriminating between one intuition and another. Most importantly, the Errickers' approach forecloses the debate about modernity and postmodernity by requiring the adoption of a non-realist stance as a pre-condition, marginalizing children holding realist views of religious truth.

The treatment of 'provisional data', in the form of *any* conception of religious tradition or any type of curriculum material, as what Erricker calls 'metanarrical' knowledge misrepresents those who see criticism of sources as being a vital component of education, and denies children the opportunity to review the relationship between individuals and wider religious groupings in ways that are informed by scholarship. Moreover, the process of facilitating personal narratives in the Errickers' scheme is not pristine, and should be open to the same methodological scrutiny as other forms of interviewing. Despite these criticisms, we can agree wholeheartedly with Clive and Jane Erricker about the importance of making pupils and their concerns a key element of religious education, reducing the amount of 'content' that the subject has, making time and space for reflective activity and dealing with the emotional as well as the rational. Their involvement of children as agents in the process of religious education is refreshing. One can gain important insights from their work without adopting its non-realist theoretical framework. Moreover, their work could provide the basis for an alternative form of education for those subscribing to their views. The Errickers – like Wardekker and Miedema – also remind religious educators not to lose sight of general debates in education, and the importance of maintaining a critique of general education policy and its relation to economic and other socially instrumental goals. Finally, their arguments against views that confine religious education to the study of religions point to a need for further debate about the nature and scope of the subject (see Chapters 8 and 10 below).

Chapter 5

Religious education as religious literacy

A further reaction to the modernity/postmodernity debate in religious education has been the development of an approach emphasizing the goal of religious literacy in the subject. This position rejects phenomenological and experiential approaches as embodying varying degrees of liberalism and romanticism. Although other writers have emphasized the importance of language and concept analysis in religious education (e.g. Cooling and Cooling 1987; Jackson 1997), the religious literacy approach results specifically from the work of Andrew Wright. While his approach might be described as post-liberal, Wright is highly critical of postmodernist approaches, such as Erricker's (Wright 2001).

Andrew Wright defends a form of neo-modernism, associated with a critical realist stance to epistemology, and advocates the development of what he calls religious literacy. Wright is interested both in religious education and spiritual education, and some of his recent work has emphasized the latter (e.g. Wright 1998, 1999). He is concerned about what he sees as an uncriticized liberal consensus in British religious education. In reaction, his work seeks to challenge this and to defend a form of post-liberal modernism over against romanticism and postmodernism. He sees the latter pair as a continuum, both reacting to the rationalism of eighteenth-century modernism, promoting the image of the dislocated self and the idea of freedom as emancipation from constraint (Wright 1998: 57). Romanticism attempted to recover natural reason – the individual's relationship with the natural order – and to show the superiority of feeling and intuition over rationality. Postmodernism is seen as 'a radical extension of the romantic tradition' (Wright 1998: 61), especially radicalizing romanticism's assertion of externally constrained human freedom.

Wright sees much contemporary writing about spiritual education and religious education as an expression of the Romantic critique of modernism. For example, the work of David Hay on spirituality, which seeks empirical evidence for religious experience as a universal human biological attribute (e.g. Hay 1982, 1990), is seen by Wright as essentially neo-Romantic. Wright would take the same view of any position on religious education that assumes a universal religious experience expressed in different ways through passing through a variety of cultural and linguistic filters (e.g. Smart 1971).

Both romanticism and postmodernism seek the emancipation of the individual, with the latter offering freedom from romanticism's transcendent ultimate reality as well as from pre-modern superstition and modern rationalism, empiricism and idealism. Postmodernism offers absolute freedom through the deconstruction of any system of thought or truth claim. It offers freedom through using language and culture in the game of constructing or de/reconstructing images of reality based on personal preference or choice. The extreme relativism of postmodernism denies the possibility of any ultimate reality, but facilitates the celebration of freedom to construct personal and disposable worldviews.

So where does Wright place himself in relation to the positions he rejects? He adopts a 'critical realist' position, regarding linguistic competence rather than 'experience' as the basis for understanding religions:

> ... experience does not constitute an autonomous realm of private meaning, but is always informed by, and dependent upon, public discourse.
>
> (Wright 1996a: 167)

This is public discourse in the widest sense. Meaningful discourse is not confined within forms of life or language games. 'To understand language', says Wright, 'requires reference not to the closed worlds of private communities, but to the open and universal nature of human interaction' (Wright 1996a: 172). Wright thus glosses over the conceptual difficulties that might be encountered in intercultural or inter-religious communication. For Wright:

> The meaning and truth of religious language is ... located not in its ability to enhance inner experience, but in its ability to picture the actual nature of reality.
>
> (Wright 1996a: 173)

Religion, argues Wright, is at its base concerned with claims to truth. For Wright, contemporary religion is not grounded in universal, but variously expressed, religious experience. Rather, it is 'a set of ambiguous, competing and often overlapping narratives about the true nature of reality' (Wright

1996a: 173). Thus, it is not *experience* that children need as a tool to understand religion, but 'religious literacy', '... an immersion ... in the various public linguistic traditions that seek to account for the ultimate nature of reality' (Wright 1996a: 174).

Rather than allowing pupils to construct their own religious or spiritual mix, Wright would aim to enable them to learn how to differentiate and interpret their raw experience in the light of public discourse. They would need to gain linguistic competence in a range of religious discourses in order to achieve an appropriate level of religious literacy. The process of religious education would seek:

- to raise the student's awareness of his or her latent or partly articulated tradition or worldview.
- to help the student move from this pre-understanding to dialogue with the narratives and language of relevant primary religious traditions and key secular traditions that deny religious truth.
- to raise the student's awareness of the tension between their present worldview and challenges to it (developing both a hermeneutic of faith and of suspicion), exposing them directly to religious ambiguity, and to help students to develop their interpretative skills in order to engage with this.

Pupils would not be indoctrinated into a religious or non-religious viewpoint, would not be *expected* to form a 'pick and mix' postmodern position and would not be exposed to a purely descriptive, non-evaluative 'liberal' study of religions. Rather, they would be helped to form well-reasoned positions on religious truth claims.

> The mark of the religiously educated child ... would be his or her ability to think, act and communicate with insight and intelligence in the light of that diversity of religious truth claims that are the mark of our contemporary culture.
>
> (Wright 1996a: 175)

> ... the aim of religious education need be no more complicated than the process of producing religiously literate individuals. This is an aim in itself that has intrinsic importance and has no further need of justification.
>
> (Wright 1993: 63)

Wright is tough on what he sees as liberalism in general and on liberalism in religious education in particular. To protect the autonomy of the individual, liberalism distinguishes objective public knowledge from subjective private belief. Individuals have absolute freedom in the latter within the limits of tolerance. Beliefs and values are seen by liberals, says Wright, as optional extras, based on personal preference. Religion and morality are relativized and privatized – there is no necessary linkage of moral and religious beliefs to any external reality. Liberals, says Wright, also over-emphasize tolerance and respect for any religious position, attempting to sidestep issues of conflict:

> … [S]ociety needs to accept the reality of unresolved tensions within its plural diversity, tensions that are unlikely to disappear overnight and which liberalism is not capable of papering over.
>
> (Wright 1993: 39)

With regard to religious education, he equates liberal and 'neutral' approaches that tolerate religions so long as they remain within a Western, liberal framework (1993: 37). He sees such liberal approaches as distorting, reductionist, sanitizing and patronizing, failing to recognize the ambiguity of religions – their negative and dark sides as well as their positive features. Unfortunately he does not identify any of these 'liberal' writers, and I am hard pressed to find examples of this restricted view of uncritical liberalism. Perhaps he is thinking of those advocating a phenomenological type of religious education in the manner of Ninian Smart's Schools Council Project for secondary schools (Schools Council 1971). This would be unfair, since Smart clearly saw criticism and a concern for truth as part of the process of religious education (Smart 1968). Perhaps Wright is simply noting his observations of bland official syllabuses or of teachers who encourage no critical element in their classes in an attempt to encourage tolerance of every viewpoint.

For Wright, liberal and emergent postmodern approaches marginalize more traditional positions, such as the critical realist Trinitarian Christianity which he embraces. Wright makes a case for the dissociation of this tradition from Romantic, universal ideas of religious experience and from postmodern reformulations of Christianity (Wright 1998: 69–79).

> The fundamental issue at stake … is not whether the Christian religion is justifiable or true, merely the assertion that, if Orthodox Christianity is understood within its historical and doctrinal integrity, it is revealed as being fundamentally incompatible with the spirituality currently

taught to children in the majority of schools. It is then necessary to accept the reality of a diversity of contrasting and conflicting spiritual traditions.

(Wright 1998: 78)

The passionate way in which Wright argues his case for his view of Trinitarian Christianity, with its legitimation in terms of internal theological and doctrinal orthodoxy, might convey the impression that Wright is setting out to promote this particular view as *the* correct one. However, Wright's personal views need to be distinguished clearly from his views about the nature of religious education. Wright insists that religious education should consist of an analysis of *competing* spiritual narratives, of which the critical realist Trinitarian Christian (in its various cultural and denominational forms) is but one. His use of Trinitarian Christianity is an example of the type of narrative that current liberal religious education orthodoxy and liberal work in spiritual development, he maintains, tend to omit.

The classroom

So what would religious education (or spiritual education conducted in the RE classroom) be like in schools according to Wright? Wright does not get *too* close to the classroom, but he does have a schematic model. This has three stages, dealing respectively with:

- the horizon of the child
- the horizons of alternative spiritual stories
- the emergence of spiritual literacy.

Thus religious/spiritual education starts with the child's own perspective. All children and young people, maintains Wright, can be located within some or other religious or secular spiritual narrative, even though they may not be aware of this. Children should be allowed to identify and articulate their already held spiritual values, commitment and worldviews. Interestingly, this first stage has close similarities with our Warwick interpretive approach. Teachers need to create space and time for this and need to be able to teach young people the skills and methods to enable this form of expression. 'From the start children are expected to identify, own and take responsibility for their own world-view narratives' (Wright 1999: 44). The process must not be coercive, and children must feel secure.

The second stage involves young people in engaging critically with the process of clarifying and refining their spiritual commitments. Here the key questions are:

- Are their views internally coherent? Do their stories actually make sense?
- How do they relate to alternative worldviews – both the worldview of the school within which they are being nurtured, and the worldviews on offer within broader society? (1999: 45)

Wright has a rough taxonomy of possible worldviews to help young people to place their personal positions. These are:

- Specific religious systems
- Universal pluralistic theology
- Secular atheism
- Postmodern relativism.

The teacher's role is to help students to relate these in a structured way to their own provisional positions.

In the final stage:

> … the process of conversation between and across the various horizons can begin to take place. It is through the quality of this conversation, and through the ability of the teacher to equip children with the skills to take part in the dialogue for themselves, that genuine spiritual literacy will begin to emerge.
>
> (Wright 1999: 45)

This process is informed and deepened by drawing on the various disciplines – history, anthropology, philosophy, theology etc. – as academic tools. The process involves both getting close to and being critically distant from one's own and other positions, and is fundamentally linguistic. Wright wants 'more articulate, informed, literate conversations' (1999: 45). The process is not grounded in any heightened spiritual experience, and spiritual exercises of any kind are regarded with suspicion. 'Gratification', says Wright, should be 'deferred'.

To sum up, in Wright's words:

> Education will inevitably nurture children into a particular world view. The question is not whether this will happen, but how: consequently a primary task of spiritual education is to ensure that the spiritual tradition in which children are nurtured is appropriate and that the process of nurture is effective.
>
> (Wright 1998: 95)

In addition to nurturing pupils within a particular spiritual tradition the school also has the duty of allowing them critical access to alternative traditions so that informed insight and wisdom may flourish through the development of spiritual literacy.

(Wright 1998: 97)

Critical discussion

Wright's approach assumes agreed narratives for whole religions and philosophies, what he calls the '... various public linguistic traditions that seek to account for the ultimate nature of reality' (1996a: 174). Given his attention to the formation of modernity and its intellectual background in the European Enlightenment, it is surprising that he does not discuss the construction of these 'wholes' during that period. I have alluded to this in Chapter 1, and have written about it in more detail elsewhere (Jackson 1996a; 1997: Chapter 3), pointing out that there is a considerable literature on the reification of religions as systems of belief in the contexts of the rise of rationalism and of cultural encounter through colonial expansion, especially during the eighteenth century (e.g. Fitzgerald 1990; Halbfass 1988; Marshall 1970; Oberoi 1994; Said 1978), or, in the case of Africa, the European denial and containment of African religion (Chidester 1992, 1996a, 1996b, 1999). Little attention is given by Wright to contested representations within traditions or to disputed borders. To use a linguistic metaphor, Wright does not pay much attention to the range of dialects and sub-dialects, and none to creole dialects and even elements of bilingualism (e.g. Geaves 1998 or Nesbitt 1991, which examines caste specific congregational practice showing the indeterminacy of boundaries between Sikh and Hindu traditions and identities). In this respect, Wright provides a new linguistic version of nineteenth- and early twentieth-century comparative religion, in which religions are compared as separate whole narratives. Wright's approach is much more even-handed than the kind of comparative religion that assumed the truth of Christianity and compared other religions unfavourably with it. However, in trying to provide 'standard', homogenized religious languages, Wright reifies the religions (or particular strands within them) as clearly separate and distinct 'systems'. Perhaps, in his desire to give the doctrinal formulations of Trinitarian Christianity a fair hearing, he is imposing an equivalent systematic structure on other traditions. In Wright's version of the religions, the fuzzy edges of real life are trimmed off, and the personal syntheses and multiple allegiances revealed by ethnographic study (e.g. Jackson and Nesbitt 1993) are interpreted as deviations from doctrinally pristine religious narratives. Thus he writes (partly in relation to our work at Warwick):

> A growing number of ethnological studies stress the particularity of children's assimilation of their primary religious culture, pointing out how the 'pure' version of a religious tradition is rarely, if ever, embraced in its entirety by religious adherents. How far does such empirical research open up the possibility of the inference that, because of this, the traditional religious systems do not actually exist, merely individuals who utilise a similar set of religious symbolism? Such an inference rests on the reductionist fallacy, that the whole, because it cannot be perceived in any uncontaminated form, is merely the sum of its parts; a fallacy central to postmodernity.
>
> (Wright 1996b: 22)

One does not have to be a postmodernist anti-realist to point out that an individual may (and often does) have a set of personal beliefs and values shaped by experience and through interaction with others (including groups such as sects or denominations) and yet relating to some wider narrative. That personal or group narrative may, nevertheless, include beliefs that are true or false. It seems likely that, in his desire to place students within a neat schematic framework of spirituality, with its clear and distinct 'pure' models, Wright filters out idiosyncrasy and hybridity, as well as playing down differences that are group tied. With regard to the latter, among children from Christian families who were involved in a research project at Warwick (Jackson and Nesbitt 1992),[1] there were both similarities and quite striking differences in children's perception of Christianity.[2] Baptism and holy communion were factors in the children's experience and understanding of their congregations' priorities. This was true even for the Salvation Army and the Religious Society of Friends, groups in which children learned to define themselves partly by reference to their denominations' omission of these rites. Yet with regard to holy communion, there were differences in nomenclature, emphasis, atmosphere and detail across the groups studied. In talking about the Christian tradition, children tended to use the idiom and vocabulary of denominations or sub-traditions to which they and their families belonged, using in-group terminology, such as 'junior soldier', the 'dedication' of infants and 'meeting for worship'. Group language was also used to describe religious experiences such as 'asking Jesus into their life' or 'having a vision'.

All the case-study children said that they believed in the existence of God, some picturing God in a human form, with others understanding

God to be 'spirit', regarded as powerful, incorporeal and formless. Their evident realism coheres with that observed by Ipgrave in her school based research on children from different backgrounds (Ipgrave 2001, 2002, 2003). However, while belief in God, Jesus and the authority of the Bible was common to all groups, belief in the Holy Spirit was much more varied. Most children did not refer to the Holy Spirit unless they were prompted, and the most explicit references came from three Jamaican Pentecostals who mentioned speaking and singing in tongues as evidence of 'being filled'. One girl belonging to a 'New church' spoke of 'gifts of the Spirit', especially speaking with tongues, done more at home than at church.

With regard to belief in saints and angels, the Roman and Ukrainian Catholics mentioned their existence while the Orthodox reported their activity in the present. The latter's literal belief in the current activity of angels perhaps had more in common with the beliefs expressed by Julia Ipgrave's Muslim interviewees than with many of the Christian children in our study (Ipgrave 1999). Belief in the devil, while not general, united children from the Orthodox and Pentecostal, Charismatic and Evangelical congregations.

With regard to examples of hybridity and idiosyncrasy, the most striking case was in relation to beliefs about life after death. More than in any other subject, children revealed the way in which they sifted different beliefs and arrived at individual conclusions. Some children held different ideas concurrently, rejecting or adopting beliefs as their own in the light of personal experience (such as the death of a grandparent) or the teaching of their parents and churches (Nesbitt 1993b).

One wonders how Wright would classify these children or those British Anglican Christian children whose belief in reincarnation is documented in Leslie Francis's research (Francis 1984: 75). With regard to the latter, would Wright help them to understand that their belief was perhaps (though not necessarily) a synthesis of Indian and Christian ideas, or would he feel a duty to wean them off unorthodoxy?[3] Perhaps Wright is simply using conceptual overviews of religions as a rough framework, a tool to help children to see the relationship between their own 'dialects' and other related viewpoints, but his reference to 'pure' religions suggests otherwise (Wright 1996b: 22).

The internal plurality of religious traditions, and the diversity of discourse within them, is recognized even by some theologically conservative empirical researchers. For example, in his discussion of the insider/outsider issue in relation to the empirical study of religions, Martin Stringer writes of his faith as a traditional Catholic being an obstacle to understanding Quaker theology of 'God within', even though the two theologies are located within the same broad tradition. For Stringer, God is always 'out there', and he feels that his own position overlaps more with elements from other religious traditions that emphasize the 'exterior' character of the divine. Similarly, Stringer's traditional view of the 'power' of the Latin mass – as having great religious significance even to those who could not understand its language – helped him understand similar positions within other traditions, such as the *gongyo* rituals in Soka Gakkai Buddhism. Here it appears that the understanding of the texts used in the rituals by participants does not matter. It is the attendance at the rituals that is of key importance. In reflecting on discussions at a conference on the insider/outsider debate, Stringer writes:

> I have no difficulties with the stance of the Soka Gakkai Buddhists. I can understand their position and can make sense of their ritual, as I attend a Catholic Church in which the liturgy is still celebrated primarily in Latin. Other participants at the conference, however, found the whole idea of attending a rite conducted in a language that they did not understand utterly incomprehensible. These particular participants were themselves committed members of their own faith tradition, primarily Christian and including a number of Quakers. The Muslim participants on the other hand, as well as those of no specific faith, who had studied Buddhist and other rituals, tended to side with the Soka Gakkai and myself.
>
> (Stringer 2002: 10)

Returning to Wright's views, his critique of liberalism is flawed in the sense that he creates an unnamed generalized liberal with all the characteristics he disapproves of, and proceeds to attack that stance. Although there are likely to be some who occupy this position, they are very difficult to find. Although the work of, say, Michael Grimmitt, John Hull, Ninian Smart or myself differs in various ways, all would want to include both sympathetic understanding *and* critical elements in religious education, and all would want pupils to address questions of truth. None would want teachers to take an aloof and neutral stance (e.g. Grimmitt 1981; Hull 1982; Jackson 1997; Smart 1968).

A further point is the apparent heavy rationalism of the process of religious and spiritual education as Wright sees it. He seems so concerned that the expression of feeling might lead to error that the emotions do not appear to figure in classroom religious education. This is rather like being told that one must go through the discipline of learning chords in jazz before being allowed to play or sing, or having to do a course in the history of art before one's enjoyment of a picture can be authentic. For Wright, religious and spiritual education is to do with clarifying one's position, facing critical challenges to it (by thinking about its coherence and its relationship with other positions) and restating it. Any spiritual practice or exploration of emotions is regarded as potentially misleading. Emotional expression must follow intellectual clarification. Thus Wright's total framework for helping children to develop and express their position on spirituality is very much influenced by the neo-modernism he has sought to defend. There is a suspicion of the emotional as leading to simplistic answers – especially leading easily to a position that sees all spiritual experience as being fundamentally the same – either in touch with the same transcendent reality conceived in different ways, or being an expression of the deeply affective side of a universal humanness. If Wright is happy to present children with different intellectual positions and to encourage them to challenge their own positions from different stances, I cannot see why he should be so concerned not to do this with the affective dimension. One does not have to adopt a strongly relativistic postmodern position in order to see the emotions as crucial to religious and spiritual education, as the work of Anne Krisman (discussed in the next chapter) illustrates. This is an area that has been neglected in the field of RE, although writers in both religious and moral education have recognized its importance, for example John Wilson (1971) and to some extent Harold Loukes (1961, 1973). Wright's concern is understandable, for a teacher wishing to propagate a particular view might seek to manipulate children's emotions. Moreover, particular resources encouraging an emotional, experiential response might seek to promote a particular view. However, it was this kind of fear that led some to advocate the purely descriptive form of religious education that Wright rejects in favour of exposing the young to a variety of positions. If the starting point is children's personal narratives, then we have to accept that there will be a strong emotional dimension to them that is just as important to explore as any other dimension. To be fair, Wright has responded recently to the criticism that his approach is too rationalistic, pointing out that his method involves not only a quest for knowledge and truth, but also the search for wisdom. The hermeneutical nature of his approach, argues Wright, collapses 'the established distinction between "learning from" and "learning about" religion, thereby enabling religious understanding to become simultaneously academic and personal' (Wright 2003: 284). Thus, 'When taught effectively the academic study of religion should not be a passionless affair, since it engages with fundamental existential concerns of immediate relevance to us all' (Wright 2003: 288).

Finally, despite Wright's move towards the classroom, it is hard to see his approach working over all the years of schooling. The approach appears to be demandingly academic. His own experience is very much in secondary education, and it is difficult to imagine his project working with younger children or with less able young people (see the discussion of Krisman's work in Chapter 6 below).

Moreover, despite his assurance that children should not be coerced and should feel secure, there will be young people who do not feel psychologically ready to face the tensions involved in resolving inconsistent intellectual positions. It would be instructive to see the results of a project in which Wright collaborated with primary and secondary teachers so that they could develop strategies to adapt his ideas to particular situations. The work of Susanna Hookway, a secondary teacher who has developed an approach influenced by Wright's ideas, suggests that such a project could be very fruitful (Hookway 2002).

Conclusion

I have made a number of criticisms of the religious literacy approach as advanced by Andrew Wright. These cover his tendency to reify religions, his attack on a generalized liberalism in RE, his insufficiency of attention to emotional elements in religion and the feeling of distance from the classroom (especially in relation to young or less able pupils) that comes across in some of his writing.

Having made some critical remarks, I should emphasize that there are many strengths to the religious literacy approach, one of which is its inclusiveness. Wright reminds us that the conversation of religious education should involve everyone and should embrace plurality. No one should be marginalized from the subject because their position is conservative or radical, secular or religious, and no methodology for the subject should take any stance that suppresses conversation between students holding different views or forecloses debates. His ability to combine such a view with a strong personal religious commitment is a powerful antidote to the type of 'confessional' view advanced by Thompson (Chapter 2 above). Importantly, he also reinforces the centrality of language as an issue in religious education and rightly insists on the application of critical skills to data from religions as an essential element of the subject.

Chapter 6

Interpretive approaches to religious education

This chapter presents a further response to the modernity/postmodernity debate as it figures in religious education, especially in publicly funded schools of democracies. The approach rejects the idea that it should be the common school's goal to induct children into a particular religious world-view, whilst at the same time being critical of other approaches that seem to lock children into a particular epistemological stance. The aim is, rather, to help children and young people to find their own positions within the key debates about religious plurality. In this sense, it has some key features in common with Andrew Wright's view of religious education as religious literacy. Unlike Wright's position, however, the approach recognizes the inner diversity, fuzzy edgedness and contested nature of religious traditions as well as the complexity of cultural expression and change from social and individual perspectives. The approach was outlined in my book *Religious Education: An Interpretive Approach* (Jackson 1997), and draws on methodological ideas and debates from ethnographic research. The approach was illustrated through a curriculum project, the Warwick RE Project. In the present chapter, the approach is discussed in relation to religious education pedagogy more generally and is not tied to the use of school books. It is essentially an approach to understanding the ways of life of others and is intended as a complement to other aspects of religious education, such as the application of philosophical techniques or thinking skills to RE or the use of the arts in religious or spiritual education. The interpretive approach has been applied to RE practice by a number of teachers and researchers and has sometimes been combined with other methods. Examples of these will be discussed below.[1]

Following some comments on the view of religious education advanced in *Religious Education: An Interpretive Approach*, the chapter introduces a suggestion as to how the approach could be developed in order to introduce a historical dimension, and goes on to discuss four case studies of recent and current research and development in religious education that give further insights into various aspects of the interpretive process.

An interpretive approach to religious education

In *Religious Education: An Interpretive Approach*, I argued that if religious education at least includes understanding the religious worldviews of others, then a range of issues about the representation of religious material and methods for interpreting them need to be addressed (Jackson 1997). In particular, I pointed to the dangers of representing religious worldviews as bounded systems of belief and proposed a more personal and flexible model allowing for the uniqueness of each person, while giving due attention to the various influences which help to shape any individual's sense of personal and social identity.[2]

I also developed some methods for interpreting religious material, especially drawing on insights from various strands of social anthropology. Rather than expecting students to set aside their own presuppositions when studying other positions (as required in many phenomenological approaches), these methods made direct use of their concepts and past experiences. Since interpretation involves the learner in comparing currently understood concepts with those of others, the student's own perspective is an essential part of the learning process. This matter is very important from the point of view of teaching, since educators need to be sensitive to students' own positions in devising strategies for teaching and learning about the worldviews of others.

Finally I also discussed various elements of reflexivity, broadly understood to refer to different aspects of the relationship between the experience of students (or researchers) and the experience of those whose way of life they are attempting to interpret. I have drawn attention to three aspects of reflexivity:

- learners re-assessing their understanding of their *own* way of life (being 'edified' through reflecting on another's way of life).
- making a constructive critique of the material studied at a distance.
- developing a running critique of the interpretive process – being methodologically self-critical (Jackson 2000b).

These points too have implications for pedagogy. There needs to be an approach to teaching that encourages reflection and constructive criticism and which sets out to equip pupils to make their own judgements about religious claims. As with dialogical approaches (see Chapter 7 below), the more the teacher is aware of the religious and ideological backgrounds of students, the more sensitive and focused the teaching can be, whether it be through discussion or the setting of activities. The pedagogy for this approach to religious education also requires methods that allow students to gain insight from their peers and to be able to examine different ideas of truth held within the classroom. The 'content' of RE is not simply data provided by the teacher, but includes the knowledge and experience of the participants and an interactive relationship between the two. The specialist religious education teacher, working with children from diverse backgrounds, needs the professional skill to manage learning that is dialectical. If teachers can have the right degree of sensitivity towards their students' own positions, as well as to the material studied, and can develop appropriate pedagogies, then a genuinely conversational form of RE can take place which can handle diversity.

'Insiders' and 'outsiders'

The issues of representation, interpretation and reflexivity are closely related. Edward Said's seminal work on *Orientalism* (1978), for example, provides a historical dimension, showing how aspects of Islam were constructed and represented stereotypically by Europeans in their own interests. For Said, Orientalist interpretations are to do both with self-definition and with giving stereotyped portraits of the 'other'. A major fault with such interpretations was their lack of *self*-criticism, leading to an institutionalized view of knowledge, reflected in literature of various kinds and perpetuated through the influence of such established texts on future writing. Thus, for example, various stereotypes of Islam or representations of 'Hinduism' have been perpetuated in some Western literature.

Clearly, one's position on interpretation depends on where one stands in relation to the debate about the relationship between insiders and outsiders in the study of religions and cultures. At one extreme, there are those who see religions and cultures as organic 'entities', changing over time, but maintaining a bedrock of core values and beliefs, and having distinct boundaries (e.g. McIntyre 1978). Here the distinction between insider and outsider is clear and sharp. At the other extreme, there are those who would make a case for the complete deconstruction of religion(s) and cultures. The focus is solely on individuals and their personal narratives. Vincent Crapanzano's study of a Moroccan Muslim tilemaker (1980), for example, concentrates on the connections made between aspects of his subject's psychological life and theoretical material from modern European cultural studies, setting aside the broader religious and cultural context of Morocco. This work has been criticized for saying more about its author than about Tuhami, the subject of the book (Geertz 1988: 95). In the field of religious education, the work of Clive and Jane Erricker deconstructs religions and cultures, conflating religious, cultural, moral, emotional and other aspects of affective education (Erricker and Erricker 2000a, 2000b and Chapter 4 above). In the case of both 'religions' and 'cultures' I would argue for a middle way. The European Enlightenment view of 'religions' as clearly distinct and internally consistent belief systems should be abandoned in favour of a much looser portrayal of religious traditions and groupings, variously delimited and politically contested by different practitioners and non-practitioners, and in which some individuals may locate themselves or be located by others. Individuals they are, but they need to be seen in relation to a range of contextual group influences, some of which may be outside the religious tradition (Jackson 1997: Chapter 3).

Similarly, individuals might be seen as part of a cultural tradition, in the sense that they maintain or modify certain practices (perhaps in a climate of contest or conflict). However, they also may utilize a range of cultural resources available to them from a variety of locations. This is especially so if they live in plural and globalized societies where they may experience complex interactions and mutual influences with others, as well as being open to influence from the media and the internet. With this position, no single metaphor is capable of capturing the complexity of cultural experience. The categories of 'insider' and 'outsider' are hard to apply with consistency. There may be some areas where religious and/or cultural, social, political and gender experience overlap and thus are shared, but others where a distinction between insider and outsider is clearer. Moreover, the social context in which an interview is conducted or a conversation is held determines to some extent which elements of a person's identity are in the foreground.

In late modern pluralistic societies, individuals might identify with aspects of a cultural tradition, argue with other aspects and also draw creatively on new resources in reshaping their own cultural identities. We have already noted that Gerd Baumann's research demonstrates that much cultural reshaping and creativity takes place when people of different backgrounds interact at sites of mutual or overlapping interest (Baumann 1996; see also Chapter 8 below). As well as seeing a person as part of a continuing, yet contested cultural tradition (Clifford 1986; Said 1978), it is *also* possible to observe that person drawing on and being creative with new cultural material. What are of particular interest are the processes of cultural change, and the influence of context on cultural expression.

To make this outline of a middle position more concrete, Eleanor Nesbitt's longitudinal study of young British Hindus reveals some very different individuals having a sense of 'being Hindu' as an important part of their personal and social identity, and yet drawing eclectically (and in their own different ways) on religio-cultural material outside as well as within Hindu tradition (e.g. Nesbitt 1998a, 2001). One young woman, 'Mina', interviewed at ages 12 (when a school girl) and 21 (when a psychology student), drew on her family and personal experience as a devotee of Sathya Sai Baba as well as on sources such as Western music in developing her own exploratory spirituality. This young woman, at 21, still connected with her experience of Hindu *bhakti* tradition, especially through meditative practice. She also maintained a strong social concern, consistent with Sathya Sai Baba's teaching. However, she had abandoned ritual practices that she followed as a 12-year-old in the context of family life, preferring the expression of a theistic spirituality rather than what she regarded as the practice of a religion.

The identities of Nesbitt's interviewees emerge as complex, utilizing a range of elements, yet well integrated.[3] They relate to each other through a common sense of connectedness with Hindu tradition (and thereby display a family resemblance). However, in some ways, the young people are very different from each other. Interestingly, Nesbitt's own experience as a member of the Society of Friends, with a strong interest in the spiritual quest, especially 'overlapped' at some points with that of 'Mina', facilitating the interpretive process. The encounter affected both of them (Nesbitt 2001).

Julia Ipgrave's classsroom-based research with primary school children also challenges the insider/outsider distinction. Rather than conveying an 'insider' perspective to an 'outsider' researcher, the act of communication engaged both researcher and researched in a process of mutual understanding. Children's perceptions resulted from a *negotiation* between their own understanding and the researcher's presence. As Ipgrave remarks, 'In this process the clear distinctions between "self" and "other", "insider" and "outsider" break down. In their place is a more dialogical and constructive paradigm of research'. As with the previous example, the context of increasing globalization also placed researched and researcher in a dynamic interaction between many ways of life (Ipgrave 2002: 33).

So far I have pointed to the dangers of reifying religions and cultures, yet defended the usage of the terms with certain caveats and in particular contexts. I have also pleaded for a high degree of flexibility in portraying the individual as part of religious or cultural space, and for using a range of metaphors to portray religious or cultural identity. I have further presented both qualitative research and classroom learning as circular, interpretive processes, involving comparison and contrast of concepts and experiences, personal reflection and self-criticism with regard to method. All these processes can contribute significantly to students' on-going exploration of their own identities in relation to wider social structures (Skeie 1995, 2002).

Experimental curriculum development

Many of the above points were used in a curriculum development project, the Warwick RE Project (WREP), in which a team of writers and researchers attempted to apply them in the production of texts for use by children aged 5–13 (Barratt 1994a, 1994b, 1994c, 1994d, 1994e; Barratt and Price 1996a, 1996b; Everington 1996b, 1996c; Jackson *et al.* 1994; Mercier 1996; Robson 1995; Wayne *et al.* 1996).[4] In designing experimental curriculum materials to help teachers and pupils to use this approach, the WREP team drew on ethnographic research on children related to different religious communities and groups in Britain, and on theory from the social sciences, literary criticism, religious studies and other sources (Jackson 1997: Chapter 5). The intention was to provide a methodology that was epistemologically open and, within the limits of using books as learning resources, conversational in tone. The framework for teaching and learning encouraged sensitive and skilful interpretation, opportunities for constructive criticism (including pupils' reflections on their own use of interpretive methods), and reflection by students on what they had studied. Of course, the materials had the inherent disadvantages of the textbook format. There could be no *actual* dialogue between learners and those portrayed in the books, therefore there could be no genuine negotiation of meaning. Moreover, ethnographic material, however well chosen, cannot offer more than snapshots of past experience. All ethnographies are therefore close in form to historical texts or biographies rather than presenting opportunities for live encounter. Understood in this way, the texts nevertheless have value in portraying individual children and young people in religious contexts and in reporting some of their activities and commitments.

Introducing a historical dimension

The Dutch philosopher of education, Wilna Meijer, has recently suggested how the interpretive approach might be augmented in order to introduce a historical dimension (Meijer 2004 (in press)). Whilst approving of the approach in general, Meijer points out that the three level model of individual, group and tradition as expounded in *Religious Education: An*

Interpretive Approach (Jackson 1997) does not make full use of the idea of 'tradition'. What can be added is a discussion of pupils themselves as part of tradition(s) in relation to their own pasts and futures.

Meijer uses the term 'tradition' in a general way, not employing it (as in Jackson 1997) as a technical term specifically in relation to religion. For Meijer, one's tradition includes those assumptions, values and prejudices that arise from one's personal and social history. On this definition, one's tradition may well include assumptions about religion. One of Meijer's concerns is to find ways of helping students to uncover the preconceptions they derive from 'tradition'. This is seen as a key element of reflexive learning, vital to understanding and dealing with 'difference', in religious education or intercultural education, for example. In discussing this view of tradition, she draws on the work of two writers from the hermeneutical tradition, the German philosopher Hans-Georg Gadamer and the French philosopher and critic Paul Ricoeur. Meijer refers specifically to Gadamer's book *Truth and Method* (Gadamer 1975) and volume 3 of Ricoeur's work *Time and Narrative* (Ricoeur 1988). Essentially, Gadamer argues that the study of something radically different – in cultural terms, for example – helps learners to identify their own preconceptions or prejudices, derived from their own 'tradition'. Gadamer points out that preconceptions are in our eyes, not in front of our eyes. We can only identify (and perhaps correct) them indirectly – in grasping how they contribute to our understanding or misunderstanding of something. For Gadamer, preconceptions cannot be known directly. They can only be recovered through the experience of negativity – being alert to and concentrating on the strange and unfamiliar. This process uncovers previously unasked questions. Meijer thus argues that an important element in the study of the unfamiliar is reflection upon one's own responses to it. This can both reveal a good deal about the learner's assumptions, and open up the possibility of change. The process is close to what I have described as 'edification' (Jackson 1997: 130–1).

Meijer also identifies two key concepts from Paul Ricoeur's work in *Time and Narrative* (Ricoeur 1988). These are temporality and historicality. Temporality is an awareness characterized by anticipation of the future. When we look forward and make plans, in a sense, we bring the future into the present. In contrast, historicality is the recovery of the past through reflection. Through this process we can discover something about our own identities. Reflection allows the possibility of new interpretations of the past and can reveal new potentialities for the future. The creative application of these ideas from Ricoeur to pedagogy in religious education might help young people who have been cut off from their past traditions, or are at odds with them, to reinterpret them or to see them in new ways. New pedagogical strategies developed from Meijer's readings of Gadamer and Ricoeur might help those children, researched by Linda Rudge, who could not make personal contact with any background tradition (Rudge 1998).

Interpretive pedagogies

What follows are brief accounts of some developments of the interpretive approach, one dealing with a textbook, the others covering research and development in classrooms. All illustrate religious education's contribution to the discussion of issues relating to identity. Religious education is seen as a forum for discussion where children and young people can be encouraged to engage critically but sensitively in key debates about religion and culture that help them to clarify their own sense of identity. Although the pedagogies described here have dialogical elements, some cognate approaches concentrating on processes of face to face dialogue in the classroom are discussed in the next chapter.

The four variants on the interpretive approach discussed below are complementary to the work of the Warwick RE Project. Two are related to developments that have taken place under the auspices of the Warwick Religions and Education Research Unit in England (the work of Krisman and O'Grady). The others are from colleagues in South Africa (Stonier, Kwenda and Mndende) and Sweden (Eriksson). Each case study has its own emphasis and methodology, but all have in common the view that religious education should both promote an understanding of religious material and help students to develop their own views and insights.

The first is an example of a pedagogical stance developed in response to an issue about the representation of African Religion in post apartheid South Africa. The second is from the work of a teacher of religious education in a special school in London, England.[5] The third is an example of starting religious education from a consideration of values and issues considered important by a group of Swedish secondary school students. The fourth is an example of research in an English secondary school that combines the interpretive approach with action research methods.

As well as illustrating variations on the interpretive approach, each case study illustrates a different approach to research and development in religious education. As will be discussed in Chapter 9, which focuses on research in RE, there has been a debate in Britain about educational research since around the mid-1990s. The key underlying question was whether or not such research offers information and ideas directly relevant to the improvement of practice in schools in order to raise the quality of learning and teaching (Tooley and Darby 1998; Hargreaves 1996; Hillage et al. 1998).

All the cases discussed below have in common some clear insights relevant to educational practice. The research and development activities all have practical and transferable methods that could be utilized in different international settings.

Each case study involves writers who take different roles. Stonier, Kwenda and Mndende are *academics with an interest in applying insights from religious studies to religious education*, in the context of a rapidly changing social and political climate in which social justice is high on the agenda. Krisman is a *reflective practitioner*. She does not engage in empirical research as such, but her writing consists of reflections on her practice and on the processes involved in linking material from religious traditions to the experience and questions of her pupils in a special school. Eriksson, a former teacher turned teacher-trainer, has the role of *researcher as teacher*. His research takes him into the school in order to use his teaching as a means to collect research data on students' values. O'Grady takes the role of *teacher as researcher*. He sets out to discover elements that were most significant in a Year 8 (aged 12–13) class's interpretation of religious education. He is especially concerned with identifying the factors which pupils saw as motivating and engaging.

The oral and the written: text as a chorus of voices

The first example of an interpretive approach comes from the Institute for Comparative Religion in Southern Africa (ICRSA), based at the University of Cape Town. Here there is an engagement with the politics of representation, through attempting to counter the colonialist suppression and containment of African Religion. There is also an attempt to bridge the experience of home and school culture of Black African students by affirming the value of oracy as a means of communication and oral tradition as a valid source of knowledge. Paradoxically, these values are encouraged through the medium of a particular style of textbook.

Religious education in South Africa

In South Africa, between 1948 and 1994, when the new democratic government was elected, a Biblically oriented Christian National Education reinforced apartheid divisions and encouraged the construction of particular racial and ethnic identities. African religious traditions were denied the category of religion and derided. Children classified as Indian were given separate moral instruction, intended to defuse tension between Hindu,

Muslim and Christian groups, but actually reinforcing other social boundaries (Steyn 2003; Stonier 1999).

In preparation for a new policy that fairly reflects South Africa's cultural and religious diversity, educators have been debating the kind of religious education that is appropriate in South Africa's publicly funded schools (Chidester 2003b; Chidester *et al.* 1992; Du Toit and Kruger 1998; Ferguson 1999; Mitchell *et al.* 1993; Roux 2000; Stonier 1999).

Representing African Religion

A particular issue has been how to represent and teach African Religion, both to Black and to other students, in a context where pupils and teachers alike have been taught to downgrade knowledge from traditional African sources. Scholars from the field of religious studies have worked on the history of the representation of African Religion, showing how, in the seventeenth and eighteenth centuries, it was denied by European observers and, in effect, defined out of existence (e.g. Chidester 1992, 1996a, 1996b, 1999). The European denial of African Religion continued into the nineteenth century. When religion *was* recognized (as with J.C. Warner's 'discovery' of the religion of the amaXhosa in the 1850s), it was deemed to fulfil the functions of security and stability, duplicating the aims of the colonial administration, and becoming a strategy for colonial containment (Chidester 1996a: 73–115). As Chidester points out, the strategies of denial and containment were perpetuated in much twentieth-century literature on African Religion (Chidester 1999).

Chidester's colleagues at the Institute for Comparative Religion in Southern Africa (ICRSA) have taken account of this historical work in experimenting with approaches to African Religion for schools that attempt to provide sound methods for its portrayal. In particular, Janet Stonier, Chirevo Kwenda and Nokuzola Mndende have attempted to write a text for students which deals both with issues of representation and interpretation. The text, *African Religion and Culture Alive!* (Kwenda *et al.* 1997) attempts to deal with African Religion as an *oral* tradition, with knowledge presented through myth, biographical and autobiographical stories, discussion, question and comment. The book, aimed at the upper secondary age range (16–18), is based on an edited transcript of audio-taped oral interchanges between the three authors (two South African women, one Black and one White, and a Black Zimbabwean man). Using a simulated, dramatized format, the book provides a context for using teaching and learning strategies employed in an oral tradition, but within the Western institution of the school.

We hoped in this way to mirror and mediate a situation in which many South African students find themselves: at the interface between a home underpinned by an oral tradition, and a school underpinned by a written tradition.

(Stonier 1996: ii)

In order to produce a text that the authors hoped would be acceptable to different varieties of African religious practice, and to encourage the collection of oral traditions, they included a primary research component. This requires students to seek out traditional elders within their communities and to collect material on the details of particular practices.

The production of the text was itself a creative exercise, using Stonier's skills as a curriculum developer, Mndende's as a teacher and practitioner of African Religion and Kwenda's as both a university lecturer in African Religion and as a Shona Chief. The fact that Kwenda's personal experience of African Religion was outside South Africa was regarded as an advantage, since the possibility of bias in favour of any particular South African tradition was minimized. In producing the text, Stonier and Mndende played the role of first year university students taking a course on African Religion, and Kwenda that of 'professor'. The format of the text was a series of unrehearsed question/answer sessions between the students and the 'professor', which were audio-taped and transcribed. Final amendments and refinements were also based on oral contributions. Thus the text utilized traditional African ways of learning, teaching and knowing within the context of a Western university. The choice of using autobiographical material as part of the interaction within a simulation was influenced by Karen McCarthy Brown's ethnographical study of 'Mama Lola', a Vodou priestess (Brown 1991). Brown describes her own book as a 'chorus of voices' – autobiographical, biographical, fictional and theoretical – and this polyphony is echoed in *African Religion and Culture Alive!* and in the voices of the elders via students' research.

Inevitably, the negotiations undertaken in the production of the text result in some unresolved tensions. For example, in compensating for the assumptions of the Bantustan policy of the Nationalist government (1948–94) that deliberately separated South Africans into 'own nations', regarded as synonymous with language-based cultures, there is sometimes a tendency in the responses from the 'professor' to present a generic 'Africanness'. However, the book includes field research as a key element for students and builds in the opportunity for acknowledging and re-valuing diverse oral traditions at the local level. This project may not be the last word on representing African traditions and on taking account of the family traditions of students. However, the book is South African religious education's first creative experiment in facing issues of the representation and interpretation of African Religion in a society adjusting to massive political and social change. It will provide much food for thought for future researchers and curriculum developers.

Responding to religion: speaking from the heart

The second example is from the work of Anne Krisman, a teacher in a secondary school for young people with moderate learning difficulties in Greater London, England. Krisman's main text is a reflective account of her experience of teaching religious education and was written during a Teacher-Fellowship at the University of Warwick (Krisman 1997; see also Krisman 1999).

Religious education in the special school

All the pupils in Krisman's class had problems reading and writing and several had speech and communication difficulties. Personal experiences of physical disability and illness, surgical operations and bereavement were common. The class included young people from a variety of ethnic backgrounds, many of them from families with a religious affiliation. As Ursula McKenna points out, some writers and syllabuses see special needs pupils as concrete thinkers, whose work in religious education can be based on materials prepared for younger pupils in mainstream schools (McKenna 2002). Krisman takes a different view, having become aware that her pupils' history of difficulty and struggle helped them to relate to and understand some of the deeper spiritual themes of the subject more than many more able and physically well young people. Her pupils' awareness of themselves as having distinctive needs shaped their personal understanding, both of religions and human experience. Krisman tells of Harry, for example, who was drawn to Buddhism through his personal experience of suffering and his association of Buddhist traditions with calmness. Krisman remarks:

> Mainstream pupils may be able to read about religious figures who renounce wealth for spiritual gain, but these messages might be contradicted as soon as they reach their Business Studies lesson. Harry has a deep belief, based on his experience of ill-health, in the importance of family and love beyond wealth. When asked to list his needs in life, he wrote 'Parents who love you', 'a home' and 'warmth'. He says, with

conviction, 'If I win the lottery, I would give half to the Royal Free [Hospital] and half to Great Ormond Street Hospital … because they have done so much for me in my past and in my future'.

(Krisman 1997: 11)

Adapting the interpretive approach

Krisman adapted the interpretive approach to meet the needs of her pupils. In particular, she found that the concentration on a study of *individuals* aroused their personal interest far more than attempts to deal with a body of knowledge about religions. Children could move from a personal story to a universal issue or fundamental human question, however much they struggled with written (and sometimes oral) language.

Krisman made use of a number of points from our work at Warwick. She took the idea of using pupils' previous knowledge and experience to make comparisons with the views being studied, seeing RE as 'two-way', with the pupils' knowledge and insight contributing to new understanding and the understanding of something new sometimes 'edifying' the student. Pupils might struggle in giving clear *overviews* of religious traditions, but they could connect their own concepts and experience with those of others, often identifying concepts that went to the heart of the tradition. She remarks that her special school pupils frequently had a sensitivity towards the 'organic, personal and changing' nature of religion (Jackson 1997: 47), because they were fascinated with the way in which real people lead their lives. They were drawn to the lives of religious figures 'that have an echo in their experience'. They were therefore more interested in the ways in which individuals practise religion than in a list of facts about faiths.

> Children in a special school will often have difficulties in coping with a mass of information. However, this will lead them to draw heavily on their inner resources, and to use the messages from their own lives to understand religion. This emphasis on knowledge coming from within, will often lead to them developing a questioning approach and a philosophy of life. Therefore, the special school child's sensitivity to feelings, which leads to an engagement with the meaning of symbols for individuals, can promote a deeper understanding of religious tradition than a dry historical overview or an over-emphasis on facts and information.
>
> (Krisman 1997: 17)

Just as the Warwick RE Project materials attempt to build conceptual bridges between pupils and those studied in the texts, Krisman used her pupils' own spiritual vocabulary to make connections with the characters she introduced, often through story and personal anecdote rather than textbook. Krisman noted that pupils often used a vocabulary that seemed to reflect their needs, using terms such as heart, soul, spirit and love with a powerful personal meaning.

> After hearing the story of Guru Nanak, who accepts a meal from a poor carpenter, Lalo, but rejects the rich merchant's feast, Kathleen said, 'The rich man had a heart of gold but the poor man had a heart of God'. In another story from the Sikh tradition, a rich merchant is presented with a needle by the Guru, to give back to him when he meets him in Heaven. Immediately the pupils' discussion moved into the language they felt secure with. 'You can't take money to Heaven, but you can take your soul', remarked one boy.
>
> (Krisman 1997: 17)

When appropriate to the meaning of the story, Krisman built the pupils' vocabulary into her own version.

> When I told the story of the woman who comes to the Buddha with her dead baby in her arms, asking him to bring the child back to life, I chose relevant words that had been used by the pupils and therefore had a significance for them: 'A woman came to the Buddha and asked him *with all her heart and soul* to bring her baby back to life again.'
>
> (Krisman 1997: 19)

Krisman notes that this seemed to heighten pupils' sympathy with the mother's plight and, in turn, to stimulate pupils' own use of symbolic vocabulary. One girl remarked, after a role-play based on the theme, 'the mother feels like part of her heart has gone; it is like having a hole in the heart'. The use of language acting as a bridge between the pupils' experience and the experience of the mother in the story, enabled a deeper understanding of the story's wider meaning – the acceptance of death and the nature of suffering.

Krisman gave status and recognition to pupils' responses by using what she called the 'Wall of Wisdom', part of a wall in the classroom where pupils' comments were displayed in speech bubbles for all to read. Kathleen's observation, 'Don't judge a book by its cover, don't judge a face by its colour' or Darren's words on racism, 'You can get up from being beaten up, but you can't get up from hurt in your heart' are typical of the comments displayed on the wall. The display of these often profound comments and questions, says Krisman, 'encourages pupils to see themselves as part of a construction of understanding in RE' (1997: 19).

Krisman's own background in the arts, her teaching skills and her own spirituality (nourished by her Jewish life and by other influences) are important ingredients of her particular approach in the classroom, but she is convinced of the transferability of her methods. Her presentations to students in training make a strong impact.

Connecting with young people's values

We now turn to a piece of Swedish school-based research conducted by Keijo[6] Eriksson on the direction and character of pupils' basic values (Eriksson 1999, 2000). The context for Eriksson's research is the Swedish national curriculum for comprehensive ('basic') schools, which includes providing pupils with opportunities for learning about and reflecting on different religions and views of life as an aid to forming their own views. Religious Studies is seen partly as a means to expand and deepen pupils' experience and to provide opportunities for reflection on religious and ethical questions (Swedish Ministry of Education and Science 1994, 1995). Eriksson is particularly interested in how religious education might connect with and spring from those issues that young people feel to be most important.

School-based research on values

Eriksson conducted his research in one secondary school over a year. The classes he taught included 30 boys and 40 girls with average academic records, all aged around 16, in their final year of compulsory schooling. The numbers were augmented sometimes through joint teaching of the whole year group. Although he had a few 'immigrant' pupils in the group he studied, most students were White, middle class and native Swedish (with nearly all the religiously affiliated ones connected to the State Church of Sweden) and they came roughly equally from urban and rural home backgrounds.

Eriksson's principal aim was to determine the central values of life held by the pupils he studied. These are defined as 'those basic goals which students consider to be essential: that is, what one strives for and aims to manifest through action' (1999: 191). Eriksson attempted to explore values with the students in a teaching environment that encouraged democratic participation, with plenty of pupil-pupil as well as pupil-teacher interaction. The starting point was written work, with students completing statements such as 'When I think about death, I think …', 'When I think about the meaning of life, I think …' and 'When I think about God, I think …'. The pupils' reflections on these topics then formed the basis of classroom discussions that were followed by more written work. Eriksson collected all the written material produced over the year as part of his data, but focused on an analysis of essays written at the end of the course by 45 volunteers in response to the title 'What is most important to you in your life?'

The data were analysed in a series of stages. First, text was categorized under headings concerned respectively with ontological statements, human relationships, society/politics and concepts of God and religion. Next, the essay material was further categorized using the question 'What do these pupils think about in this context?' In order of popularity among pupils, the following categories emerged: family, education, social concerns, leisure time, sympathy and understanding, the environment, health and keeping fit, religion, death, joy of growing up/satisfaction of making progress, peace, and security in one's social environment (Eriksson 2000: 120). Further analysis showed that students had difficulty in expressing themselves on ontological questions, their reflections being incorporated into discussions concerning individuals and their relationships, society and religion/theology.

Eriksson found some differences – especially along gender lines – but also some common themes: his respondents were supporters of family life, found education valuable, were inclined to a work ethic, and had a well-developed ability to reflect on existential questions. Moreover, their opinions encouraged action: values and a readiness to act were connected for these young people.

With regard to gender differences, thoughts about love and about secure relationships with others were expressed almost exclusively by girls, and more girls than boys reflected on the importance of solidarity with the weak, asserting a belief in the fundamental equality of all human beings. More girls than boys also wrote about religion and about death, as distinct from the care of the elderly, on which boys wrote as frequently as girls. Boys tended to write about objectivity, uncertainty in matters of faith, atheism and the supernatural. Eriksson was cautious in drawing any strong conclusions from these gender differences, noting that it was impossible to discern whether they were due to the varying capabilities in expressing themselves in writing (girls wrote more than boys and were more open about emotions) or to differences in the way they thought.

What Eriksson did conclude was that the act of writing helped young people, especially boys, to clarify and formulate their ideas, even if they struggled with the process and did not write at length. This was especially so with written work that required pupils to explain and defend their convictions and opinions. He thus recommends this type of written work, in addition to more reflective writing. Eriksson made a comparison of his own findings with earlier work done by Sven Hartman with 5–13-year-old pupils (Hartman 1986). The comparison shows that although younger and older pupils express their reflections on fundamental questions differently, the content of what they say shows many similar features.

The value of Eriksson's findings lies especially in their relevance to pedagogy in RE. His suggestions for the practitioner include:

- Recognizing the importance of encouraging pupils to reflect.
- Using knowledge about pupils' needs, cognitive skills, experiences and thoughts in planning lessons.
- Including work that requires pupils (especially boys) to write in order to explain and defend their ideas.
- Including pupils' written reflections or 'inner dialogue' in teaching material.
- Using pupils' own problems as a starting point for lessons.

Eriksson's work illustrates the efficacy of active learning methods and the positive motivational effects of using pupils' own reflections as the basis for the content of lessons. He also outlines possible ways in which the concerns of pupils can be linked to the study of material from religious traditions (Eriksson 2000: 124–5).

Involving pupils in planning RE

Kevin O'Grady's central concern was also poor motivation among secondary pupils. His research was on younger pupils than those studied by Eriksson, namely Year 8 pupils (aged 12–13) in the mainly White, urban comprehensive school where he taught. Thus, O'Grady set out to use classroom-based research to identify factors which his pupils saw as motivating and engaging (O'Grady 2003). He designed a project in which he studied a particular class over one term using ethnographic methods (participant observation, interviewing and textual analysis) together with methods derived from action research. The action research element involved pupils as participants in the research, contributing their own interests and preferences in helping plan work on Islam, keeping diaries providing fresh ideas and a running evaluation of work in progress, and responding to questions in semi-structured group interviews. The broad topic in the syllabus was Islam. The pupils used their diaries to contribute their own ideas about studying Islam that related to issues about life which interested them. Pupils were also challenged to consider how their studies could be made more challenging and more interesting than their earlier work in RE. O'Grady then analyzed the diary entries and redrafted the scheme of work to take account of the pupils' ideas. They contributed further diary entries at two points later in the term, identifying the most important things they had learned, and the most and least helpful and interesting features of lessons. O'Grady drew on these comments in modifying the redrafted scheme of work as the term progressed. A research diary was kept, recording O'Grady's observations of lessons during the term, while semi-structured interviews with small groups of pupils were audio-taped during school lunchtimes. Overall, the approach increased student motivation and participation. The first diary entry provided information on the types of activities and questions which the pupils found motivating. Creative activities such as art, creative writing and discussion of videos were listed as important, but drama was the most popular activity of all. Interestingly, the questions raised were both about Islam (Muslims, Islamic beliefs, Allah) and about the individual and society (personal and religious questions, and questions about society and the wider world). As an example of the convergence of the two interests, O'Grady cites the pupils' particular interest in Islamic dress, later confirmed as reflecting their fascination with fashion. Interests such as these were incorporated into lesson planning.

> Interpretive work on the students' attitudes to clothes, and comparison with Islamic codes, was planned; the topic as a whole was informed by the aim that Islamic material would prompt a re-assessment of students' attitudes, whether to clothes, family life, or any questions they had raised.
>
> (O'Grady 2003)

This holistic and integrated approach to learning avoided the sharp distinction between 'learning about' and 'learning from' religion made in many syllabuses. The second and third diary entries confirmed the importance pupils gave to learning about themselves as well as about Islam, as did O'Grady's own log of observations. Questions were also raised by pupils about race and ethnicity, and the opportunity was taken to explore these. Here RE made a direct contribution to intercultural and antiracist education and to education for citizenship. Other topics were dealt with in order of popularity. Interestingly, most of the elements of Islam listed in the Agreed Syllabus were covered, but not in the systematic order given in the official document.

O'Grady records examples of increased student motivation, illustrated by imaginative activities designed by the pupils themselves, including – in the instance of Islamic dress – analyzing the relationship between bullying and dress, researching Islamic dress codes and using drama to explore the ban on Muslim girls wearing 'headscarves' in French schools. O'Grady notes the maturity of the plenary discussion following the sharing of these activities.

Discussion

Each of the case studies sees religious education as a hermeneutical process. All are concerned with interpretive approaches that aim to bring together well crafted representations of religious material with a concern that students should have opportunities to engage with it at a personal level and relate it to their own experience. Each has a different emphasis. If we think of learning in religious education as an unbroken hermeneutic circle, then the case studies begin at different points on its circumference.

Stonier, Kwenda and Mndende start with the data of religion and find ways of interpreting it to students who themselves are part of the history of African Religion's denial and containment. They confront the issue of representation – both in terms of the representation of African Religion and through using the written word to capture the character of oral tradition and to raise awareness of the value of oral traditions. Although they consult historical sources on representing African Religion (notably David Chidester's work), the authors utilize Kwenda's and Mndende's personal knowledge and experience of African ways of thinking and expression in their representation of African Religion. The to-ing and fro-ing between the concepts and experiences of 'insider' and 'outsider' was here a matter of negotiation within the group, rather than between ethographer and informant (Geertz 1983).

The authors' connection with students is indirect. They design activities to develop students' skills in collecting qualitative data; these research tasks also reinforce the importance of oral traditions in the minds of students, potentially raising self-esteem, as well as providing data on the diversity of practice and myth. Perhaps their material takes insufficient account of religious and cultural fusion (a criticism that equally could be levelled at some of our Warwick RE Project materials). In wanting to restore African Religion to the consciousness of South Africans, they chose to leave aside a range of religio-cultural hybridities which synthesize African Religion with ideas and practices from other traditions, notably Christianity.

Their work is close to that of the Warwick RE Project in the sense that they begin with an issue of representation and then move to methods for interpretation. As with the curriculum developers in the Warwick RE Project, their focus was on producing material to be used by others who were not part of the development process. Extensive trialling in schools was beyond the remit and the budget of both projects.

Stonier, Kwenda and Mndende developed a creative approach to representing African Religion, carried out in an atmosphere of academic freedom. However, they were working in a society in which the politics of education is part of the history they were attempting to re-present. In the wider social context in which they work, the issue of representation is not just a matter of academic debate. In educational systems that attempt to get educators and religious bodies to *co-operate* in achieving educational aims, the representation issue becomes deeply political. Specific groups often come with ideologically charged agendas for promoting or resisting certain forms of representation. Educators need to be highly sensitive to this. Representation in educational materials becomes negotiable, provisional, and strategic. This political factor is evident in the social context of both the Cape Town and Warwick examples. The educational debates relating to the development of policy on RE in South Africa reveal that the nature and status of African Religion is still a highly contested matter (e.g. Stonier 1999). Similarly, the well-intentioned but politically expedient view that 'insiders' could define the content of their traditions, while educators provided the methodology for teaching it, resulted in the generation of essentialized and schematic versions of the 'principal religions' in Britain in national model syllabuses (SCAA 1994a, b and c). A side effect was inadvertently to marginalize alternative approaches to representation (Jackson 2000a).

Just as Stonier, Kwenda and Mndende address the denial and containment of African Religion in the cultural traditions of students, so Krisman challenges the containment of children with learning difficulties within stereotypes of 'special needs', empowering them to articulate and express their understanding and insight. Krisman moves around the circle in both directions. In order to meet the needs of her students with learning difficulties, she avoids schematic overviews of religious traditions, using vivid human stories from religious settings as a means both to give insight into the spiritual depths of the traditions and to engage her pupils personally. Thus she enables them to relate the material to their own experience and vice versa. Her identification and use of language to bridge the experience of her students and characters in her stories enhances this process. The students' own reflections and aphorisms are both creative responses *and* important data for the edification of anyone who reads them in context.

While Krisman is deeply concerned with connecting religious material to the spiritual needs of her special needs pupils, and with their creative responses, Eriksson's starting point is the affective concerns of his students.

Through a study of his students' values, he aims to develop a form of teaching which encourages them to reflect on existential questions and to provide a basis for making connections with material from wider religious and non-religious sources. His findings demonstrate the motivational force of using pupils' experiences and reflections as the first point on the hermeneutic circle. O'Grady's approach reverberates with both Krisman's and Eriksson's work. Like Eriksson, he asks pupils to identify questions and issues that are of concern to them, but (like Krisman) he introduces explicitly religious material at an early stage. O'Grady and Eriksson both involve students in planning, the selection of topics to be covered and in designing methods of working. Like Krisman, O'Grady finds that the creative arts are a powerful means to explore ideas and present findings. All three writers find that the approaches they use are motivating to pupils.

Eriksson's particular students were adolescents from a fairly homogeneous and middle class background, one with an association with a national church. O'Grady's pupils were from working class urban communities, including some areas of relative deprivation; nearly all pupils were from White and mainly secular families. Krisman's pupils were from different multi-religious social situations. It would be instructive to replicate Eriksson's and O'Grady's research in more culturally plural settings. That would raise issues of dialogue and communication between pupils from different religious and cultural situations that are introduced in the next chapter.

Although O'Grady's pupils were from a mainly White and secular background, he managed to engage them in the study of religions. A further approach has been developed in an all White, mainly secular and working class school by another teacher-researcher based at Warwick. Sarah Edwards was particularly concerned with religious education in relation to the cultural development of her pupils (Edwards 1999). Whereas O'Grady made links directly from students' concerns and interests to material from the religious traditions, Edwards utilized her own pupils' negative attitudes towards religion by making them the focus for debate in RE lessons. Through raising their awareness of cultural choices, her approach sought to challenge pupils' assumptions about religions. Her approach engages students in critical debate, potentially releasing them from confinement within static cultural identities. O'Grady and Edwards both provide practical ways to involve pupils from relatively 'monocultural' and secular backgrounds in religious education, addressing some of the concerns raised about the relevance of religious education to such children (Rudge 1998).

Perhaps Eriksson under-interprets his findings about gender. The differences he identifies certainly suggest a need for more research in this field, especially since gender difference is not covered specifically in any of the other case studies, or in the Warwick RE Project. Eriksson's findings about the discipline of writing, as a means to record personal reflections and to clarify and formulate arguments, are highly suggestive for practitioners. They resonate with Krisman's techniques for encouraging less able pupils to write, for example by transforming oral contributions into written ones and then encouraging pupils to review and edit them before inclusion in their books or display on the Wall of Wisdom.

Conclusion

The interpretive approach is not confined to the use of ethnographic methods or to the use of school books and can be developed in new directions, as with Meijer's discussion of the approach in relation to history and tradition. The four case studies introduced above illustrate how the interpretive approach can be adapted creatively to suit different classroom situations. Such approaches include the possibility that students might have their own views deepened through the study of other positions, whether outside or related to their own traditions. They also offer opportunities for pupils to apply their critical faculties skilfully and sensitively to material studied and for creative approaches to presentation.

The case studies also recognize that pupils' own religio-cultural experiences, reflections and interactions can and should be part of the subject matter of religious education. Pedagogically, the more aware teachers are of beliefs and values embedded in the experience of students, the more they can take account of pupils' concerns and can provide teaching and learning situations which are designed to foster communication between students from different backgrounds. The classroom-based case studies provide evidence that such an approach to teaching is more likely to motivate pupils to participate with enjoyment and fulfilment in RE than approaches which are less personally engaging.

The interpretive approaches outlined here are intended to provide opportunities for different religious and cultural positions to be understood in a methodologically sound and self-critical way. They also acknowledge the potentially transformative character of religious education. The various studies show that teaching and learning can begin at any point on the hermeneutic circle, with a critical overview of a representation of a religious tradition, with a study of an individual person or case study, with pupils' experiences or interactions in the school or with a concern or question from students.

Chapter 7

Dialogical approaches to religious education

The interpretive approach to religious education, discussed in Chapter 6, allows learning to *begin* at any point on the hermeneutic circle, according to need. For example, it could start with an overview of key concepts, if that suited the needs of a class, or it could start with the experiences and assumptions of class members, or with some activity designed to sensitize pupils to studying a way of life that might be very different in some ways from their own. There are thus dialogical elements in the approach – dialogue between pupils, between pupils and material studied and between pupils and teacher. In recent years, several pedagogical approaches have been developed which concentrate on dialogue in the classroom, in which the students are the starting point as well as the key resources and actors. Some approaches have emphasized co-operative learning – for example, research in Germany that experiments with bringing children of different denominational backgrounds together for RE (Schweitzer and Boschki 2004). Others, notably the Dutch researcher Carl Sterkens, have applied principles from inter-faith dialogue to religious education in a rather 'top-down' way (Sterkens 2001). Dialogue, in Sterkens' work, is not so much seen in terms of children's interactions with each other, but as their response to a multifaith curriculum. The 'dialogue' is not between child and child, but between child and teaching material designed to present the internal diversity and dynamism of religions. Sterkens argues for an inter-religious RE aimed at 'stimulating dialogue between religious "voices" with a view to establishing a religious identity in the form of a religious polyphonic self' (Sterkens 2001: 122). This identity is understood as a continuation of the children's religious history, grounded in their inherited traditions, as well as being open to constant change as a result of contact with religious diversity.

In Sterkens' research, a number of Catholic and Protestant schools took part in an experiment in which children were given a programme of 'interreligious studies' dealing with some central themes from Christianity,

Hinduism and Islam. The purpose of the research was to assess the effectiveness of an inter-religious approach to identity formation. Questionnaires were given to the children before and after the lessons and their responses were used as indicators of the influence of the teaching material on the pupils' cognitive, affective and attitudinal relationship with their own and other religious traditions. Sterkens converted questionnaire responses into qualitative data, classifying the children according to their religion or worldview, and using numerical values to indicate the changes in their responses to their own tradition (religious in-group) and other traditions (religious out-group). Pedagogically, Sterkens argues that an inter-religious curriculum supports the development of the autonomous individual by engaging pupils in a continual re-examination of life from fresh angles and enabling them to establish their own identity through dialogue with others.

In his chapter on RE, Sterkens presents a dialogical model of religion as a dynamic, changeable totality. When he uses the term 'interreligious', he is not referring to a dialogue between fixed bodies of religious ideas, norms and values but rather to the internal dynamics and internal plurality of religious traditions. However, this internal plurality and religious dynamism are not fully reflected in Sterkens' empirical research. The children were not given the opportunity to express their agency by taking their understanding of religious ideas in new directions. Rather, their responses were limited to four options in a series of multiple choice questions. In the instructions the children were told that there was only one correct answer to each question. Thus, the openness of religious dialogue was denied by the closed nature of the questions. The questionnaire tested the children's ability to absorb what they had been taught in the teaching material provided, but not their readiness to *engage* with it.

Here I shall discuss three dialogical approaches that do recognize the agency of children and young people, treating them as co-learners, co-designers of curriculum and even as co-researchers. In this regard, these dialogical approaches have much in common with interpretive approaches discussed in Chapter 6, but emphasize the child both as actor and processor of ideas from others engaged in dialogue. There are also certain features that overlap with the personal narrative approach discussed in Chapter 4, although the approaches discussed in the present chapter are not grounded in an anti-realist epistemology. The contributions discussed show a high degree of awareness of the social influences on children in family and other contexts, but also the diversity of positions that children themselves take on epistemological issues with regard to religion.

The approaches discussed here have been developed by Heid Leganger-Krogstad, initially in Alta, Norway, Wolfram Weisse and his team in

Hamburg, Germany and Julia Ipgrave in Leicester, England. These dialogical approaches were developed in specific local contexts – a highly rural situation, far from the national capital, and two rather different cosmopolitan, urban settings. In each example, however, the approach is seen as adaptable and transferable. As might be expected, dialogical approaches are not amenable to rigid syllabus requirements. Compromises have to be made in order to cover the requirements of syllabuses that prescribe a very specific 'content' (compare the discussion of O'Grady's work in Chapter 6). Leganger-Krogstad's contextual approach, for example, led her to become critical of what she sees as an overly prescriptive national syllabus introduced in Norway in 1997.

Heid Leganger-Krogstad

Leganger-Krogstad's contextual approach was developed through her research and teaching in a very particular multicultural context in northern Norway (Leganger-Krogstad 1998, 1999, 2000, 2001, 2003). Between 1980 and 1996, she was a lecturer at Finnmark University College in Alta, educating teachers mainly for work in the largest, most sparsely populated and most northerly of Norway's nineteen counties. Finnmark has had a culturally diverse population for centuries, long before new immigration made southern Norway 'multicultural'. Finnmark's population includes a mixture of people with Norwegian, Sami ('Lapp'), and Kven background, which religiously means a combination of old Sami shamanistic, animistic religion and Christianity – both the national and Laestadian varieties. The Laestadian tradition, named after Lars Levi Laestadius (1800–61), a Swedish Sami Christian minister, classicist and botanist, was a northern Scandinavian revivalist movement, combining the restoration of Sami and Finnish language and traditions with a Biblical Christianity. Thus, Leganger-Krogstad found that a national syllabus and textbooks reflecting national (urban and southern Norwegian) concerns did not meet the needs of children in a very specific cultural situation in which there was suspicion of public education. Her views about the nature of religion and education were challenged. She became convinced that the fundamental resource material for her work should be the children's own life-world and concerns in the context of local culture.

> Religion, as I experienced it through travelling all over the county visiting schools, was so different from my previous knowledge and experience that, with colleagues from our department at the university college, I had to do research to describe religion in this context. Some

did historical studies, others concentrated on contemporary life, through contextual studies. My own research was done in order to develop new approaches to education. Since this diverse culture was nearly invisible in the local curriculum, I had to look for an alternative approach to religious education, giving the local culture value and public acceptance by making it part of the syllabus.

I combined ethnographic field studies with action research, carrying out experiments together with my students. These ideas were then implemented in schools. I taught my students to deal with religion in the same way. In Alta, the municipality where I did the experiments, I also saw the need for co-operation between schools, the different religious communities and the local secular humanist organization. I initiated work with local curriculum plans and collected information to enable co-operative work in practice. This included providing information on local contacts for arranging visits to places of worship and for representatives of communities to visit schools, as well as giving background information on the religious communities and their history in Alta, including evidence of that history in the locality. The idea was to make all children familiar with religion in the local environment through visits to places of worship, meeting representatives, looking at religious artefacts and art and hearing about local religious practice and outreach. This enabled the children to report back to their classmates about local religion and culture.

(Leganger-Krogstad, personal communication, 2003)

However, Leganger-Krogstad did not see local culture in isolation, but as affected by global issues and concerns. Her experiments accepted children as participants in local cultural life, but she also taught them gradually to distance themselves from local culture and to be able to analyze it. In this respect she taught children basic ethnographic techniques for collecting and analyzing local cultural material. Local culture became a common arena for the pupil, the teacher, and the subject.

Leganger-Krogstad thus developed a contextual approach to religious education that she hopes can be taught in any location. Through interacting with each other and a variety of source materials, pupils are encouraged to see themselves in relation both to the past and the future, at various points looking 'inwards' to draw upon their own life-worlds and 'outwards' in relation to the wider society. According to need, RE moves between the children's personal experience and wider social experience and between the past (in terms of tradition and history, especially the children's own 'roots') and the future. Over time, there is a gradual broadening of children's experience as they relate their own concerns to wider cultural material, extending their horizons beyond family and locality to the region and nation and to wider European and global issues. In doing this, the RE teacher is expected to complement ethnographic skills with a range of methods, especially textual, phenomenological and philosophical techniques. Textual and phenomenological methods are used in looking backwards in time, while philosophical methods – whether existential in emphasis when reflecting on personal views and choices, or social-ethical when considering and forming views on wider social issues – are emphasized in looking towards the future.

Pupils' individual concerns and questions, raised through their first and second hand experiences, are related to wider social and cultural issues, with 'local' issues acting as a bridge. The issues of social plurality and identity raised at the theoretical level (Skeie 1995, 2002) are connected to the life-worlds of individual pupils at their own level through a practical approach to religious education (Leganger-Krogstad 2000, 2001, 2003). Leganger-Krogstad's goal is to develop what she calls metacultural awareness and competence in pupils. Drawing on the work of Skutnabb-Kangas, she sees this generic skill in handling cultural material and issues as:

> ... an understanding of the distinctiveness and relativity of one's own culture and other cultures, consciously being able to reflect over one's own and other cultures, at times distancing oneself from them and looking at them as objects. A precondition for being able to do that is at least some knowledge of other cultures with which to compare and contrast one's own.
>
> (Skutnabb-Kangas 1987: 21–3)

Children's dialogue, whether 'within' their own culture – in recognizing its internal diversity – or 'between' cultures, is seen as a key element in developing metacultural competence. Leganger-Krogstad distinguishes between the dialogue of children in the classroom and that of adults, for example, in ecumenical or inter-faith dialogue. The autonomy of children is seen as relative; they are both part of the family culture, yet can exercise some independence from it. The school is seen as affirmative of children and their backgrounds – and in this sense provides a nurturing role – but also provides space for children to interact with each other and the teacher and with wider issues and ideas. At the same time, their skills to analyze and reflect on new cultural material are developed:

Dialogue between children in the classroom is tentative and shows signs of curiosity. Children often argue on behalf of their parents, their religious community and their customs, but not always on behalf of themselves. The child in the classroom is both a part of different groups he or she identifies with and free and distant from those groups. The child has the right to pursue meaning independently …

Children at the age of 6–10 are very open-minded and it is important that they meet education that gives them both support for their own background and information about others. This means that making religion into a school subject serves both the purposes of supporting each child in his or her background and of providing orientation and insight in relation to the religious plurality in the class. This diversity is often less complex on a local level than on a national level.

(Leganger-Krogstad 1999)

In Leganger-Krogstad's scheme, religious education for children in the primary years (age 6–10) focuses on the geographical area where children live, concentrating on the exploration of similarities and differences between people who live in the locality. Thus, in the middle years (age 10–13), children begin to study different cultures, while in the upper secondary school, young people engage with religious and cultural issues at a personal level, sometimes using indirect methods of communication such as role-play and drama. In this way, young people can 'bridge' first hand and second hand experience and 'experiment' with different lifestyles at a distance. Enabling children to express and reflect on personal views without necessarily having to share them publicly is an important element in the method, and she uses various kinds of writing, role-play and drama as tools to help pupils to distance themselves from issues of personal concern.

Leganger-Krogstad now works in the Education Department of Oslo University, and applies her ideas in the context of teacher education. Her students identify features of religion in the environment of the schools where they do teaching practice. The starting point of RE is how religion is made visible in the school (through its organization, the school building, school traditions, school rules, the timetable, school subjects etc.), in the local environment and in the city more widely. Bridges are then built between this and the children's own life-worlds, in engagement with media and music, for example.

Wolfram Weisse

Weisse's dialogical approach to RE developed from his experience as an educator in Hamburg, involved in inter-religious studies, educational research and city politics. His approach essentially combines religious education and education for citizenship in a multicultural setting. The Hamburg approach is unusual in the German system in bringing children and young people from different religious and cultural backgrounds together in the same class for religious education. Most Länder (federal states) have either Protestant or Catholic religious education, with an opt-out clause allowing withdrawal on the grounds of conscience. Within this system, however, especially in Lutheran RE, there have been various experiments that show openness to children of different religious and ideological backgrounds and which have liberal educational goals. For example, a recent project on co-operative learning was referred to above (Schweitzer and Boschki 2004), and the work of researchers such as Hans-Günter Heimbrock, Heinz Streib, Peter Schreiner and Christoph Scheilke gives close attention to issues of religious and social plurality in considering approaches to religious education (e.g. Heimbrock 2001, 2004; Rüpell and Schreiner 2003; Scheilke 2001; Schreiner 2001; Streib 2001).

However, a different approach evolved in the federal state of Hamburg where RE has been taught to all pupils in an integrated way with no separation of students by denomination or religion (Weisse 1996c). Weisse and his research team have had a strong influence on the development of the subject in Hamburg, through their school-based empirical research (e.g. Knauth 1999; Leutner-Ramme 1999), their experiments with curriculum and dialogue (e.g. Weisse 1996a, 1999; Weisse and Knauth 1997) and their involvement in the politics of education and policy making (Weisse 2003).

Weisse distinguishes between 'ecumenical learning' and 'intercultural/ interreligious learning', the former being a Christian theological approach used especially in the 1970s and 1980s in Germany. His own approach, that of 'intercultural/interreligious learning', is seen as a different but comple-mentary pedagogy, with a theoretical base that is international and with Christian theology as only one of its various sources. 'Intercultural/inter-religious learning' aims at communication within multicultural societies, and uses a variety of pedagogical strategies according to context and the composition of the class. Weisse's empirical studies illustrate how teachers and pupils favour RE in which pupils of different religious and worldview backgrounds participate jointly in one class. Problems of undermining faith, relativism and threatening absoluteness of Christianity are all seen as part of the debate that should be engaged in by young people themselves. Dialogue, in this context, especially involves learning to listen to others – learning to know when to stay in the background – and goes beyond the basic demand of 'tolerance'. Weisse describes the approach as follows:

Our approach refers to an experience-orientated understanding of dialogue ... In this approach, it is the dialogue in the classroom which is important: a dialogue in which pupils can participate with their different and various religious and ideological backgrounds and during which they can form their own views and positions. Questions about the meaning of life and death as well as ethical questions about justice, peace, and the integrity of creation are covered in such lessons. While the spectrum of topics points to the many similarities between the religions, dialogue in RE is also designed to demonstrate the differences between religious traditions. Individual positions are not found by mixing different views, but by comparing and contrasting them with one another. Religious education should make dialogue in the classroom possible by allowing participants to refer to their different religious backgrounds, while not requiring differences. Dialogue in the classroom fosters respect for other religious commitments, can confirm pupils' views or help them to make their own commitments whilst also allowing them to monitor their commitments critically. This kind of religious education does not set out to mirror or even increase social divisions in the population, but rather to develop mutual understanding and respect.

(Weisse 2003: 193–4)

The socio-political justification for Weisse's view of dialogue is grounded in the kind of 'humaneness' that is embodied in declarations of human rights, such as the United Nations Charter on the Rights of Children. The theological influence comes especially from the Christian theologian Hans-Jochen Margull (1925–82) and the Jewish scholar Martin Buber. Biblical themes such as the idea that all people are children of God are also invoked. Weisse's ecumenical theology of dialogue draws especially on Margull's ideas, including the view that all religions are 'incomplete' and that genuine dialogue involves the endurance of the 'griefs' that result from the particularity of each of the religions. Dialogue, even in the classroom, can sometimes be a painful process. He also adopts Margull's view that the starting point for dialogue should be common human experience, not the similarities and differences of religions. *Personal* encounters are decisive (Weisse 1996b: 273). Another insight from Margull is that religious education should study religious and cultural life together, and should not attempt to separate these elements. For Weisse, 'living religiosity', with both its religious and cultural elements, should be the centre in a religiously and culturally plural class – not the ascription of pupils to particular religious systems. Moreover, the interactive and reflexive nature of dialogical RE is paramount. Pupils need to practise the skills of comparing and contrasting their own views with those of others, aiming to understand the others as they understand themselves. Difference must be recognized, and no particular epistemological view should be imposed on pupils. In any classroom, there will be different claims to truth which cannot be reduced simplistically to 'common ground'. There is a recognition that dialogue and encounter in school can lead to conflicts and even to temporary breaking off of relations. These experiences need to be worked through as part of religious education. Situations of unsettled differences are inevitable (Weisse 1996b: 275–6).

One way in which Weisse's version of dialogue differs from some 'world religions' approaches in England and Wales is in its emphasis on themes of social justice, peace and human rights as well as on understanding and learning from religions and the exploration of existential questions. There is an overtly political dimension: RE aims to help pupils to come to terms with various religious, ideological and political beliefs. It is also action-oriented, encouraging an 'active acceptance of responsibility towards society'. It has a central social goal – to be a means for communication and thus to encourage people to live together peacefully in the city. The general pedagogical method is dialogical and personal, with young people learning about others' positions, and clarifying their own, by comparing and contrasting their views with one another. Much responsibility is devolved to pupils to explore particular issues of concern (Weisse 1996b: 275–6, 2003).

Julia Ipgrave

Like Weisse, Julia Ipgrave's work on dialogue relates to her educational experience in a multicultural city, in this case being prompted by her experience as a primary school teacher in Leicester in a Community primary school with over 85 per cent Muslim pupils.[1] She became interested in the interactions of children from different backgrounds and she developed research on the religio-cultural and theological influence of children from her class upon one another, and their formation of new ideas through encounter (Ipgrave 2002). It was this research that stimulated her pedagogical work on dialogue.[2]

The research concentrated on the minority of non-Muslim children and was informed by small discussion groups in which these children were free to explore and share their own ideas. Ipgrave took part in conversations held in and around the time of the festival of Id ul Fitr in 1997 and 1998 during which the Muslim children were not present. Her research methodology was ethnographic, drawing on ideas and methods used in various home and community based studies of children conducted at Warwick University (e.g. Jackson and Nesbitt 1993; Jackson 1997). The research was based on work with 35 children from Years 4–6 (aged 8–11), 20 of whom self-identified as Hindu, and were of Gujarati family background, and 15 of whom self-identified as Christian, including children whose ethnic backgrounds were White and Afro-Caribbean, and whose families ranged from practising Christian, to Christian in a mainly 'cultural' sense. She developed a form of group interview in which small groups of children (a mixture of Hindu and Christian children in their year groups) took part in discussions prompted by 'word cards'. The children sat round a table on which were placed cards bearing some generic words associated with religion (e.g. 'religious') and some specific words from religions, commonly used by children in the class (e.g. Krishna, Jesus, Jah; haram, guna, Ramadan). The recorded discussion was used as source material by three Year 6 children who were selected to design questions which could then be used in further interviews and discussions. These children came up with questions around the themes of pressures of minority status within the school, religious beliefs in a context of plurality, religious, cultural and racial difference, and inter-religious and racial tension and relations within the school. The deliberations on these issues by the three children provided further data for analysis. The questions were used in further discussion groups to elicit more recorded dialogues for analysis.

Analysis of the dialogues showed that children's thinking was clearly influenced by their dealings with adults at home and at school. However, adult views presented the children with different attitudes and models of behaviour which sometimes conflicted with the evidence of their own experience. The children's experience of a religiously plural society, for example, did not always follow the model of mutual respect promoted by the school. In discussion, children revealed tensions and pressures of which teachers were often unaware.

Most of the children claimed to follow their parents' religion and to share their beliefs, yet some revealed attitudes towards religion which were different in various ways from those of their parents. Sometimes they showed a greater openness to the beliefs and religious backgrounds of their peers than the adults in their community would have done, bringing their religious identity into dialogue with other ways of believing and negotiating new meanings.

Ipgrave highlights three aspects of children's thinking evident in their dialogue. The first is the experience-led nature of their understanding. In their environment they had encountered religious plurality, and in their relationships with their peers they had experienced religious rivalry. These experiences led the children to explore religious issues. A second aspect is the rational basis of their thinking about religion. The children provided many examples of bringing together ideas in an attempt to synthesize them into a coherent whole. A third feature of much of the discussion is its underlying realism. Rather than moving towards a relativist stance in the face of a variety of belief systems and religious languages, many of the children maintained a realist view.

In analyzing children's discussions, with a view to assessing the influence of encounter on children's language and meaning, Ipgrave employed a theoretical framework based on Mikhail Bakhtin's concept of heteroglossia – the way language relates to diversity and change (Bakhtin 1981: 428). Following Bakhtin's view that 'One's own discourse is gradually and slowly wrought out of others' words that have been acknowledged and assimilated' (1981: 345), she 'tracked' the words of others in the children's discussions. Using Bakhtin's classification, she gave particular attention to the 'assimilated discourse', 'reported speech' and 'assimilated words' of the children.

Assimilated discourse

Ipgrave's analyses of children's discussions reveal how past interactions can be filtered through personal experiences, of conversation and reflection for example. Such discourses have their own language patterns using particular vocabularies and rules, and Ipgrave gives examples of how children were able to move easily from discourses on religion to diversity, power, race and equality. Children recognized different forms of diversity, associating religious identity with words such as 'Muslims', 'Christians', 'Rastafarians', with the names of places of worship ('church', 'mosque', 'gurdwara' etc.) and with particular forms of dress (topi, turbans, scarves). Similarly, racial diversity was recognized through the use of words associated with colour and ethnic origin.

Children's discourse of power was revealed through their sense of being at the receiving end of racist and teasing remarks from peers, through being reprimanded or in trouble from teachers, or being 'allowed' or punished by parents. Their discourse regarding power also was consistent with that of their parents. Their views about power, in relation to relative numbers of Muslims and non-Muslims in the school, overlapped with their parents' view of their own limited power in relation to the Muslim majority in the local neighbourhood, over such matters as the purchase of property and erection of buildings.

Religious discourse was dominated by 'God-talk', which Ipgrave regards as a natural product of a social setting in which the majority of Muslim children habitually used theistic language. The children's language employed religious vocabulary that could be applied across faith boundaries – 'God', 'devil', 'afterlife', 'life everlasting' etc. The use of terms such as 'real' and 'true' suggests a concern with truth and a realist view of religious language.

Reported words of others

Ipgrave reveals how the children used and processed the reported words of others. Remembered language spoken by Muslim pupils could be distinguished from their own and used, for example, to provide information about Muslim practices. It could also be used to relive and resolve tensions and disagreements. The retrospective discussion of others' 'mistaken' or 'hostile' speech gave children an opportunity to formulate a more considered response. Ipgrave also reports cases of expansion of thinking through the introduction of new ideas in a positive way. Often this happened when children were personal friends, and therefore not perceived as part of an 'other' group. By introducing 'experimental' ideas as the words of others, children could create distance from themselves, whilst at the same time showing that they judged the ideas to be worthy of consideration. If the reception was positive, then children might become more confident in the use of the words or adopt them as their own on future occasions.

Although reported speech had various functions in the children's discussions, its overall effect was a distancing or 'objectifying' of the other's words. The other's words were questioned and tested in new situations. They were not yet fully integrated into the children's language.

Assimilated words of others

In discussing the integration of others' words into their own language, Ipgrave applies Bakhtin's distinction between *authoritative* and *internally persuasive* discourse. She gives examples of how children adapted and assimilated a wide ranging, multi-sourced God-language into their own discourse, using it as a means to formulate and express their personal theological views (internally persuasive discourse). Children could also express rather formulaic statements in which they appeared to speak with an authority that was not their own, but also not explicitly attributed to others (authoritative discourse). Examples of this latter form of utterance include, 'God can make peace on earth' and 'He gave us life'. Bakhtin evaluated authoritative discourse negatively, seeing its authority 'already fused to it' (1981: 342), rather than being spoken with the authority of an autonomous person. Ipgrave is more positive about the authoritative discourse of the children, arguing that they sometimes consciously *chose* to accept the authority embedded in the language. Authoritative discourse, she argues, does not necessarily inhibit creative thinking.

Applying findings to religious education

The key pedagogical lessons from the research were derived from observations of the ways in which the children who took part responded to the format and style of the interviews and discussions. The research revealed the abilities and resources that children brought to their learning. These included children's readiness to engage with religious questions and the use of the religious language they had assimilated as well as their creativity in reworking received ideas as they negotiated their way through different viewpoints and understandings. The research also demonstrated a range of insights into the challenges of difference that children had gained through their experience of diversity, showing the 'bank' of meanings and associations they had accumulated which was available to them in developing their understanding.

Children who participated in the research showed a number of benefits they had gained from a dialogical approach. For example, children's sharing of ideas in interviews and discussion groups stimulated their interest in religious questions, and also provided a sympathetic forum for the discussion of issues that concerned them. Ipgrave found that the approach raised children's self-esteem, provided opportunities to develop critical skills, gave a voice to underachievers and generated an atmosphere of moral seriousness as children discussed fundamental human questions. The fact that children worked out solutions to problems themselves rather than accepting answers on others' authority was empowering.

The research project developed a threefold approach to dialogue which has been incorporated into the pedagogical work derived from it. *Primary dialogue* provides a context for other forms of dialogue and is basically the acceptance of diversity, difference and change – a recognition that people are in daily encounter with different viewpoints, understandings and ideas. In pedagogical terms, primary dialogue acknowledges and capitalizes on different experiences, viewpoints and influences in children's social backgrounds. *Secondary dialogue* represents a positive response to primary dialogue, characterized by an openness to difference. Bringing together different points of view is seen as a positive activity, of benefit to all participants. Pedagogically, this is represented by a class ethos in which children are willing to engage with difference and to share with and learn from others. Individual children are open to the possibility of change in their own understanding and outlook. *Tertiary dialogue* is the activity of dialogue itself – the forms and structures of verbal interchange that draw upon primary and secondary dialogue. Tertiary dialogue is enabled through methods, strategies and exercises that facilitate verbal interchange.

Ipgrave applies the dialogical model to her highly multicultural primary school in inner city Leicester. In terms of primary dialogue, the resources are the diverse intake of the school together with children from a suburban Leicester Roman Catholic school and a primary school in rural East Sussex who communicate with partners by email.[3] Further voices are introduced into classroom discussion through quotations from people holding a variety of beliefs or viewpoints or taking different positions on moral issues debated by the children. Material for discussion is also introduced from religious traditions, including extracts or quotations from texts.

Secondary dialogue encourages openness to one another's ideas. International tensions – whether the Iraq war, the Palestinian situation or the inter-religious troubles in Gujarat state in India – affect local feelings among the different communities in Leicester, and can be barriers to dialogue. Discord is countered by a school ethos that values diversity and listening to others. Children are taught the skills of listening to and learning from others as fundamental values in a plural society, and are also encouraged to engage with difference. In religious education, the pupils themselves discuss and set out the basic rules for the study of religions. They identify ideas such as respect for each other's religion, talking and thinking seriously about differences, and being ready to learn new things, including about their own religion – three principles identified by a class of 9- and 10-year-olds. Such principles are re-visited and used as criteria for success when pupils evaluate their learning at the end of lessons. A willingness to share with and learn from others also underpins the school's work on inter-faith dialogue by email. Pupils are encouraged to formulate their own questions when they engage with other religions and points of view, not least when formulating questions to ask visiting speakers.

Various strategies, activities and exercises are used to facilitate tertiary dialogue. The basic activity is discussion and debate. Different stimuli are used to raise questions and issues for discussion, including stories and other textual sources, case studies, quotations from different viewpoints, pictures, film or video extracts and examples of teachings from different religious traditions. To maximize involvement from children, sorting exercises are used in which pupils classify or sequence cards with different statements, words or pictures. These are the sorts of exercises regularly used by advocates of the development of 'thinking skills' (e.g. Baumfield 2002). These help children to organize their thoughts as they negotiate with one another or justify their positions. For example, a study of Islam by 8-year-olds began with small groups finding ways to complete the sentence 'A Muslim is someone who ...'. Children had to select four key statements from these to record on cards. All the statements from the groups were then shared and classified according to whether they applied only to Muslims or could apply as well to various categories of non-Muslims. Children are also introduced to issues of ethics, such as the pros and cons of using violence or taking animal life, or of belief, such as whether there can be life after death, and how such a belief relates to other beliefs – about forgiveness, for example. Some of these questions are discussed and debated with email partners.

Throughout, the approach encourages personal engagement with ideas and concepts from different religious traditions (How does this idea relate to my views?) and children are encouraged to be reflective about their contributions and to justify their own opinions (What are your reasons for thinking that?). They are also encouraged to consider how they arrived at their conclusions (How did you reach that answer?), to recognize the possibility of alternative viewpoints (Can you think of reasons why some people would not agree with what you have said?) and to be open to the arguments of others (Do you think X has a point here?). Role-play is used to help children to engage with different points of view. In this, children (as individuals or in groups) have to argue a case from the point of view of a particular interest group. For example, 9-year-olds took on the roles of conservationist, tourist, government official and bereaved father in discussing whether a man-eating tiger should be hunted and killed (Ipgrave 2001).

Ipgrave's approach to teaching and learning regards children as active participants in social construction, as they negotiate varied ideas of child-hood in home, community and school experience and access their previous experience, knowledge and understanding as resources for learning in class. Children are seen as collaborators in teaching and learning. Teaching maximizes pupils' input, with the teacher acting as prompter, chair, interviewer, questioner as well as providing information when required.

Discussion

The three examples of dialogical approaches discussed above were developed independently and are influenced by a variety of theoretical ideas. Leganger-Krogstad's influences include hermeneutics, ethnography and contextual theology; Weisse uses human rights theory, politics and Christian and Jewish theology; Ipgrave produces a highly creative synthesis of ideas from the sociology of childhood, literary theory, inter-faith dialogue and research on thinking skills. In each case, the development of pedagogy and practice is related to theory and original empirical research. Some of the similarities in their approaches are striking. All assert the relative autonomy of the individual, but recognize the contextual influence of different kinds of social group, such as family and peer, ethnic and religious groups. There is common agreement that the personal knowledge and experience that young people bring to the classroom can provide important data for study, communication and reflection. However, all also agree that further information and issues need to be introduced; religious education does not simply consist of an analysis and exchange of personal narratives. Leganger-Krogstad has the most sophisticated model for relating the child to wider knowledge and experience, placing the individual pupil at the crossing of a horizontal line representing the present and a vertical line representing past and future. Over time, the horizons of the student are gradually broadened, connecting personal experience and self understanding ('life-world') to local, national, European and global information and issues. At the same time, attention is given to the past and to the future – the shaping effects of 'tradition' can be analyzed, and future possibilities can be considered (compare this to Meijer's remarks about bringing a historical dimension to the interpretive approach discussed in Chapter 6).

The contextual character of the three approaches allows religion to be studied in its cultural context. Leganger-Krogstad relates cultural awareness and cultural analysis in a reflexive way, using techniques of participation (collecting information from home and family, for example) and distanciation (such as role-play and drama). Her goal of developing the generic skills to handle cultural material with all its internal diversities and fuzzy edges (what she calls metacultural competence) reverberates with the interpretive approach. Weisse too emphasizes the cultural context of religious life and the importance of avoiding stereotypes. The contextual approach also guarantees that both traditional and modern plurality are exemplified in an interactive way. Each writer finds ways to connect local and global issues.

All three writers give strong emphasis to the agency of young people in selecting and reviewing topics and methods of study, and in being given opportunities to reflect critically both on content and method. As with O'Grady's adaptation of the interpretive approach (Chapter 6 above), all note the strong motivating effects upon pupils of a high degree of personal involvement in decision making.

Weisse's picture of dialogue sees 'intercultural/interreligious learning' as a means to promote communication within multicultural societies, a process that can involve the management of conflict and a recognition that some disagreements are incapable of resolution. Ipgrave's research on language especially illuminates the processes of dialogue. She illustrates shifting boundaries between groups of children, which at times might be reinforced through conflict. She shows how, on other occasions, boundaries are crossed as children filter and rework one another's religious languages in formulating their own ideas. In my own work, I have argued (with reference to the research of Fredrik Barth and Gerd Baumann, for example) that, in plural contexts, children are able to utilize a variety of religio-cultural resources in creating new culture (e.g. Jackson 1997: Chapter 4). Ipgrave's analysis of children's language illustrates graphically how these processes occur in the multi-religious school – through interaction with others, reflection on others' language and meanings, and through disagreement with or through adaptation or adoption of others' words. Ipgrave's distinction between primary (awareness of diversity), secondary (being positive about diversity) and tertiary (engaging with diversity) dialogue is also a very useful tool for thinking about dialogue in relation to whole school and curriculum policy. Primary and secondary dialogue need to be features of school ethos and governance as well as of religious, intercultural or citizenship education.

Like the interpretive approach, all three pedagogies emphasize reflexivity. Through reflecting on difference and through comparison and contrast of their own and others' beliefs, values, assumptions and practices, students become both more educated about otherness and more self-aware.

These approaches have great potential for development and adaptation to different educational contexts. Moreover, Ipgrave's extension of her method, using email as a means to link children from different geographical locations and educational settings, has much potential for development. All the writers maintain a goal of epistemological openness, insisting on clear thinking and consistency, but recognizing that students have or will adopt a wide variety of views. However, the procedures adopted assume a framework of values consistent with a concern for democracy, social justice and human rights.

Chapter 8

Religious education's contribution to intercultural education, citizenship education and values education

So far we have argued for approaches which develop skills of communication – of interpretation, criticism and dialogue – and which give pupils agency, maximizing their active participation in the methods and practices of religious education. We have rejected both the view that Christian instruction should be the basis of religious, citizenship and moral education in the common school and the deconstructive view that the distinction between religious education and other forms of education such as citizenship, values and emotional education should simply be discarded. However, the family of approaches advocated in this book emphasizes the importance of context in religious education. At the social level, religion is approached in relation to its cultural context and the attendant debates about concepts such as community, ethnicity and nationality. All these debates can be seen in relation to a matrix of traditional and modern plurality (Skeie 1995, 2002). At the level of individual identity, each person's religious or secular beliefs or outlook can be positioned in relation to such factors. Thus religious education as a subject of study, and religious education teachers as professionals with expertise in the study of religions, have a great deal to offer to overlapping fields such as multicultural or intercultural education, antiracist education and citizenship education.

Nevertheless, there have been advocates of antiracist education and citizenship education who have attacked religious education. Some antiracists have argued that multicultural education (of which 'multifaith' RE was seen as an example) reifies religions and cultures, reinforces difference and should be replaced by antiracist education. One influential educationist has argued that religious education is out of place in the common school and should be superseded by citizenship education. This chapter responds to those arguments, showing that the approaches to religious education advocated in this book enhance both multicultural (or intercultural) education and citizenship education. Some remarks are also made about the contribution of religious education to values education. Although policy issues will be referred to, further issues of policy making with regard to religious education will be considered in Chapter 10.

Multicultural or intercultural education

Both the terms 'multicultural education' and 'intercultural education' have been used in a variety of ways by different writers over time, and they are sometimes used interchangeably. However, the term 'multicultural education' gained currency in Britain and to some extent in the USA, while 'intercultural education' has tended to be used more in continental European literature. Some writers prefer the term 'intercultural' since it seems consistent with the idea that cultures are not discrete but constantly interacting, and that cultures can learn from each other, creating new and exciting fusions – in music, for example (e.g. Kwami 1996). Something of the debate about the meaning and use of the term 'multicultural education' will be revealed in the following discussion, but the key point is the argument that the approaches to religious education advocated in this book resonate with ideas of multicultural and intercultural education that give close attention to the analysis of culture and the complexities of culture making in the lives of individuals, including pupils.

A feature of the history of multicultural education in Britain was the attack on multiculturalism in the 1980s by some of those who identified themselves as 'antiracists' (e.g. Mullard 1984). According to antiracists, the treatment of 'cultures' in the language and practices of multicultural or multiracial education was superficial (Troyna 1983). Such superficiality, it was claimed, reinforced stereotypes, and hence reinforced racism. In multicultural education, a culture was generally presented as a closed system, with a fixed and inflexible understanding of ethnicity. This emphasis by multiculturalists on distinct, separate cultures allowed them to be perceived as rivals to the national culture which, through its tolerance, allowed them limited forms of expression (McIntyre 1978). Superficial multicultural education was described witheringly by Barry Troyna as 'saris, samosas and steel bands' (Troyna 1983). Moreover, multicultural education was also judged to emphasize the exotic, the other, the different, perpetuating the approaches of early social anthropologists. Multicultural education avoided giving attention to hierarchies of power *within* different cultural groups and also neglected the academic debate about the nature of cultures. According to antiracists, advocates of multicultural education perceived racism psychologically in terms of personal attitudes that could be changed through knowledge and learning the value of tolerance. The power structures and established social practices within institutions, which were principally responsible for the perpetuation of inequality, were ignored. The antiracist critique of multiculturalism was not directed specifically at religious education, but 'multifaith' RE was seen as one subject having multiculturalist assumptions, presenting 'cultures' as bounded wholes and religions as distinct internally homogeneous systems, and diverting attention from issues of power.

For antiracists, individual beliefs about 'race' and the content of cultural traditions were not regarded as the central issue. According to antiracism it is the structures of power within institutions that produce racial oppression. Racist ideas reinforce and legitimate unequal distribution of power between different groups (Troyna and Carrington 1990: 56). The antiracist response to racism was to challenge and change these structures, not by teaching about culture or religion in the classroom. Because of its primary concern with changing structures, antiracism (especially during the 1980s) was limited in its suggestions with regard to the school curriculum. Some writers offered ideas to promote a critical awareness of 'institutional racism' and strategies to promote racial justice in the school, but did not address the complex issues of culture, ethnicity, community and religion that exist in schools and in British and other Western societies generally. Moreover, with its preoccupation with structures of power and its use of categories intended to eliminate the distinctions between groups (using, for example, 'Black' as a category to refer to all 'non-White' groups), this form of antiracism has itself tended to 'homogenize' or blur the differences between different communities. The antiracist critique was also often uncompromising, giving little opportunity for reflection and conversation with those holding different views.

A change in approach amongst antiracists began in the early 1990s. Some writers became critical of some of the assumptions of antiracism, recognizing that, in attacking superficial and closed accounts of culture and ethnicity, antiracists themselves had underestimated the importance of questions of cultural and religious representation, transmission and change. For example, Mal Leicester attempted to synthesize antiracist and multicultural education (e.g. Leicester 1992) while Ali Rattansi and some of his co-writers addressed issues of culture, 'race' and difference together (Donald and Rattansi 1992). Rattansi criticized the approaches to multiculturalism and antiracism still dominant in the early 1990s. Multiculturalism represented ethnic groups as closed systems ignoring the fluidity of cultural formation and the continual redrawing of boundaries between groups, while antiracism ignored or avoided the debates about culture. For Rattansi, both multiculturalism and antiracism had to change:

... the multiculturalists will have to abandon their additive models of cultural pluralism and their continuing obsession with the old ethnicities. Antiracists ... will have to move beyond their reductive conceptions of culture and their fear of cultural difference as simply a source of division and weakness in the struggle against racism.

(Rattansi 1992: 41)

Some writers now use the terms 'critical multiculturalism' (May 1999: 33) or 'reflexive multiculturalism' (Rattansi 1999: 77) to indicate approaches that are critical of essentialist views of culture and acknowledge the role of power relations in the formation of culture. These approaches reflect an understanding of plurality that is consistent with Skeie's matrix of traditional and modern plurality (Chapter 1 above). This understanding is reinforced by an increasing amount of empirical evidence showing multiculturalism to be the outcome of collective negotiations and on-going power struggles of cultural, ethnic and racial differences (Baumann 1996, 1999; Modood and Werbner 1997).

Multicultural societies

Gerd Baumann's reflections on his field studies in Southall, west London, are especially helpful in unpacking the subtleties of the discourse of religion, culture, ethnicity and community in relation to multicultural societies, demonstrating that, in Skeie's sense, 'traditional' ways of representing these ideas are to be found alongside the complex kind of culture making and boundary crossing referred to by writers such as Rattansi. Baumann describes the processes of cultural negotiation and change in terms of the interaction of two kinds of discourse, creating ambiguities in the use of terms such as 'community' and 'culture'. He identifies these as 'dominant discourse' and 'demotic discourse'. 'Dominant discourse' reifies cultures, seeing 'communities' as defined by ethnic and religious identity. This is the kind of language used by the media and politicians (using expressions such as 'the Muslim community' which blur differences between Muslim individuals and groups), but also by 'insiders' when it suits their interests, for example when engaging in contests regarding group rights. 'Demotic discourse', however, is the language of cultural interaction on the ground, so to speak. It is the language of culture making, and characteristically becomes used when people from a range of backgrounds focus together on topics of common concern or interest. Thus 'culture' can be seen as both a possession of an ethnic or religious 'community', and also as a dynamic process relying on personal agency, in which community boundaries are renegotiated and there is the possibility of redefinition of the meaning of 'community' in particular situations (Baumann 1996).

Models of a multicultural society, and of multicultural education, need to acknowledge both forms of discourse. Some views of multicultural education – the varieties criticized by writers such as Rattansi, Leicester and May – are couched *entirely* in terms of dominant discourse, picturing cultures as bounded entities, with subordinate cultures functioning in their own private space, and depending on the values of the dominant culture for their continued existence. John McIntyre's views (1978) are a good example of this position, as are the views of Burn, Hart, Coombs and Thompson discussed in Chapter 2 and of Hargreaves (1994) discussed below. Empirical evidence from qualitative research shows that this idea of a multicultural society is not sustainable (e.g. Baumann 1996; Jackson and Nesbitt 1993; Østberg 2003a, b and c). The way we picture a multicultural society needs to be more flexible.

More needs to be made, for example, of the fact that some degree of cultural plurality in a society is not dependent on the presence of ethnic minorities who are descended from migrants, nor on indigenous peoples, but on other forms of local diversity. The anthropological studies of local British communities conducted by Anthony Cohen and his co-writers show no single homogeneous national culture but, rather, many diverse cultures often founded on a sense of local belonging. Cohen illustrates how members of local communities manipulate symbols in sustaining boundaries, with individuals investing common features (from everyday speech to watching TV soap operas) with 'local meaning' (Cohen 1982a, 1982b, 1986). For Cohen, 'local experience mediates national identity'; the latter cannot be understood without a knowledge of the former (1982a: 13). In terms of pedagogy, there are interesting possibilities for developing methods for pupils to explore their own sense of identity in this respect. It is also evident that cultural conditions in different countries result in different views of national identity, and this affects the ways in which multicultural societies are described (e.g. Skeie 2003 on Norway, Weisse 2003 on Germany and Steyn 2003 on South Africa; see also the discussion of civil religion in relation to religious education in Chapter 10).

It also needs to be recognized that minority cultures, religions and ethnicities are themselves internally pluralistic, and the symbols and values of their various constituent groups are open to negotiation, contest and change. Moreover, individuals from any background may identify with values associated with a range of sources and may draw eclectically on a variety of resources in creating new culture. A young person might be a 'skilled cultural navigator' (Ballard 1994) or display 'multiple cultural competence' (Jackson and Nesbitt 1993) or possess an integrated plural identity (Østberg 2003a, b and c). At the same time, in the context of groups, there will be those claiming a more bounded religious and cultural identity. In Gerd Baumann's words, 'A multicultural society is not a patchwork of five or ten fixed cultural identities, but an elastic web of crosscutting and always mutually situational identifications' (Baumann 1999: 118).

Of crucial importance for the maintenance and development of such societies is the provision of mechanisms that raise awareness of the debates and maximize dialogue and communication, identifying common or overlapping ideas and values, but also identifying and addressing difference. There is a need for structures that enable and foster these interactions, including educational structures. Interpretive and dialogical approaches to religious education are consistent with forms of multicultural or intercultural education that take account of the factors discussed above, incorporating the debates within the social sciences about culture and cultural change as well as synthesizing multicultural and antiracist concerns, such as having a direct role in countering 'cultural racism', and promoting the cultural development of individuals. It is interesting that a project on intercultural education across the member states of the Council of Europe, current at the time of writing, is giving close attention to recent developments in religious education (see Chapter 10 below).

Religious education and citizenship education

The topic of citizenship is very much on the agenda of education systems in many democracies. Whether influenced primarily by fears of the young's disengagement with political processes, as in England and Wales, or by concerns about social cohesion in multicultural societies, as in South Africa's commitment to nation building, citizenship education has emerged, either as a curriculum subject in its own right or as a dimension of the wider school curriculum (Paludan and Prinds 1999). In those societies where the *term* 'citizenship' (or its equivalent) is not used, other elements are emphasized such as democratic values, virtues and political literacy (Skeie 2003). For some societies, including Britain, citizenship education is seen as the field through which intercultural issues can be explored.

If religious education can contribute positively to multicultural or intercultural education, can it do the same for citizenship education? At least one influential educationist thinks not. In the mid-1990s David Hargreaves, at that time Professor of Education at Cambridge University and, until 2001, Chief Executive of the Qualifications and Curriculum

Authority, contributed to the debate about citizenship in relation to issues of religion and education. In this discussion, Hargreaves relates his arguments directly to specific recommendations for policy change (Hargreaves 1994). Hargreaves' views on education have been highly influential on the policies of the current Labour government. His ideas about educational research, his advocacy of the expansion of state-funded religious schools and his plea for the introduction of citizenship education have all contributed to current government policy. His views about religious education have not been adopted, although some commentators are concerned that they could be in the future (Gay 2001). It is thus important that Hargreaves' arguments should be considered.

Hargreaves recognizes that, in a secularized and pluralistic society, religion can no longer be the basis for a socially cohesive civic education. He points out that

> the problem of Britain as a pluralistic society is how to find some social cement to ensure that people with different moral, religious, and ethical values as well as social, cultural and linguistic traditions can live together with a degree of harmony.
>
> (Hargreaves 1994: 31)

Hargreaves proposes a threefold solution.

First, there should be an expansion of religious schools within the state system. These should have a distinctive ethos, asserting the links between religious faith and morality and should express a joint commitment by home and school to 'the transmission and living experience of a shared moral and religious culture' (Hargreaves 1994: 35).

Second, religious education should be abolished in all other schools – what Hargreaves calls 'secular schools'. Hargreaves argues that, since religious education has a moral purpose, there is no point in attempting to provide it in schools reflecting a secularized, religiously diverse society where there is no consensus about the relationship between religion and morality. As Hargreaves puts it, 'The notion of a non-denominational core RE to be offered in all schools as a buttress to moral education is becoming less and less viable and should now be abandoned' (Hargreaves 1994: 34). 'Multi-faith' religious education is no answer according to Hargreaves.

> The multi-faith pick 'n' mix tour of religions easily trivialises each faith's claims to truth. As an academic discipline, it has little appeal to most children and comes before they are mature enough to engage in the necessary historical and philosophical analysis.
>
> (Hargreaves 1994: 34)

For Hargreaves, religion is no longer a 'first language' in society. It is a 'second language' to be spoken in the home and the faith community (including the faith-based school). However, argues Hargreaves, religious and cultural groups do provide bridges between the individual and the state, and are thus vitally important. Such groups should express themselves through the participation of representatives in a range of public institutions. Third, religious education in 'secular' schools should be replaced by citizenship education. Hargreaves' argument is that, whereas Christianity formerly provided a moral basis for civic life, now the 'public language of citizenship' provides the necessary social cement, also functioning as a bridge to the 'second languages' of the distinctive moralities of the various religions now actively present in our society. The first language of religion is thus replaced by the first language of common values associated with citizenship. Hargreaves also argues for citizenship education in religious schools, as a complement to religious education.

Hargreaves thus sees more or less homogeneous religious communities providing state supported faith-based education in which their children inherit the beliefs and values of particular religions. Meanwhile, key adults from the communities participate in the democratic process, representing the beliefs and values of their constituents, and identifying values shared with other members of society in order to promote social cohesion.

Hargreaves' analysis is flawed through its particular assumptions about the homogeneity of religions (and implicitly cultures and ethnic groups), about the nature of secularity in society and (a related point) about the nature of social plurality. I will argue that, rather than being an outmoded subject to be replaced by citizenship education, religious education (though not as understood by Hargreaves) has a vital contribution to make to various aspects of education for citizenship in the common school.[1]

How far do community leaders and faith-based schools represent religious communities?

First, there are problems with Hargreaves' view of the homogeneity of religions. This creates difficulties for his view of the role of faith-based schools and his claim that community representatives should act as the bridge between the 'second languages' of faith groups and the 'first language' of public institutions through which democracy functions. Religious schools are seen by Hargreaves as havens for particular moralities, in which home and school are jointly committed to 'the transmission and living experience of a shared moral and religious culture', while key adult members of religious communities are regarded as their spokespersons and negotiators. This exhibits an over-uniform view of the nature of religious or religio-cultural groups. Many ethnographic field studies confirm the diversity of belief and practice within religions that appear superficially to be monolithic, often challenging conventional views of religious boundaries (e.g. Geaves 1998; Nesbitt 1990a, 1990b, 1998a, 2000a). This diversity is not simply the product of different cultural influences on homogeneous belief systems. As we noted in Chapter 5, a considerable body of scholarship in cultural history (e.g. Marshall 1970; Said 1978) and the study of religions (e.g. Chidester 1996a; Fitzgerald 1990; Jackson 1996a; King 1999; Oberoi 1994; Smith 1978) provides evidence that the representation of religions as bounded systems with an essential core of beliefs is a product of the rationalism of the European Enlightenment coupled with and shaped by encounters during the colonial period.[2]

Moreover, ethnographic field studies of children and young people also reveal how religious and cultural elements interact and change over time. Young people might utilize the religious and cultural resources of their historic family traditions, but they are likely also to import elements from a variety of sources, thereby generating new religious and cultural positions. This is especially evident in situations where families have migrated from one society to another (e.g. Barth 1996; Jackson and Nesbitt 1993), and in which influences on the formation of identity are plural and complex (e.g. Østberg 2000a and b, 2003a and b). The riots in Oldham, Burnley, Bradford and Leeds in England during the summer of 2001 provide a graphic example of the gap in perceptions of personal and social identity that can exist between community leaders and groups of young people, ostensibly from the same religious or ethnic 'communities'. Putting the point another way, treating religious and cultural groups as homogeneous allows the possibility for 'leaders' to invoke traditional authorities and practices in order to impose restrictions on their own members – a point often made by feminist writers in relation to discussions of women (Kassam 1997; Lister 1997: 37; Tobler 2003), but equally relevant to other groups such as children or those whose traditions diverge from an abstracted norm.

The difficulty for individuals to speak and negotiate authentically on behalf of those who identify themselves with a particular religion is clear. Individuals could act in the interests of a particular sub-group, perhaps to promote a particular ideological viewpoint, or in their own interests. Furthermore, the issue of representation in this context raises an issue of gender. As feminist discussions of citizenship have pointed out, the political institutions associated with such formal representation in the public arena have been traditionally understood as male domains (Tobler 2003). For example, it is perhaps not a coincidence that the faith group representing different elements of 'the Hindu community' in advising on the content of national model syllabuses for religious education in England had an entirely male membership (SCAA 1994c).

When Hargreaves' points are considered in the light of Baumann's analysis of 'dominant' and 'demotic' discourse discussed above, it is clear that he focuses *entirely* on 'dominant discourse', reinforcing the idea of bounded and homogeneous cultures and religions. In doing so, he is simply doing what politicians and the media often do. As Baumann puts it:

> ... the civil religion and political culture of Britain encourages so-called minorities to strive for emancipation as if they were sports teams: They are approached as so-called 'communities', and politicians, the media and almost everybody else thinks of them as tightly knit 'cultural groups' held together by the same traditions, value system and history.
>
> (Baumann 1999: 76)

Baumann goes on to point out that groups collude with this, since they can only hope to achieve civil emancipation by accepting such reifications when state agencies try to 'help' them and, anyway, co-operation might suit the personal agendas of some of those identified as community leaders. This compounds the problem with regard to the reification of cultures and communities. Baumann identifies the stages in the encounter between the state and minority communities in Britain. First, a group is identified (it could be a temple, mosque or association of some kind) as the representative of a community or culture. Next, the state provides resources and therefore assists in forming new, more tightly bounded groups. Third, the state devolves some of its functions to the 'community'. This is exactly the cycle that Hargreaves recommends in relation to faith-based schools, and which is now being applied as government policy. In pointing this out I am not condemning the idea of faith-based schools in principle (see Chapter 3 above), but am attempting to raise awareness about the dangers attendant on the processes through which they are often established. Similarly, I am not arguing for the marginalization or exclusion of community leaders or representatives, but for the kind of 'differentiated citizenship' advocated by Iris Young (Young 1990), who argues for more institutions through which individual voices can be represented.

The key point is that dialogue should not be *confined* to the participation of official representatives of groups in public arenas. As Baumann's research shows, there are many possibilities for dialogue, exchange and negotiation in social life. However, what Hargreaves especially misses by wanting to shunt religious education *only* into faith-based schools is the opportunity for dialogue and interaction between young people from different backgrounds in the common school (see Chapter 7 above). The community school is a rare, structured social forum for debates about religion and culture, and for bringing different perspectives to bear on religions or issues of common concern, such as the environment, gender and the rights of children – topics that cut across reified views of religions or cultures. The issue of the homogeneity of religions applies also when considering faith-based schools. Rather than being clear partners with families, promoting shared community values, faith-based schools could set out to promote a particular view of orthodoxy or the views of the school's sponsors rather than reflecting the diversity of tradition represented by pupils and their families. It is equally clear that, while religious schools may have some very positive features, there can equally be a downside (see Chapter 3 above).

The nature of religious education

Hargreaves' key reason for dismissing religious education from the curricula of common schools is that the subject has ceased to be relevant to issues of morality and citizenship for the majority of members of a largely secular society in which there is no consensus about the relationship between religion and morality. This view is based on his assumption that religious education has a moral purpose achieved through the promotion of a religious view of life. In maintaining this view of the subject, Hargreaves ignores over thirty years of British scholarship and research in the field of religious education in which alternative models of the subject have been advanced that take account of secularization (from Cox 1966 onwards) and religious plurality both globally (from Smart 1967, 1968 onwards) and locally (from Cole 1972 onwards). The only alternative to a religious and moral formation model Hargreaves countenances is what he calls a 'multi-faith pick 'n' mix tour of religions', which he regards as trivializing claims to truth, and as inappropriate for those who have not reached a state of intellectual maturity. This glib dismissal of multifaith religious education echoes – in word as well as sentiment – attacks on the subject by lobbyists from the political radical right in the late 1980s (Burn and Hart 1988; Hull 1991; Jackson 2000a; see also Chapter 2 above), and ignores discussions informed by scholarship and research (see Chapter 9 below). There is some evidence that Hargreaves' view is largely based on his experience as Chief Inspector of the Inner London Education Authority (Hargreaves 1986). At the time, ILEA had a heavily content laden religious education syllabus with little reflective and critical work built into it, and it is not surprising that he was sceptical about the effectiveness of this highly diluted version of phenomenology, and found the subject to be unpopular with young people in schools. His view also seems to be coloured by the on-going political debate about the nature and purpose of RE, and he is clearly irritated with the various fudges and compromises that have weakened legislation and non-statutory advice. One can but sympathize. Yet Hargreaves fails to offer convincing evidence for rejecting the possibility of a genuinely open and pluralistic religious education that promotes dialogue and communication across boundaries, that takes issues of truth seriously, that is appropriate to the age, aptitude and family background of pupils and that engages them intellectually and emotionally. The interpretive, dialogical and religious literacy approaches to religious education discussed above do provide this combination of elements, and there is evidence of teachers employing them, or variants on them, with a high degree of success. There are thus strong grounds for rejecting Hargreaves' easy dismissal of multifaith religious education.

Secular schools or plural schools?

In Hargreaves' scheme of things, there would be religious schools and secular schools, with religious education confined to the first. The assumption is that secular schools would reflect the secular climate of the greater part of society. There would be an interest in moral education in secular schools (which, says Hargreaves, could be dealt with by subjects such as English), and there would be civic education. However, Hargreaves' characterization of the common school as secular in contrast to religious schools misunderstands the plurality of Community schools.

First, there are plenty of individuals, families and groups practising religion who do not favour separate education for children. Some of these see real dangers in separate schooling, and wish their children to learn with others from a range of backgrounds in the Community school (see, for example, Connolly 1992; Humanist Philosophers' Group 2001; Jackson 1987; Jackson and Nesbitt 1993; Chapter 10 below). Second, Hargreaves assumes that young people not practising religion in a formal way have little or no interest in religious or spiritual issues or in being informed about religion (see Blaylock 2001 for a report of evidence to the contrary;[3] see also the survey of secondary pupils in Pocock 2000; see also the discussion of the Bradford shadow SACRE in Chapter 10 below). Third, he assumes (because of his view of the nature of religious and moral education as forms of socialization) that religious education hijacks moral education rather than complementing it (see Hawke 1982, for example, for a completely different analysis). Fourth, his view of plurality in society is limited to overt religious diversity and secularity. He largely omits the dimension of what in this book (following Skeie 1995) we have called 'modern plurality', the intellectual climate of late modernity or postmodernity that currently provides the context for religious and ethnic diversity and provides a backdrop for all education (see Chapter 1 above). When different positions on modern plurality are brought together with religious diversity, a wide variety of spiritual and moral responses and syntheses becomes possible, many not being directly identifiable with orthodoxies of the major religions. Similarly, the debate about citizenship is broadened when modern plurality is considered, taking on board the debates about rights and duties at local and global levels as well as the level of the nation state. It is Hargreaves' restricted view of plurality that mainly accounts for his sharp distinction between the religious and the secular. This is also probably true of his view of citizenship, seen as purely a set of duties and rights related to one's place within the state, rather than as a wider debate about the relationship of the individual to a broader range of collectivities, including global responsibilities and rights.

The common school should not be secular in the sense that Hargreaves uses, that is as the direct opposite of 'religious'. Rather, Community schools should be secular in the Indian Constitutional sense of 'secular' – that is maintaining impartiality towards different religious and non-religious truth positions. The Community school can provide a genuine forum for dialogue between students and teachers from different religious and non-religious backgrounds and for learning the skills to interpret, reflect upon and gain insight from different worldviews. However, Community schools should provide space for the exploration of debates, whether about religion, culture, morality or citizenship or about modernity and postmodernity, as well as opportunities for encounter and exchange with people who have different views and commitments. In this sense, the common school should be a microcosm of a democratic society, and is therefore the ideal place to explore and practise ideas of citizenship. The knowledge, understanding and skills that can be provided by religious education have a vital contribution to make to this process.

The contribution of religious education to education for citizenship

Fortunately, the national curriculum for citizenship is not seen by the UK government as a replacement for religious education or any other subject area. Rather, it envisages a core of topics covered as 'citizenship', with a range of contributions made from other subjects, including religious education. It is a pity that the cross-references to contributory subjects in official documents omit religious education, because they deal specifically with the national curriculum.[4] However, the guidance documents refer clearly to RE's potential contribution, as does Professor Bernard Crick in his personal reflections on the citizenship curriculum, emphasizing its flexibility (Crick 2000). Moreover Estelle Morris, when Secretary of State for Education and Skills, stated clearly that 'Citizenship education complements RE; it does not replace it' (personal communication 2001a).

The religious dimension to citizenship education can be covered in a variety of ways. Dialogical approaches that maximize pupil participation in religious education make a clear contribution. The knowledge and skills to be acquired and developed through citizenship education have much in common with the goals of dialogical religious education. Interpretive, dialogical and religious literacy approaches all deal with the understanding of the language of religions. Examples of inter-communal, inter-religious tension in Britain and globally demonstrate that religion is not just a private, but a public concern and that it will benefit society if pupils in our schools are conversant with its language. Interpretive and dialogical approaches to RE that challenge traditional representations of religions and cultures as closed systems reveal the issues of identity and belonging in multicultural societies and thereby contribute to citizenship education. Moreover, the reflexivity that is a vital ingredient of dialogical and interpretive approaches involves pupils in becoming aware of how some of their own prejudices or preconceptions are formed. Both approaches also link the experience of pupils to wider issues, from local to global, opening up issues of human rights (Gearon 2002, 2003a, 2003b; Plesner 2002) and global environmental issues (Christian Aid 2000; DfEE 2000; Oxfam nd) as well as issues of duties and rights within the state. Finally, the very nature of religious thought – its engagement with 'ultimate questions' and the different answers it presents – makes religious education an ideal forum for the development of the skills of dialogue and negotiation, and of the intellectual and moral awareness that is a key element of the citizenship ideal. Here, philosophical approaches and methods employing 'thinking skills' have a particular role (e.g. Baumfield 2002; Robinson 1988).

Pragmatically, religious education on its own may not have sufficient time available to deal with all the relevant issues (Everington 2001), while citizenship education or social studies would need expertise from specialists in religion. Collaborative and inter-disciplinary approaches would seem to be most appropriate for citizenship education. Especially important is the insight that both religious education and citizenship education should engage students and not be reduced to an externally imposed body of knowledge.

Values education

Hargreaves' views on the relationship between religious, citizenship and moral education raise the issue as to whether religious education can contribute to the dimension of values within citizenship education, or indeed values education more generally. In Britain, the Crick Report identifies social and moral responsibility as one of the three strands running through education for citizenship, and the national curriculum documents on citizenship make reference to the promotion of spiritual, moral and cultural development of students in order to foster self-confidence and responsibility. The wide ranging international literature in the broad fields of moral and values education debates how far and in what ways publicly funded schools should promote particular values or moral positions and how far they should help pupils to develop their own skills of moral thinking and decision making (Halstead and Taylor 2000). The issue is the role that religion might play in either process in state-funded schools that are not religious foundations. The approaches to religious education advocated in this book reflect the plurality of late modern democratic societies, which includes diverse religious and secular positions. It is no longer appropriate to promote particular views of religious truth in schools that reflect such a plurality of views and beliefs. Schools should help to develop an understanding of religions that is both critical and reflective, with students being given the opportunity to gain insight from their studies as well as knowledge and understanding. The ethical teachings of religions and spiritual movements are thus source material for study and reflection rather than sources of authority which all pupils are expected to follow. In the dialogical approaches to learning, discussed above in Chapter 7, pupils' own stances on moral issues – some of them grounded in religion – become material for analysis and reflection, while students from different religious and non-religious backgrounds might work together in exploring and developing positions on particular moral or social issues. There is the possibility of pragmatic agreement on moral issues from participants whose values 'overlap'. The school can provide opportunities for 'conversation' and 'negotiation' within a broadly democratic framework. Thus the framework for values education is not 'neutral' or 'value free', but mirrors the values and procedures of democracy (see Chapter 10 below).

There is another relevant issue that has largely been neglected in the debate on values education. Whilst it is inappropriate to promote the teachings of any particular religion or philosophy in publicly funded common schools, it is arguable that there are certain generic skills and activities derived from or associated with religions and spiritual movements that might offer an experiential dimension to moral development and citizenship education. Activities such as 'stilling' or sitting quietly whilst concentrating on an idea or value have features in common with some forms of prayer or meditation. There is an argument that such activities can be used legitimately for all pupils, but away from the context of a particular religious worldview. An account of one school's use of such techniques suggests that they can be highly effective in promoting a sense of responsibility, humanity and maturity amongst pupils (Farrer 2000). The fact that some schools adapt materials influenced by religious or spiritual movements to help children to experience calm and stillness or to explore values may also indicate a need for this type of experiential activity. Recent research on this interface between religious organizations and schools needs to be discussed as part of the debate on the relationship between religions and values education (Arweck and Nesbitt forthcoming a and b; Nesbitt and Henderson 2003).

Conclusion

This chapter has argued that religious education can make an important contribution to intercultural education, citizenship education and values education, especially in terms of understanding various aspects of social plurality in relation to the experience of individual students. This social plurality combines traditional and modern/postmodern dimensions, connecting local, national and global elements. By participating in discussions related to these issues, students should be helped to examine their own and their peers' assumptions and reflect upon their own identities.

Specifically in relation to multicultural or intercultural education, religious education can deal with questions of religious and cultural identity, taking account of the different ways in which the term 'culture' is used, in the media, by politicians, by community leaders and by people engaging with one another – including children and young people – in social life, including the life of the school. RE can also explore with pupils their own sense of identity in relation to place and personal and family history. In addition, religious education can analyze the religious elements in racism, an important aspect of what Tariq Modood calls cultural racism (Modood 1992), bringing together both multicultural and antiracist concerns.

With regard to citizenship education, the skills of listening, negotiating and formulating a position that are part of dialogical approaches to RE are essential to good citizenship. Similarly the skills of dealing with difference, interpreting unfamiliar religious language, constructive criticism of another's stance, and personal reflection all contribute to education for citizenship, as well as facilitating an understanding of religion in society. Moreover, religious education can deal with the role of religion in global issues, such as human rights, the distribution of wealth and environmental issues. Rather than taking place in a moral vacuum, religious education should be conducted in a context that upholds a democratic social morality, reflected in the ethos of the school, respecting the rights of freedom of religion or belief within the law as advocated in Article 18 of the Universal Declaration of Human Rights (http://www.un.org/Overview/rights.html), Article 18 of the International Covenant on Civil and Political Rights (http://www.unhchr.ch/html/menu3/b/a_ccpr.htm), and the 1981 United Nations Declaration on the Elimination of All Forms of Intolerance and of Discrimination Based on Religion or Belief (http://www.unhchr.ch/html/menu3/b/d_intole.htm). Ethical teachings from religious, spiritual and secular sources are material for study and reflection, not automatically authorities for all pupils. Values education also promotes collaborative exploration of moral issues by students with different religious and non-religious outlooks. There is the possibility of respectful disagreement as well as agreement on moral issues from pupils whose values 'overlap'. Thus, pupils' personal moral stances, whether secular or set in a religious framework, are not a matter of whim, but should be internally consistent and justified rationally in the context of conversation, negotiation, discussion and debate with others.

For all this to happen, the voices of pupils need to be heard within the structures of the curriculum and school. As Iris Young says:

> ... we require participatory structures in which actual people with their geographical, ethnic, gender and occupational differences, assert their perspectives on social issues within institutions that encourage the representation of their distinct voices.
>
> (Young 1990: 116)

In promoting this idea of 'differentiated citizenship', the common school is a vitally important forum for discussing religious, cultural and moral issues. The dialogical, interpretive and religious literacy approaches illustrated in this book are seen as contributing theoretical and practical ideas for helping students to interact with one another and with a variety of source materials in developing and refining their own stances.

Chapter 9

The relevance of research to religious education

This chapter discusses some of the current issues facing research in religious education, partly in the light of the debate about educational research in general which began in England and Wales in the late 1990s. One intention is to argue that theoretical and empirical research is vital to the healthy development of the subject. Another is to stimulate further discussion about RE research in relation to practice in schools and policy making. A further intention is to encourage more collaborative research and research networking, whether involving researchers from different institutions (in higher education or otherwise), higher education researchers working in complementary fields or academics working with practising teachers. Finally, international networking and collaboration in research in religious education and related fields are seen as essential in an increasingly interdependent world, whether in the context of Europe or wider society.

RE and educational research

Since the mid-1990s, there has been a debate in Britain about the quality and relevance of educational research. The debate was prompted by David Hargreaves in a lecture for the Teacher Training Agency (Hargreaves 1996). Hargreaves' critical comments precipitated the reviews of educational research which resulted in the Tooley and Hillage Reports, sponsored respectively by The Office for Standards in Education and the Department for Education and Employment (Tooley and Darby 1998; Hillage *et al.* 1998). The key underlying question in the debate was whether or not educational research offers information and ideas directly relevant to the improvement of practice in schools in order to raise the quality of learning and teaching.

Educational research can be of a range of types and have a number of possible applications. It can inform public debate about educational issues and it can inform policy decisions. In the field of RE, for example, Brian Gates' research on behalf of the Religious Education Council of England and Wales provided valuable evidence of under-provision which eventually influenced government policy (REC 1988, 1990). Another application is to inform and improve educational practice in schools. Yet in the case of primary RE, although there is some evidence of improvement (Ofsted 1999: 137–40), there is also evidence that RE is a subject whose aims are a source of confusion for some teachers (e.g. Ashenden 1995) and which many teachers feel inadequate to teach (e.g. Gay *et al.* 1992) or teach in a purely informational and non-reflective, non-questioning way (Ofsted 1995). Also, there is evidence that some secondary teachers inhibit pupil progress through their low expectations and through setting trivial tasks (Ofsted 1997; Wintersgill 2000). For whatever reasons, there are issues about the impact of RE research upon practice.

Moreover, educational researchers in fields other than RE seem to have a very limited awareness of research in religious education. For example, the Tooley Report reviews a sample of educational research papers from four leading UK-based educational journals, finding weaknesses in many of them, yet acknowledging the relevance of most of them to practice and/or policy. Although the report discusses important issues relating to the quality of research, there is little reflection on the *scope* of educational research. The report discusses important issues relating to partisanship and research, methodological problems, especially in relation to qualitative research and sampling, non-empirical research and the relevance of research to practice and policy. However, the main impression made on this writer by the Tooley Report was of the marginality of curriculum research in general and RE research in particular when viewed from the perspective of general educational research. The 41 articles analyzed in the Tooley Report include historical studies, discussions of sociological research and research reports on topics such as educational management, equal opportunities and examinations. Only four articles on curriculum issues appear in the sample, one each from mathematics education, design and technology, music education and history education. It would appear that there is a communication problem, even within the field of education research. RE teachers need to communicate better both with practitioners and with the wider educational research community.[1]

What is religious education?

One of the difficulties in discussing religious education research and applying its findings is that researchers have operated with different preconceptions about the nature and aims of the subject. As we have already noted, the history of RE in the County/Community schools of England and Wales since 1944 has shown a gradual shift from types of non-denominational Christian nurture to a non-indoctrinatory study of the main religions represented in Britain with the goal of developing understanding, linked to reflection by pupils on their studies, geared up to the promotion of personal development (Jackson 1990). In addition to a shift of meaning in the County/Community school sector, researchers operating within the Roman Catholic system, or writing about RE in Church of England Aided schools, generally have had different views of the nature of the subject and its aims, corresponding to the parallel legislation for RE in the Voluntary sector. Also, educational systems in different countries have differing and changing ideas as to the nature and aims of the subject. Since the formation of the International Seminar on Religious Education and Values in 1978,[2] there has been a slow move towards internationalization in terms of research interest and co-operation. Researchers with common methodological interests, working on topics such as stage development and young people's attitudes towards Christianity, have benefited from mutual criticism, debate and collaboration on projects (e.g. Francis *et al.* 1991). However, since the topics they have researched have often related more closely to Christian nurture or formation than to a pluralistic religious education, the relevance of this research to practice in English and Welsh Community schools has been limited. Recently, international research agendas have been changing, with more attention being given to issues of religious and cultural plurality, and with educationists and researchers from more countries (or some of their provinces or states) aiming to develop forms of religious education that cater for a combined multi-religious and secular citizenry. Some of these developments will be discussed below under the heading 'The Internationalization of Religious Education Research'.

The ambiguity of the nature of religious education suffuses the research literature, making the application of much RE research to teaching and learning in English and Welsh Community schools especially difficult. Thus, Francis, Kay and Campbell's substantial compendium of research papers entitled *Research in Religious Education* (1996) brings together research on RE as perceived in different kinds of Voluntary and County school in England and Wales, research reports from different national systems of religious education (with a bias to psychometric research on attitudes), and research on collective worship in schools, an activity clearly distinct from religious education according to the 1988 legislation. Religious education specialists might find their way through the maze, but educational researchers on the outside of RE and non-specialist classroom teachers could be forgiven for expressing some confusion. The tensions between the needs of classroom practitioners in the UK and the wider interests of international RE research can also be detected in research journals. *The British Journal of Religious Education*, the main specialist journal in the field in Britain, has a policy of considering serious academic work for publication from any educational system, although current editorial policy gives priority to empirical and scholarly research of clear relevance to RE practitioners in the United Kingdom. However, an increasing number of international contributions are closely relevant to developments in religious education in the UK, covering generic issues such as national or regional policy (e.g. Mager 2002), religious plurality (Skeie 1995, 2002) and classroom dialogue (Schweitzer and Boschki 2004).

From research to classroom practice

Lest the impression be given that relating RE research to classroom practice is purely a matter of narrowing focus to particular types of research, it should be pointed out that the shift from research findings to policy and practice carries its own dangers. It could be argued that the strong influence of Ronald Goldman's research on primary RE in the 1970s resulted in the deterioration of the subject at primary level for well over a decade. Goldman's work (1964) was very influential, partly because in the early 1960s he was one of very few people engaged in British RE research. The work, heavily influenced by Piaget's research on cognitive development, was based on interviews with a small sample of pupils using three Bible stories. Goldman's findings indicated that religious thinking went through a series of stages of increasing complexity (intuitive; pre-operational; concrete; abstract) and developed in ways similar to all other thinking. His conclusion that abstract religious concepts should be excluded from RE until children had attained a mental age of thirteen led over-zealous followers to excise much explicitly religious material from primary school RE. In due course this genre of work attracted critics from several quarters. For example, Gates' study distinguishes between children's intellectual capacity for handling religious concepts and their ability to understand before they can think in an adult fashion, questioning whether developmental researchers have measured what children really understand (Gates 1976). Merlin Price's research, importing insights from the work of Jerome Bruner and Margaret Donaldson, goes further in showing that young children's degree of understanding of a religious story partly depends on constructing the correct language approach and providing a framework of meaningful activities which enable a thorough exploration of their responses (Price 1988). Other critiques include Ainsworth (nd), Ashton (1997), Greer (1972), Kay (1996), Murphy (1977) and Slee (1986). Why did Goldman's research have so much influence on primary RE? Reasons may include the fact that there was little other empirical RE research about at the time, that there was a coherence between his findings and the types of liberal Christian theology then in vogue and that Goldman himself gave serious attention to dissemination and applying his work to school-based RE. He wrote a popular book giving a simplified account of his research (Goldman 1965), and there was a widely used series of curriculum books based on his work (Goldman 1966–8). Also, many Agreed Syllabuses picked up the approach. The fact that there was little serious criticism of the research at the time serves to illustrate the danger of accepting ideas and findings on authority. This points to the importance of promptly delivered critical debate in RE scholarship, in order to address theoretical and methodological issues, as part of the dissemination process. Brian Gates' critical discussion of attitudes research in RE in his review of Francis *et al.* (1996) (Gates 1996) and Adrian Thatcher's critique of David Hay and his colleagues' approach to experiential RE (Thatcher 1991), taken together with Hay and Hammond's response (Hay and Hammond 1992), are examples of rigorous critical discussion of aspects of research which have aired reservations about theory in relation to empirical research methodology.

Parameters of research

What might be counted as RE research? We have already noted the ambiguity implicit in the term 'religious education'. There are also different types of research when looked at from a methodological point of view. Derek Webster's review of research in religious education for the *Dictionary of Religious Education* confined it to empirical studies, sometimes linked to the curriculum (Webster 1984). Both the Tooley and Hillage Reports use wider definitions of educational research, neither limiting it purely to empirical studies. Tooley includes the category 'non-empirical' research and Hillage draws on Michael Bassey's classification of educational research as including empirical, reflective and creative research, theoretical, evaluative and action research (Bassey and Constable 1997). For present purposes, I will use the two basic categories of non-empirical and empirical, dividing the latter into quantitative and qualitative, but will also refer to research from outside RE that has a relevance to RE development and to pieces of RE research which combine more than one category, or combine one or more category with curriculum development. It is not possible here to present a systematic taxonomy of varieties of RE research, and the following account is selective and impressionistic.

Non-empirical research

There is more non-empirical or scholarly research done in the field of religious education than empirical research. In a field which is inherently controversial and which draws on a range of disciplines, each importing its own theoretical debates, perhaps this is not surprising. Although some work of this genre is not always immediately translatable into classroom method or policy, its importance lies in its keeping debates about the nature of the subject open, often contributing insights from theoretical research in other fields. Some writing on theory also integrates empirical work (e.g. Chater 1997; Jackson 1997). Theoretical discussions include debates about the aims of the subject, with writers taking different stances on issues such as the extent to which RE should concentrate on the understanding of religious material in relation to the degree to which content might be seen as instrumental to the goals of some form of personal development of students (e.g. spiritual or moral development). Grimmitt's work (1987), for example, takes a mainly instrumental view with regard to religious 'content', whereas Slee (1989) and others argue for approaches which balance accurate representation of religious material with goals related to personal relevance. Other discussions reflect on the relationship between the processes of religious education in pluralistic contexts and religious nurture or formation (e.g. Chater 1997; Nesbitt 1998b).

Many discussions apply different aspects of wider debates about religious and ideological pluralism. Andrew Wright, for example, seeks to avoid both liberal and postmodern presuppositions in arguing for a religious education grounded in linguistic competence (see Chapter 5 above). John Hull, in his more recent theoretical work, integrates insights from economics, critical theory, geo-politics and theology in reflecting upon issues relating to pluralism and globalization (e.g. Hull 1996a and b, 1997, 2002). My own theoretical and methodological work draws on fields such as anthropology, social psychology, philosophy, ethnic relations, cultural studies and religious studies to address issues of the representation and interpretation of religious material (e.g. Jackson 1996b, 1997, 2000b; Chapter 6 above).

Theoretical work has also been done on the interface between RE and other fields, such as the arts (e.g. Starkings 1993; Tickner and Webster 1982; Miller 2003a), moral education (e.g. Bennett 1994; Richards 1986) and citizenship education (Jackson 2003a). Historical research on RE in

England and Wales includes general surveys (e.g. Copley 1997; Bates 1994) and studies of particular contributors, periods and topics (e.g. Bates 1992; Greer 1985). Needless to say, there needs to be a continuing high level debate about the nature of religious education in relation to publicly funded schools. The nature of the subject also needs to be debated in the light of research in relation to cognate areas of the curriculum or fields of study such as moral and values education, spiritual development, citizenship education, education in human rights and intercultural or multicultural education.

Empirical research

A substantial survey of empirical research in religious education, emphasizing psychological studies, is Francis (1996), while an updated and more wide ranging survey, covering qualitative and quantitative research, is to be found in Francis (2000a and b). It should be noted that assumed dichotomies between quantitative and qualitative methodologies are increasingly open to criticism, with more holistic approaches combining different research styles emerging (Brannen 1992). However, research in religious education, so far, has been typically either quantitative or qualitative.

The work of the pioneers of quantitative empirical work in RE in England and Wales is well documented. Ronald Goldman's work on stage development has already been referred to. Aspects of his work, as well as those of Kenneth Hyde and Edwin Cox, who also applied methods and theory from psychology, are reviewed by William Kay (1996).[3] The work of the Northern Irish scholar John Greer, which covers themes such as 'readiness' for religion, sixth form religion, moral values, attitudes to religion and religious thinking, is reviewed by Leslie Francis (1996). Religious education research which draws on theory and method from psychology is reviewed by John Greer (1984a and b) and Kenneth Hyde (1990). Leslie Francis and his associates have produced a formidable amount of psychometric research, mainly on attitudes to Christianity, much of which has more immediate relevance to the voluntary sector than to the practice of RE in community schools (e.g. Francis 1979, 1984, 1992). Quantitative research which addresses issues of teaching and learning directly includes Astley *et al.*'s piece on RE teachers' views of the relationship between aims and methods in religious education (Astley *et al.* 1997) and Kay and Linnet-Smith's work on avoiding pupils' confusions and monitoring pupils' attitudes towards religions in relation to the methods used to study them (Kay and Linnet-Smith 2000; Linnet-Smith and Kay 2000).

Qualitative work relating to RE has included research both in school and community settings and has made use of methods such as observation (with varying degrees of participation), various approaches to informal, semi-formal and structured interviewing, action research, the recording and analysis of discussion and dialogue, video analysis and biographical research. Harold Loukes was an early qualitative researcher in religious education, recording and analyzing classroom discussions by students aged around 14. Loukes followed this up by using extracts from respondents' contributions as a stimulus for written contributions from over 500 further pupils which in turn were subjected to analysis. Working before qualitative methods had been well developed and applied in educational research, Loukes was keen to use an approach which recorded the genuine voices of adolescents (Loukes 1961).[4] Loukes certainly picked up the concerns of a particular group of young people and, in consequence (and very probably influenced by his own theology), recommended a form of RE that concentrated on human questions such as relationships, responsibilities and the problems of evil and death. Had he had the methodological expertise that has been developed in qualitative educational research since that time, his findings might have been more applicable and have stimulated further research (see Eriksson 1999, 2000 and Hartman 1986, 1994 for more sophisticated approaches to Loukes' type of research). There were also qualitative elements (interviewing and analysis of responses) in Gates' research (1976) referred to above. Small scale qualitative research on classroom RE has also been carried out by Norcross (1989) which involved analysis of children's responses to evaluative questions posed after lessons on Islam, by Short and Carrington (1995) which analyzed the responses of two groups of children following lessons on Judaism, by Hookway (2002) which applied ideas from RE theory to classroom practice and by O'Grady (2003) which used ethnographic and action research methods to enhance children's motivation in lessons on Islam. The first part of Julia Ipgrave's research on Muslim pupils consisted of semi-structured interviews with Muslim pupils from four primary and four secondary schools; part two consisted of classroom observations of religious education lessons and interviews with heads and teachers. Ipgrave (1999) discusses the second part of the research.

Jackson and Nesbitt's work, using a range of ethnographic methods, is based mainly in religious communities, but explores the interplay between RE and religious nurture in the interactions with young people during research (Nesbitt 1998b), through children recounting their experiences of RE (e.g. Jackson and Nesbitt 1993) and through using ethnographic material on the upbringing and experience of children from religious groups as source material for curriculum development (Jackson 1997). Nesbitt's work provides a great deal of empirical data on the worldviews of children and young people who relate to various religious communities in Britain (e.g. 1991, 1993a, b and c, 1995a and b, 2000a). This is complemented by Østberg's ethnographic studies of identity issues in relation to Pakistani Muslim young people in Oslo (Østberg 2000a, 2003a, b and c). Ipgrave's doctoral research on children's dialogue is a model of creative ethnographic research in the classroom (Ipgrave 2002, 2003; see also Chapter 7 above for discussions of dialogical research by Ipgrave, Leganger-Krogstad, Sterkens and Weisse). There has also been a move towards biographical research with student teachers (Everington and Sikes 2001; Sikes and Everington 2001, forthcoming a and forthcoming b) and teachers (e.g. Haakedal 2001a) that, for example, informs debates about teacher commitments in relation to pedagogical issues. Weisse's team in Hamburg and Heinz Streib in Bielefeld both make use of video analysis (e.g. Knauth 1999; Streib 2003), while Hans-Günter Heimbrock and his colleagues in Frankfurt employ phenomenological methods in studying young people's life-worlds (e.g. Heimbrock 2004). Other examples of qualitative work relevant to religious education include Erricker et al. (1997), Erricker (2001; see also Chapter 4 above) Hay (e.g. 1990) and Rudge (1998).

One innovation of the 1990s was the linkage of qualitative empirical research with curriculum development in religious education. For example, the Warwick RE Project drew on recent ethnographic studies of children and young people in Britain from a range of religious backgrounds (see Jackson 1997, the references to Nesbitt above and Chapter 6 above, for example), setting up 'conversations' between children from religious communities and children in school. The project used an interpretive approach derived from hermeneutics and ethnographic theory in creating a balance between careful representation of religions and the personal and critical development of the student (Everington 1996a). Similarly, Hay and his colleagues' research on religious experience informed the Religious Education and Experience Project which sought to sensitize students to spiritual experience which, it is claimed, underlies universal human experience and is filtered in different ways by the religions of the world (e.g. Hay and Nye 1998). This element provided an experiential basis for phenomenological study (Hammond et al. 1990). Other curriculum projects drawing on theory and scholarship, but not empirical research, include the Gift to the Child Project and the Stapleford Project. The Gift to the Child Project used content as an instrument to further the personal development of the pupil, employing techniques for helping children both to empathize with and distance themselves from aspects of religious life (Hull 1996c). The Stapleford Project focused specifically on Christianity, using an approach that familiarizes pupils with the 'grammar' of the Christian tradition through an exploration of key concepts (Cooling 1997b). Ipgrave also continues to apply her classroom research to developmental work on children's dialogue within and beyond the classroom (Ipgrave 2001, 2003).

Note should also be taken of empirical research conducted outside the field of religious education which is clearly relevant to teaching and learning in RE. One good example is a study of children's concept of an afterlife conducted by a team led by Richard Lansdown, a consultant psychologist based at Great Ormond St Hospital for Children (Frangoulis *et al.* 1996; Lansdown *et al.* 1997). The researchers studied over 100 5–8-year-old children in three schools. Children who said they believed in an afterlife were asked, for example, 'How do people get there? What does it feel like to be there? What does the "place" look like? What do people do there? Can they come back to life again? Can we communicate with people who have died?' The responses were then analyzed and discussed. Findings include that for many children who believed in an afterlife heaven could be boring or even frightening.

Theory and empirical research

Empirical research should not be conducted without attention to theoretical issues and debates, otherwise findings can be easily misinterpreted. For example, Malone's empirical work in Australia on the impact of a world religions syllabus finds that a study of a particular religio-cultural group (for example, Australian Aborigines) can increase negative attitudes towards that group (Malone 1998). A crude interpretation of the findings might be to recommend that one should cease to cover other traditions, if one of the intentions is to increase positive attitudes. However, the wider theoretical debates about the representation of religions and religio-cultural change are relevant to the interpretation of Malone's findings. The recommendation might be to represent the pluralistic and changing nature of religio-cultural groups better, rather than not to represent them at all.

Issues in research

Who should do RE research?

Traditionally, the main providers of RE research have been academics in higher education and their research students. The possibilities for interaction and exchange among researchers in higher education have recently been enhanced through the formation of the Association of University Lecturers in Religions and Education (AULRE) in 2002. This body came into existence following a merger of the Conference of University Lecturers in Religious Education and the Religious Studies section of the National Association of Teachers in Further and Higher Education. In terms of research, the key point is that the association is now big enough to organize an annual conference at which research papers are presented and issues of research discussed.

With regard to the broadening of RE research beyond the work of professional academics, there have been a number of developments. These include the introduction of a number of taught masters level courses in religious education, some of them involving research methods training and a requirement to conduct a small scale piece of research for a dissertation. There continues to be a steady flow of PhD research in religious education, and some research conducted for more professionally oriented EdD degrees. Government-related bodies such as Ofsted, and the QCA (formerly SCAA and previously the NCC) have contributed to educational research, and occasionally to research in RE. Independent bodies such as the National Foundation for Educational Research (Taylor 1991) and the Culham College Institute (Gay *et al.* 1992) also make a contribution as do professional bodies such as the Religious Education Council of England and Wales (e.g. REC 1988, 1990). Other bodies have furthered the cause of RE research in different ways. The Farmington Institute for Christian Studies has enabled RE research through the organization and provision of opportunities for teachers to participate in small scale research projects, while independent charities, for example the St Gabriel's Trust, the All Saints Educational Trust, the Westhill Endowment Trust and the St Peter's Saltley Trust have contributed through the provision of funding for projects or through giving financial support to teachers doing higher degrees. There is scope for more collaborative work bringing some of these bodies and researchers from higher education and schools together.

The idea of teacher as researcher should be welcomed in principle, but not turned into a credal statement. Many excellent teachers do not want to be – and do not have the time to be – researchers. Teachers should have as part of their repertoire the capacity to read reports of research critically and some teachers have become highly competent researchers. In order to provide the necessary support, there does need to be a partnership between scholars in higher education institutions and school-based researchers. This can be through research methods training and supervision as part of a higher degree programme or could be through a teacher fellowship or through working as part of a research and development team. At Warwick, for example, teachers work with university staff on research and development projects before, during and after studying for higher degrees.

These developments are to be welcomed. The broadening of the range of bodies and individuals researching in religious education helps to demystify research, opening up the possibility for various types of collaborative work. However, a number of issues are raised to do with quality and training, scale, funding and dissemination of research.

Quality and training

On the issue of quality, all methodologies have their weaknesses; there is no perfect piece of research. This truism should not deter us from pursuing the best research we can do, given the limitations of funding and of the various methods for data collection and analysis. Take the Ofsted (Office for Standards in Education) database, just as one example. This gives access to a wide range of inspection reports which are available for study and analysis. However, these reports contain judgements made by a large number of different people. In research terms, this means that there is an unquantifiable amount of measurement error in the data. Then there is the context of Ofsted inspections. The inspection week is unlikely to be a typical week in the life of the school. There are thus some intrinsic weaknesses in research drawing solely on the Ofsted database. Yet it does not follow that useful research cannot be done using that database, despite its limitations. The analyses of Ofsted reports on religious education which have been published at intervals (e.g. Ofsted 1995), Ofsted's more focused study on the impact of new Agreed Syllabuses on the teaching and learning of religious education (Ofsted 1997) and Ofsted findings on teaching RE at Key Stage 3 (Wintersgill 2000) have been very useful general indicators of trends in RE practice. Moreover, they can be used in conjunction with different types of study. For example, Ofsted's 1995 findings on primary RE cohere with findings from Ashenden's study – a fairly small scale piece of qualitative work forming a contextual part of a larger PhD field study on the internal plurality of Christianity (Ashenden 1995). Ashenden's qualitative study gives some indicators as to the reasons why some primary teachers tend to teach a narrowly 'culturally Christian' form of RE, which are useful in considering Ofsted's quantitative data.

Perhaps the main point about quality is that of transparency. Researchers need to be frank about any deficiencies in their data or weaknesses in their methodology, as well as being judicious in interpreting results. Researchers also need to be trained in appropriate techniques. With regard to training, there is now a huge literature on research methods, and there is no reason why potential researchers from different types of organizations, including schools, should not get the kind of critical research methods training that was elusive when researchers such as Harold Loukes were doing their fieldwork. That a special issue of the *British Journal of Religious Education* in 2001 (vol. 23: 3) was dedicated entirely to the discussion of research methods in RE shows how much has changed. Many university education departments currently offer wide ranging research methods training to masters and doctoral students.

Scale

In recent years there has been a recognition that useful research does not have to be large scale. Well conducted small studies can contribute cumulatively to the totality of RE research and can have their own impact on policy and practice (e.g. Hanlon 2000). Mention has already been made of taught masters degrees in RE, and some students who have completed high quality dissertations are now contributing to the research literature (e.g. Colson 2004; Hookway 2002; Ipgrave 1999; O'Grady 2003). Small scale research studies have also been the fruit of Teacher Fellowships sponsored by the Farmington Institute (e.g. the work of Krisman discussed in Chapter 6). Under the Farmington scheme, gifted teachers of religious education have been seconded to higher education institutions full time for a term. Some have followed subject studies or conducted pieces of curriculum development. Others, however, have pursued research which has been made available to others (e.g. Wilde 1998). (The studies produced by Farmington Fellows are available on the Farmington website at www.farmington.ac.uk/documents/reports/index.html.)

Funding

The issue of research funding is difficult. So far, the number of successful applications from RE researchers to research councils and other government funded bodies has been small. The unfamiliarity with religious education as a curriculum subject in many countries makes funding from European and other international sources still more problematic. The one successful application to the Economic and Social Research Council (ESRC) to date was via the social anthropology panel rather than the education panel (Jackson 1996b), while successful applications to the Arts and Humanities Research Board have concentrated on the interface between religious studies and education, rather than religious education specifically (Arweck and Nesbitt forthcoming a and b). The shift of interest in the ESRC towards teaching and learning might redress the balance, but one of the problems may be a lack of communication between curriculum researchers in RE and the generic educational researchers who tend to be the gatekeepers of funding. Charities, especially some of the Church College Trusts, are also playing an important role in supporting RE research and development, through funding small and medium scale projects and, very importantly, through supporting teachers receiving a training in research methods during their masters or doctoral programmes.

Dissemination

The issue of dissemination of research findings needs to be addressed. Currently the priorities of the HEFCE Research Assessment Exercise in the United Kingdom militate against academics spending time reflecting on the importance of their work for practice and writing for non-refereed professional journals, magazines and websites. The Hillage Report's conclusions that educational research tends to be presented in such a way as to be unaccessible to a non-academic audience and to lack interpretation for a policy-making or practitioner audience should be well taken by RE researchers.[5]   However, British politicians and other policy makers give little or no attention to the findings of research in RE, perhaps influenced by the negative view of educational research in general in the spin associated with the Tooley Report. This is in contrast to the generation of policy in Council of Europe projects which involve researchers and other experts as well as practitioners and other end users (see Chapter 10 below).

In 1997, the Teacher Training Agency took the initiative to support the dissemination of masters and doctoral dissertations considered to be especially relevant to teaching and learning. Julia Ipgrave's MA dissertation on the religious education of Muslim pupils was selected for funding, and she wrote a summary of her work which was made available by the TTA in a form easily accessible to busy teachers (Ipgrave 1998). This scheme was superseded by the DfES best practice scholarship programme, but the Department for Education and Skills has announced that it will not be funding further rounds of the national BPRS scheme. Rather, it will increase schools' baseline funding. In theory this will give schools greater flexibility to support research and development activities which meet local priorities and the needs of their teachers. Whether the funding actually will be earmarked for research is an obvious issue.

The growing use of ICT in RE is assisting the dissemination of research, and gateways, such as the Lancaster-based Philtar (http://philtar.ucsm.ac.uk/) and RE-XS (http://re-xs.ucsm.ac.uk/), are already becoming a means to disseminate, criticize and apply religious education research. At the level of refereed journals, wider dissemination in generic education publications as well as specialist religious education outlets needs more attention. The *British Journal of Religious Education* has had an 'online' version for institutional subscribers since January 2004, potentially widening access to RE research significantly (see http://www.tandf.co.uk/journals/).

The internationalization of religious education research

Reference was made above to the internationalization of RE debates, especially through the work of the International Seminar on Religious Education and Values (ISREV) and publications related to it (e.g. Francis *et al.* 2001; Bates *et al.* forthcoming). In addition to this, a number of smaller international research networks and workshops have emerged. For example, the European Network for Religious Education through Contextual Approaches (ENRECA) brings together researchers and research students from a range of northern European countries. ENRECA was set up in 1999 in order to bring together scholars engaged in empirical and theoretical research in aspects of religion and education in relation to intercultural issues. The group is committed to research on the educational implications of the changing patterns of religious and secular plurality in European countries. ENRECA operates as an on-going research seminar and currently includes scholars from Germany, the United Kingdom, the Netherlands, Norway, France and Estonia. Seminars include the presentation and critical discussion of current research, the exchange of research findings and discussions of common issues relevant to the European context. A key element of the group's work is its concern to ensure that research findings are relevant to educational policy makers and practitioners. The group is committed to involving practitioners in the research process and includes teachers and teacher educators who are engaged in research as well as academics from various relevant fields, professional researchers and PhD students. The group's first book was published in 2001, and includes critical essays and research reports relating to diversity as a challenge for education in Europe (Heimbrock *et al.* 2001). ENRECA plans to make available summaries of research findings to policy makers and practitioners and to provide contributions to conferences and seminars on inter-religious and intercultural education as well as consultancy on issues of research, theory and pedagogy.[6]

Another group, the International Network for Inter-religious and Intercultural Education, brings together northern European and South African scholars. The Network was set up in 1994, soon after the election of a democratic government in South Africa, and had its first meeting in

September in the Faculty of Education at the University of Hamburg. The aim was to promote links between South African and northern European research groups working in fields connecting religion and education in culturally diverse democratic societies. The seminar brought together members of research and development groups working in the fields of religion, education and cultural diversity in order to share insights and to learn from one another. Subsequent meetings have been held at the Universities of Utrecht, Cape Town and Warwick, with the 2004 seminar scheduled to meet in Stellenbosch. Books based on the seminars are Weisse (1996d), Andree *et al.* (1997), Chidester *et al.* (1999) and Jackson (2003a). There are also productive international collaborations in relation to doctoral research. For example, Sissel Østberg's PhD on Pakistani Muslim children in Oslo was supervised from the University of Warwick, while research on religion as a part of intercultural education in Dutch primary schools is being supervised at the University of Frankfurt. Several comparative studies are currently being done by doctoral students, including two Norwegian-English studies on aspects of religious education practice in primary and secondary schools. Meetings of PhD students in religious education from the UK, Germany and Norway are also planned.

Another form of internationalization is through consultation over the development of policy. For example, debates about the development of religious education policy in the Canadian province of Quebec (Milot and Ouellet 1997), South Africa (Chidester *et al.* 1999; Steyn 2003), and Norway (e.g. Haakedal 2001b; Skeie 2001) have all involved international consultation. Discussions about the inclusion of studies of religion in French schools, following the publication of the Debray Report (Debray 2002), also have an international dimension.

Conclusions

There needs to be more clarity and precision in the use of the term 'religious education' in the research literature, and religious education researchers need to interpret their work to other educational researchers, perhaps disseminating some of it through generic educational research journals. More 'basic' types of research, whether theoretical or empirical, are entirely legitimate and their importance might be appreciated in the longer term; they have the potential for challenging institutionalized received wisdom. However, relatively speaking, there has been a neglect of research giving direct attention to issues of teaching and learning in RE within the English and Welsh educational system. There are notable exceptions, but the implications of all such empirical work need to be debated in the context of theory, methodology and other empirical studies before new policy is generated. Projects linking theory, empirical research and classroom practice or RE teaching have been a welcome innovation. There has also been empirical work done outside the field of RE which has potential relevance to practice. More should be made of such studies by religious educators.

Research need not be large scale and, with appropriate research methods training, serving teachers can make a strong contribution to the development of the subject, working on their own, or in collaboration with academics. The growth of taught masters degrees in religious education, which include courses in research methods and the requirement of small scale pieces of research, have been a benefit in this respect, together with more conventional MPhil and PhD research, and newer EdD programmes. In some universities, there has been a recent flowering of doctoral research in RE which should gradually result in a good deal of work relevant to practice in schools.[7] International contact between doctoral students, to compare projects and discuss methodological questions, will also enhance RE research considerably.

There is no reason why research should be confined to higher education, and government-related bodies, independent institutes and trusts, and professional bodies all have a role to play, either in sponsoring or conducting research. More collaborative work between such bodies and higher education institutions would be welcome. Another way to collaborate is through joint research workshops and publications focusing on research topics which have a bearing on religious education pedagogy. Michael Grimmitt's compilation of accounts of different research-based religious education pedagogies was a welcome contribution to this type of co-operative venture (Grimmitt 2000b).

The opportunity is there for religious education researchers to pull together in conducting studies that make a positive impact on practice. We have seen that some networks are being formed in order to focus on key issues. The provision of research funding to cover different types of RE research remains a key issue. Religious education researchers need to make their findings more accessible to politicians and other policy makers, but politicians need to recognize the value and relevance of RE research and make efforts to consult it.

Finally, the gradual internationalization of research in religious education is to be welcomed. Religion is a very evident factor in international relations and in processes of globalization and no country can afford to see its educational provision in isolation. There are already international initiatives such as the Council of Europe's project on religious diversity and intercultural education in Europe, and the Oslo Coalition's work on religion, education and human rights (Larsen and Plesner 2002; see Chapter 10 below). Such projects need to be informed by both theoretical and empirical research in religious education if they are to introduce significant developments, rather than recording examples of good practice retrospectively.

Chapter 10

Towards a pluralistic religious education

To sum up so far, I have drawn upon research and scholarship in attempting to describe the different dimensions of plurality experienced in the contemporary world, introducing the debates about modernism and postmodernism and the analysis of religion in relation to culture, ethnicity and nationality. The distinction was made between plurality as a descriptor and the normative concept of pluralism. I went on to discuss some different responses to plurality from those thinking, writing and researching about religious education.

The position that religious education in state-funded Community schools should be taught from a Christian perspective in order to inculcate Christian belief was rejected, as were the views that it is justifiable in such schools to teach Christianity as true in order to foster a particular brand of personal and social morality or for historical and cultural reasons. The standpoint that religious education should be confined to the study of Christianity was also held to be unsustainable in the light of social plurality locally and nationally and the forces of globalization. With regard to the role of the Christian teacher of religious education in the Community school, the view that the only possible professional stances were Christian confessionalism or 'procedural neutrality' was rejected. The traditionalist Christian approach to religious education was seen as a nostalgic attempt to insulate young people in the common school from the inevitable influences of plurality, rather than helping pupils to engage with them, and as over-emphasizing the influence of schools and teachers on the formation of pupils' identities.

The trend towards an increase in the provision of faith-based schools was interpreted as a second type of reaction to plurality. Although there are important arguments against such provision, forms of faith-based education that respect the voice of the child and maintain a stance of openness to others in society were judged, pragmatically, to be legitimate. The view was advanced that *all* schools should promote social justice (including religious tolerance), knowledge about religions, the development of pupils' skills of criticism and independent thinking as well as dialogue and interaction between young people from different backgrounds. The radical postmodernist 'personal narrative' approach to religious education was seen as a third response to plurality. The fundamental problem with this approach is the stipulation of a thoroughgoing anti-realism as its epistemological foundation. The anti-realist ideology suffuses its pedagogy, discriminating against children holding realist views of religious language, and depriving pupils of opportunities to scrutinize published resources introduced by the teacher. In contrast, the 'religious literacy' approach responds to plurality in an inclusive way, seeking to help young people from all backgrounds to clarify, criticize, formulate and justify their own positions. Its deficiency lies principally in treating religions as internally homogeneous systems.

The interpretive approach, like the religious literacy approach, was seen to have the aim of helping children and young people to find their own positions within the key debates about religious plurality. However, the interpretive approach recognizes the inner diversity, permeable boundaries and contested nature of religious traditions as well as the complexity of cultural expression and change from individual and social perspectives. Having originated in ethnographic studies of children and young people from different religious backgrounds, the interpretive approach reflects debates within social anthropology, emphasizing issues of representation, interpretation and reflexivity. It utilizes pupils' own beliefs and values as a resource and encourages their active involvement in the design and evaluation of learning activities. The process of reflexivity, for example, includes pupils reflecting on their understanding of their own way of life through encountering 'difference', criticizing constructively religious material studied at a distance, and developing a running critique of study methods. Case studies illustrated how the approach can be adapted to meet the needs of children in different situations and combined with elements from other pedagogies. In the classroom situation, teaching and learning can begin according to need at any point on the hermeneutic circle with, for example, a critical overview of key concepts, a particular representation of a religion, case studies of individuals or groups, or pupils' experiences, concerns, questions or interactions within the school.

Three related dialogical approaches were seen to have much in common with the interpretive approach, but placed even more weight on pupils' personal knowledge and experience as a source of material for study, exchange and reflection. However, in contrast to the postmodernist 'personal narrative' approach, all agreed that further source material should be introduced by teachers, such as locally based material, textual and historical sources, and material relating to ethical and human rights issues or existential questions. The relative autonomy of individual pupils is acknowledged in these approaches, but in the context of influences from the family and other social groups. A key element is an emphasis on the agency of pupils in selecting and reviewing topics and methods of study, and in being given opportunities to reflect critically both on content and methods of study. As with the interpretive approach, much attention is given to the development of skills and appropriate attitudes for the study of religions and religious and values issues. Pupils are seen as co-learners, joint designers of methods of study and as co-researchers with their teachers. Finally, I discussed the contribution that RE can make to the fields of intercultural, citizenship and values education and reflected on the role of research in enhancing religious education.

I will now discuss the agency of pupils in relation to religious education and go on to consider epistemological, political and ethical foundations of pluralistic approaches to the subject. I will then discuss issues of general school policy and, with some reference to international projects, the role of RE in promoting social cohesion. A discussion of patterns of civil religion in relation to religious education follows, leading to a final consideration of ways in which law and policy might develop in England and Wales in support of a pluralistic religious education.

Pupils as agents

The personal narrative, religious literacy, interpretive and dialogical approaches all recognize the agency of children and young people as an important ingredient of religious education. O'Grady's and Ipgrave's research studies, for example, show how the involvement of pupils in planning and evaluating teaching and learning processes in RE at primary and secondary levels can be strongly motivating and can bring out a high level of maturity in young people. This is consistent with research in the sociology of childhood (e.g. James and Prout 1997) and research completed recently by the 'Consulting Pupils about Teaching and Learning' research network, funded by the Economic and Social Research Council. Findings of the ESRC research confirm that consultation with pupils over teaching and learning produces practical ideas and strengthens pupil self-esteem, leading to an enhanced commitment to learning and to the school on the part of pupils. This is sustained by teachers' increased awareness of pupils' capacity for constructive analysis which, in turn, leads to changes in pedagogy and more active and collaborative relationships between teachers and pupils (e.g. Flutter and Rudduck 2004).

I have already alluded (in Chapters 3 and 8) to Iris Young's view of 'differentiated citizenship' that requires structures to enable individuals at the grass-roots level to bring their own perspectives – whether based on religion, culture, ethnicity, gender or geography – to the exploration of social issues, and to express their own voices (Young 1990: 116). Ipgrave and O'Grady, for example, organize their religious education classrooms in ways that encourage this form of participation, and the wealth of evidence from the ESRC project referred to above supports forms of education that maximize pupils' involvement. The formation of a youth shadow Standing Advisory Council for Religious Education (SACRE) in the city of Bradford is another example of responsibility given to young people to participate more fully in planning and monitoring religious education. Initially, a one day conference was held with the purpose of giving young people the opportunity to share their views and opinions on RE, mainly at the post-16 level. The meeting was modelled on an Agreed Syllabus Conference, with different groups being given particular tasks to complete in relation to RE's aims, content and mode of delivery and the types of skills they thought they could develop through the subject. Joyce Miller, Strategy Manager of RE and Citizenship for Education Bradford, writes:

> They wanted unbiased RE, covering a range of religions, addressing issues they were concerned about so that RE would make a real contribution to their thinking and their lives. The sixth form syllabus should allow for flexibility, including day conferences, work in the community and the use of technology such as video conferencing. They wanted opportunities to meet with sixth formers from other schools to share ideas and debate because they were aware that Bradford was a very diverse district and that all too often their own experience was limited ... They wanted the full complexity of the topics they dealt with to be explored and acknowledged and they wanted to be taught by specialist teachers.
>
> (Miller 2003b: 34)

The sixth formers agreed at the end of the conference that they would like to continue their participation, so funding was sought to set up a permanent shadow SACRE. This is now in operation, and meets each term, supported by LEA officers and SACRE members, to discuss issues relating to religious education and related fields, and the more general theme of working and living together in a plural society. Each meeting has a specific goal, such as a press release to the local newspaper or a letter to the managing director of Education Bradford. The shadow SACRE elects its own chair and secretary, will have its own annual conference and will also produce an annual report. Although its main function is to advise on RE, the students want to develop their own thinking and opinions. For example, the students held an 'Any Questions' session, in order to discuss RE, race relations in the city and wider social and moral issues with a panel including a young Muslim woman, a male Sikh community worker and the Bishop of Bradford (Miller 2003c).

Foundations of pluralistic approaches

The religious literacy, interpretive and dialogical approaches to religious education are not neutral. They acknowledge the inevitable influence of plurality upon young people, and help them to engage with it. They do not set out to promote or to erode particular beliefs, including those of children in school, but they do acknowledge that pupils should be given the opportunity to study and reflect upon different religious and philosophical viewpoints in a structured way and to apply skills of interpretation and criticism methodically. They acknowledge the right of individuals to hold different religious or secular beliefs and that some pupils will bring to the classroom particular religious affiliations of their families and communities. The stance on pluralism shared by these approaches, at the epistemological level, acknowledges that issues concerning the truth of particular religious claims cannot be resolved publicly. Politically, they affirm the individual's democratic right to freedom of religion or belief and they actively promote tolerance of religious and ideological difference within the law. Ethically, they attempt to ensure that the practices and claims of religions are considered with sensitivity, accuracy, intellectual rigour and fairness. They are not *secularist*, and can be supported by citizens with different religious and secular viewpoints. If they are *secular*, then they are so only in the sense used in the Indian Constitution which, like Article 18 of the Universal Declaration of Human Rights and other human rights codes (see Chapter 8 above), is intended as a guarantee of freedom of religion or belief.

This political and ethical underpinning has much in common with the 'procedural values' that should be shared by all people in Britain, according to the Parekh Report:

> Procedural values are those that maintain the preconditions for democratic dialogue. They include people's willingness to give reasons

for their views, readiness to be influenced by better arguments than their own, tolerance, mutual respect, aspiration to peaceful resolution of differences, and willingness to abide by collectively binding decisions that have been reached by the agreed procedures.

(Runnymede Trust 2000, par. 4.30: 53)

These are non-negotiable values 'that underpin any defensible conception of the good life' (Runnymede Trust 2000, par. 4.30: 53). They are the fundamental human rights and duties that recognize the equal worth and dignity of all, upon which an open liberal democracy is based (Home Office 2001b, par. 3.12: 20).

Approaches to RE that have these values, according to Denise Cush, exhibit 'positive pluralism', which she distinguishes from the negative pluralism that avoids the encounter of religions by either leaving religion out of education or by teaching children in separate faith groups:

Positive pluralism actually welcomes plurality as an opportunity rather than a problem. Religions have never existed in hermetically sealed containers but have interacted throughout the centuries. Today, more than before, religions are in contact with and in dialogue with each other. Positive pluralism does not teach that all faiths are equally valid like the relativist, or all paths to the same goal like the universalist. It takes the differences and incommensurability of world views seriously, but approaches them from a viewpoint of 'epistemological humility' or 'methodological agnosticism'.

(Cush 1999: 384)[1]

This type of religious education in the Community school can appeal to people with a wide variety of viewpoints on religion. For example, it is consistent with the views of Trevor Cooling, an Evangelical Christian religious education scholar, who considers that the subject in the Community school should 'encourage debate between people of very different, and often fundamentally opposed views, and … assist in the development of strategies which enable people to work together for the common good despite their deeply held differences' (Cooling 2002). It also coheres with the views of the Muslim mother in Hamburg who wrote:

School is society in miniature, where children and adolescents can learn to live together, where awareness and attitudes are created. I hope for a religious education in school which treats and teaches all religions equally. I think that a truly inter-religious education enables children to take part in an important learning process: to learn about the other world religions and to get to know and value their peers for their religion and cultural backgrounds.

(Quoted in Weisse 2003: 192)

Moreover, it is consistent with the current policy of the British Humanist Association which proposes:

... impartial, fair and balanced teaching about all major worldviews, including non-religious ones, to give all children an understanding of the range of beliefs found in a multi-cultural society and the values shared by most religions and ethical worldviews.

(BHA 2002: 11)

Teachers of the subject can be from any religion or none, provided that they recognize that their role as educators in the common school cannot be to persuade children to adopt particular religious or non-religious views and that they are comfortable with this stance (see Chapter 2 above).

Management and school policy

Iris Young's idea of differentiated citizenship also raises the question of structures within school as a whole. Here, Julia Ipgrave's distinction between primary (awareness of diversity), secondary (being positive about diversity) and tertiary (engaging with diversity) dialogue (Chapter 7 above) is useful for considering whole school policy in relation to plurality. With regard to 'secondary dialogue', there is a need to consider school policies on religious discrimination and the mechanisms schools might introduce to eliminate it. It would be pointless to have a form of religious education that promotes religious tolerance and non-discrimination whilst having wider school policies that ignore or even work against them. In Chapter 8, I wrote about the value to society of the Community school as the 'plural school', but I also referred, in Chapter 3, to evidence of an anti-religious ethos or of religious discrimination in some Community schools (e.g. Weller *et al.* 2001; White 2003). The Community school needs to ensure that it takes a positive stance towards religious diversity, and engages with issues of plurality in all its procedures of management and governance.

The common school should not be a secularist school, but an inclusive school. It has the potential to be a forum for dialogue between students and teachers from different religious and non-religious backgrounds and for providing pupils with the skills to interpret, reflect upon and gain insight from different worldviews. It should also provide pupils with opportunities for debating issues of religion, culture, morality or citizenship and for encounter and exchange with people having different views and commitments. Moreover, it should also build bridges with parents and the communities to which they belong. The knowledge, understanding and skills that can be provided by religious education have a vital contribution to make to these processes.

These proposals are fully consistent with current government policy on educational inclusion (Ofsted 2000: 1). The policy of the British Humanist Association also supports an inclusive policy with regard to religion in schools (BHA 2002), and would be approved of by many parents, including many from religious backgrounds. The BHA policy document states that:

> We believe that inclusive community schools can provide an opportunity for people of all faiths, and none, to co-exist peacefully in an environment where their rights to their own beliefs and philosophies are respected. We believe that schools can and should respect the requirements of the religious, and the non-religious, without affecting the human rights and educational entitlements of all.
>
> (BHA 2002: 3)

The BHA's recommendations include provision of an impartial, fair and balanced approach to different religions and worldviews, with the addition of optional faith-based instruction, the recognition of a wider range of religious holidays, and respect for the religio-cultural requirements of pupils with regard to dress, diet, single sex classes and sex and relationships education (BHA 2002: 11–14).[2] As well as dealing with local outreach, the plural school can also help to open pupils' eyes to wider international issues of media representations of religion, global citizenship, human rights and sustainable development, including analysis of the negative as well as positive influences of religion (Gearon 2002, 2003a and b; Schweitzer 2001).

Social cohesion and the aims of RE

Events such as those of September 11, 2001 in the USA and their aftermath, riots in the north of England in the summer of 2001 (Home Office 2001a and b) and the atrocity in Bali in the autumn of 2002 have put religion on political, social and educational agendas domestically and internationally. Recent research in Britain has shown that, as a result of such events, religion may sometimes be a stronger motivator for discriminatory sentiment and behaviour than race or ethnicity (Sheridan 2002). In responding in terms of educational policy, specialists in religions and education have been in demand to suggest ways in which the study of religions can help to promote tolerance and thereby foster social cohesion. Some critics find dangers in this, especially in diverting religious education from its primary concerns, and in importing hidden assumptions of relativism or of theological pluralism. As Andrew Wright puts it:

> On the level of immanence we find a pragmatic approach to truth, in which religion is taught not as an end in itself, but as a tool for encouraging tolerance and mutual understanding in a culturally divided society. The hidden 'truth' here is that religion is no more than a relativistic expression of culture whose primary function is to point beyond itself to our common humanity. On the level of transcendence concerns for social cohesion have often led to the conclusion that, insofar as religion is viewed as a human response to transcendence, the only valid theological option is that of a universal theology in which all traditions are regarded as being equally true.
>
> (Wright 2003: 287)

I want to argue against this view. It is impossible to establish a necessary connection between the instrumental goal of using religious education to promote social cohesion and the adoption or propagation of relativism or theological pluralism. However, a religious education that sets out only to promote tolerance or social cohesion is inadequate. Elsewhere I have argued that a key aim for RE is to develop an understanding of the grammar – the language and wider symbolic patterns – of religions and the interpretive skills necessary to gain that understanding (Jackson 1997: 129). The achievement of this aim requires the development of critical skills, the application of which opens up issues of representation, interpretation, truth and meaning. Religious education develops self-awareness, since individuals develop through reflecting upon encounters with new ideas and experiences. Religious education is thus a conversational process in which students, whatever their backgrounds, continuously interpret and reinterpret their own views in the light of what they study (cf. Meijer 1995). Something of the flavour of this approach to learning comes across in the accounts of classroom practice discussed in Chapters 6 and 7, in the work of Krisman, O'Grady, Ipgrave and Leganger-Krogstad, for example. It is hoped that *through* these processes of learning, inter-religious and intercultural understanding will be fostered. But this does not imply a methodological assumption that religions are simply cultural facts or are equally true. Pupils will end up with a variety of views about the nature of religion and the relationship between the truth claims of religions, and the formation of these views will be influenced by various factors, many of them beyond the RE classroom.

It would equally be a mistake, however, to assume that understanding and knowledge necessarily foster tolerance; racists can be well informed. Moreover, propagandists are aware that lies and misinformation can increase tolerance, sympathy and respect. However, I would argue that knowledge and understanding are necessary but not sufficient conditions for removing prejudice genuinely. As I argued in Chapter 8, religious education specialists should welcome the opportunity to bring their expertise to programmes of intercultural and citizenship education, but with a recognition that their contribution needs to be complemented by that of others.

International projects

Whether in response to terrorism or social fragmentation or in promoting education in human rights, there is strong international interest in bringing the dimension of religious diversity to education. It is worth drawing attention to two international projects that are current at the time of writing in order to illustrate the possibilities for collaboration between religious education specialists and educators working in fields such as intercultural education and human rights education.

In the European context, and directly as a response to the events of September 11, 2001 and their consequences, the Council of Europe is, at the time of writing, encouraging the addition of the dimension of religious diversity to intercultural education, including education for citizenship, across Europe. A project on 'intercultural education and the challenge of religious diversity and dialogue' was approved by the education committee of the Council at the end of September 2002. This has the goal of producing materials for policy makers and practitioners across more than forty member states by the end of 2004.

The proposal was discussed by a meeting in Strasbourg in September 2002 that included representatives of the ministries of education of the states party to the European Cultural Convention, other statutory participants such as representatives of the Parliamentary Assembly and the EU and observer states, representatives of professional organizations concerned with intercultural education and religious education plus a number of individual specialists and members of the initial working party.

It was gratifying to see support for this project from countries with diverse views about the place of religion in the curriculum of schools. Religious education specialists from England and Germany joined specialists in intercultural and antiracist education and conflict resolution from various parts of Europe to find common ground in the cause of increasing inter-religious and intercultural understanding. The project plan includes two strands. The main concern of the first is teacher training, with the primary aim of drawing up a structured and wide ranging compendium of examples, and a guidance document based on these and on teacher-training workshops. The second is concerned with policy.

Experts in religious and intercultural education from different parts of Europe met in Paris in June 2003 in order to identify the key issues in relation to religious diversity and the religious dimension of intercultural education, to tease out the implications of these issues for learning and to make policy recommendations for the ministerial conference on intercultural education held in Athens in November 2003. Two working groups dealt with these issues. In terms of policy, the group that included members from Italy, the Netherlands, Germany, Greece, the UK, Latvia and Denmark recommended that, whatever the system of religious education in any particular state, children should have education in religious and secular diversity as part of their intercultural education, regardless of where specifically this was included in the curriculum. This element of the curriculum should include, for example, encouraging tolerance for different religious and secular points of view, education in human rights, citizenship and conflict management, and strategies to counter racism and discrimination in a religiously diverse world.[3]

In addition to these initiatives, each member state is encouraged to undertake related activities to inform and develop the project. John Keast, a member of the Council of Europe Working Party, took the initiative to convene a seminar in London in March 2003 in order to begin the discussion of ways in which educators in the UK might contribute to the project.

A second project is more global in scope. In November 2001 the United Nations Special Rapporteur on Freedom of Religion or Belief, Abdelfattah Amor, in co-operation with the Spanish government, arranged an international conference in Madrid on the Elimination of Religious Discrimination and Intolerance in Education. The main aim was to develop strategies for combating religious intolerance and discrimination and promoting freedom of religion or belief through education. The conference resulted in a declaration with key recommendations on the need to strengthen human rights education and to increase pupils' knowledge and understanding of the worldviews and religions of others. The importance of securing the rights of parents and children and the right to freedom of religion or belief in education was emphasized.

The Oslo Coalition on Freedom of Religion or Belief, an international network of academics, representatives from faith communities, non-governmental organizations (NGOs) and other international organizations, took on the role of following up the recommendations of the final document of the Madrid conference through initiating a project on 'Teaching for Tolerance, and Freedom of Religion or Belief', with a brief to develop a global interdisciplinary network. The principal aims of the project are:

- To encourage school education that increases understanding and respect between people of different religions or worldviews and that fosters knowledge about and respect for freedom of religion or belief as a human right … (and by this) …
- To combat discrimination and intolerance based on religion or belief and prevent violations of the human right to freedom of religion or belief.

A preparatory seminar was held in Oslo in December 2002, bringing together experts from different parts of the world specializing in human rights law, education about religion and belief (including religious education), human rights education, civic education and inter-faith dialogue. Papers from this seminar were published in a report (Larsen and Plesner 2002). A smaller working group met in May 2003 in Rabat, Morocco, in order to draft an action plan for the project including identifying and initiating a number of sub-projects. The plan included a conference in September 2004 as part of the implementation of the document produced at the Madrid conference, the development of databases giving an overview of resources and experts, the production of a book on different pedagogical models, material and methods used internationally in teaching about religions or beliefs, the compilation of a book of stories on tolerance and how to teach tolerance, and a manual for teacher training.

The Oslo Coalition Project is co-operating with existing regional and global networks and organizations and with governmental authorities and the United Nations. For example, the working group that met in 2003 visited the headquarters of the Islamic Educational, Scientific and Cultural Organization (ISESCO) in Rabat in order to make contact with personnel from different parts of the Islamic world and to set out the priorities of the project.[4]

Projects like these help to disseminate the ideas of religious education scholars and practitioners, as well as bringing their specialist expertise to issues of culture and human rights. In both projects, it was illuminating that some experts in intercultural education or human rights education were unaware of research and development projects on religious education in the UK, having previously dismissed RE as a subject concerned with the propagation of a religious viewpoint.

Civil religion and changing law and policy

The increasing internationalization of discussions of the role of religion in schools highlights national differences as well as issues common to many states. As we noted in Chapter 1, it is clear that each nation state has its own variety of civil religion, conditioned by its own particular history. Thus the processes through which religious and cultural diversity are accommodated – including arrangements for handling religion in public education – are likely to be different in different states. For example, in the European context, England and France have had different approaches to religion in the public sphere. However, in both cases, civil religion and national custom are changing as a result of increasing plurality.

France is a secular state, having no civic religious identity and no official relationship with religions or their denominations and sub-groups. The word laïcité connotes this independence of the state and religion. Laïcité has been the key principle for excluding the study of religion from French publicly funded schools, and the basis of controversies over the wearing of religious symbols in schools (such as Muslim girls wearing the 'headscarf'). The principle of laïcité has traditionally confined religion to the private domain, while a view of national identity that emphasizes 'Frenchness' has accounted for an assumption by some of a cultural assimilationist view with regard to immigrants to the country.

However, a debate began in the late 1980s over whether or not pupils should be informed about religions in schools. A report was published in 1989 advancing the view that education about religions should be included in the school curriculum, partly with the aim of promoting understanding between young people from different religious backgrounds, and helping to integrate rather than assimilate children from 'immigrant' families into the Republic (Prelot 2002: 6). In 1996, some study of Islam was introduced through programmes of study in French and history. In 2001, Régis Debray was commissioned by the Minister of Education to produce a report making proposals for the teaching of knowledge about religions in the secular school (l'École laïque). In producing his report, Debray consulted widely with educators in schools and higher education as well as inspectors and teachers' associations. Debray notes that majority French opinion approves of strengthening the study of religions in the state schools (Debray 2002: 13). His report contains a series of recommendations including introducing the study of religions, not as a separate subject, but as a theme across a range of subjects, including history and philosophy. Debray also recommended the establishment of a national institute of 'sciences of religion', in order to facilitate initial and in-service training of primary and secondary teachers and training of regional inspectors in the philosophy of laïcité and the history of religions. The European Institute of Religious Sciences was set up in June 2002, and steps are now being taken to prepare appropriate courses for teachers and other educationists. These developments represent a very significant shift in French government policy, but one which reflects France's particular, though changing, historical circumstances. The state's principle of laïcité is still at the heart of the policy, but not to connote secularism. In Debray's view, rather than being anti-religious, laïcité guarantees the individual's freedom of conscience to have or not to have a religion (Debray 2002: 39). As Debray puts it with regard to Islam, 'Laïcité is an opportunity for Islam in France and French Islam is an opportunity for laïcité' (Debray 2002: 42).

In England, the situation is very different with regard to civil religion in general and in relation to the role of the religions in education in particular. There has been a long partnership between the state and the Church of England, in the case of publicly funded education going back to the introduction of state schooling in 1870. The 1944 Education Act made the use of Agreed Syllabuses for Religious Instruction by state-funded County schools mandatory. Under the terms of the 1944 Act, English Local Education Authorities (LEAs) had to convene a syllabus conference consisting of four committees representing the Church of England, other denominations (in effect Protestant ones), the local authority and teachers' organizations.

Changes to religious education brought about by the 1988 Education Reform Act reflected both increasing religious plurality and secularization. Many features of the 1944 Act (provision, withdrawal and Agreed Syllabuses) were retained, but significant changes were made. For example, the term 'religious education' replaced the expression 'religious instruction' with its suggestion of deliberate transmission of religious beliefs. In recognition of the need for different interest groups to have a say in the production of syllabuses, and for local circumstances to be considered, the arrangements for producing Agreed Syllabuses were retained in a modified form. However, for the first time in law, representatives of faiths other than Christianity were given a place on Agreed Syllabus Conferences, on what used to be the 'other denominations' committee (though subsequent legislation in 1993 limited this representation to those local authorities where significant numbers of adherents were present). Also, SACREs now had to be set up with statutory functions that include monitoring the use of Agreed Syllabuses. Since SACREs have a composition which parallels that of Agreed Syllabus Conferences, it is now common, in areas where there are significant numbers, to have, for example, Hindu, Sikh and Muslim representatives both on SACREs and Agreed Syllabus Conferences. Members of other religious minorities and humanists may also be present as co-opted members. As we noted in Chapter 2, the 1988 Act also required that any new Agreed Syllabus has to 'reflect the fact that religious traditions in Great Britain are in the main Christian, whilst taking account of the teaching and practices of the other principal religions represented in Great Britain' (UK Parliament 1988: Section 8.3).

The role of faith representatives in policy making and syllabus design

In both the examples of France and England, their particular civic views of religion in relation to the state have profoundly influenced the ways in which religious plurality is accommodated within education. In the English case, just as there is a gradual incorporation of the main faiths represented in the country into national and local civic religious life, so there has been an increased involvement of religions other than Christianity in the processes relating to religious education in Community schools. However, the Church of England retains its dominant role in the formulation and approval of syllabuses for the common school, and representatives of other denominations and religions continue to have a major say in the content of syllabuses. It is significant that, in 2003, Charles Clarke, the Secretary of State for Education and Skills, consulted Christian and other religious leaders about reforming religious education before speaking to the educators who teach the subject (see also Chapter 9 above for comments on British politicians' lack of attention to research in RE). In the French case, the one set of institutions Debray did *not* consult was the religions. He consulted teachers in schools, colleges, lycées, university professors, school inspectors, and teachers' associations (Debray 2002: 10), but not representatives of the religions. The French state retains a deep suspicion of the motives of the Church, and one reason for not introducing the study of religion as a separate subject was precisely this fear.

In the longer term there would be worries of a substitution of clerical for lay [teachers]. Intervention from outside would sooner or later seek to replace the teachers with those with diplomas from faculties of theology and representatives from different confessions who would argue that they have real qualifications and centuries of experience.

(Debray 2002: 35)

In the English case, the religions – especially the Church of England – continue to have a good deal of influence on the content of religious education, while in the French case, the study of religions is seen as solely the concern of academics and teachers. Michael Grimmitt has argued passionately that the strong involvement of faith representatives in the production of syllabuses in England and Wales has allowed them to present domesticated versions of religions to pupils that work in the interests of the religions, rather than of the pupils (Grimmitt 2000b).

Grimmitt also targets the view of education held by the Thatcher government that introduced the 1988 Education Reform Act, as imposing 'a market-led, output and assessment oriented, centralised education system and a National Curriculum upon the country' (Grimmitt 2000b: 7). He sees Section 8.3 of the Act as reinforcing the market driven ideology introduced by the Conservatives, but sustained by successive Labour governments, perpetuating the predominance of Christianity and creating a competitive atmosphere among the religions. This has led to the study of religions in isolation from one another, with an emphasis on the 'teachings and practices' of religions as an organizing principle in syllabus design. For Grimmitt, the combination of the application of a market-led educational ideology and the implementation of Section 8.3 of the Education Reform Act, has led to 'the captivity of RE by the joint forces of politicians and religionists, each pursuing their own self-interests' (Grimmitt 2000b: 13).

Grimmitt is especially critical of the role of representatives of the religions in producing the national model syllabuses that were published in 1994 (SCAA 1994a and b).[5] These syllabuses are non-statutory and are for the use of Agreed Syllabus Conferences, who can choose to ignore them or can edit or borrow from them. Nonetheless, for several years (from 1997), secondary trainees in RE were required to have a detailed knowledge of them, so their influence was widespread. During the preparation of the syllabuses, six separate working groups, made up respectively of representatives of Christianity, Judaism, Islam, Hinduism, Buddhism and Sikhism, were set up in order to identify essential teachings and practices that could be included in the syllabuses. This procedure, argues Grimmitt, resulted in an emphasis in the syllabuses on content rather than process, and the study of each religion in isolation from the others. (I would add the point that the processes which brought the syllabuses to fruition did not address the important issue of the historical representation of the 'religions' in particular and 'religion' in general and also downplayed the internal diversity of religious traditions.) In Grimmitt's view, the two models were so similar to each other as, in effect, to impose a view of the nature of religious education as the study of discrete religions. Presumably, Grimmitt's scepticism about the involvement of the faith representatives in producing syllabuses extends to Agreed Syllabus Conferences, although he does not discuss this. His key educational point is that present arrangements militate against any serious consideration of pedagogy by syllabus makers and teachers. In having to use syllabuses produced in the interests of politicians and members of faith groups, 'the subject's very rich repository of pedagogical research and development' has been sidelined (Grimmitt 2000b: 15). Syllabus makers and teachers, argues Grimmitt, need to be informed by pedagogical principles that draw on theories of learning and human development.

There is a good deal of truth in what Grimmitt says, but he overstates his case. In his book, he moves on to introduce a range of research and development projects in religious education which tackle issues of teaching and learning at a serious level. However, he leaves the political aspect of religious education behind. There is no discussion of how current arrange-ments could be improved, apart from expressing the wish to take power away from politicians and representatives of religions.

Inevitably, there is a political element in the production of syllabuses, and this was especially so in the case of the drafting of the national model syllabuses. Fierce objection by politically right wing Christians to any 'thematic' model which juxtaposed material from different religions (see Hull 1991 on their fear of 'pollution'), and their wish to have a high percentage of Christian studies specified for each key stage, had some influence. The bid for percentages was defeated, but no 'thematic' model syllabus appeared (see Robson 1996). Towards the end of the process, there was a considerable amount of lobbying from the right as well as some intense political activity by members of the faith groups on the Syllabus Monitoring Group. As Grimmitt says, the outcome in this case was unsatisfactory. Political disputes involving faith representatives have also occurred in relation to the workings of some local Agreed Syllabus Conferences and Standing Advisory Councils for Religious Education.

However, it does not follow that members of faith groups cannot participate in an informed and constructive way in contributing to the processes of religious education in the common school. There is evidence from annual reports of the high value of many local Standing Advisory

Councils for Religious Education in bringing together the resources of local faith communities, teachers, politicians, and co-opted members such as humanists to work collaboratively in the interests of religious education and the pupils who study it. In contrast to the case of the model syllabuses, members of a SACRE may work together over many years, and learn to work as a team. My own experience of serving on a SACRE as a co-opted member has been one in which faith group representatives have not set out primarily to pursue the interests of their own constituencies. Generally, they have been ready to learn about the faiths of others (a regular feature of SACRE meetings is a presentation by a member of a faith group or by a humanist on their own religion or philosophy) and to pursue the interests and needs of pupils. For example, a recent presentation was on the youth shadow SACRE in Bradford. Faith group representatives also come from a range of professional backgrounds, and some of them are skilled teachers of religious education, well informed about pedagogical issues. Local politicians too have worked in the interests of pupils and of democracy within schools. Generally speaking, however, there is a need for a shift in balance towards a deeper consideration of pedagogy by SACREs and Agreed Syllabus Conferences, with more input from teachers, pupils, researchers and curriculum developers, and more flexibility for teachers and pupils to take account of local circumstances. Moreover, there is a case for restructuring SACREs and Agreed Syllabus Conferences in order to give more equity to religions and philosophies. There is also a case for including school students. In their study of prison chaplaincy in Britain, James Beckford and Sophie Gilliat have argued that the time has come to reconsider the practice of keeping ethnic and religious minorities dependent on Anglican 'brokering' of their access to prison chaplaincy (Beckford and Gilliat 1998). Similarly it may well be time for the Church of England to accept a less favoured role on SACREs and Agreed Syllabus Conferences, especially in the light of the expansion in the provision of Church of England Voluntary schools.

Currently, there is a debate in England and Wales about whether the local arrangements for designing syllabuses for religious education should be modified or changed. One proposal recommends the introduction of national guidelines for the subject, provided primarily for the use of SACREs and Agreed Syllabus Conferences in reviewing Agreed Syllabuses and offering advice for schools (QCA 2003: 15). This recommendation could be implemented under current legislation. The other recommends a single national syllabus to replace locally Agreed Syllabuses, a proposal that would require new legislation. The local-national debate will not be pursued here, but Grimmitt's point about close attention to pedagogical issues needs to be taken. For example, the critical, interpretive and dialogical approaches discussed in this book require syllabuses, whatever their provenance, to offer a balance between the acquisition and application of skills of interpretation, reflection and criticism and subject content. There needs to be far more attention to pedagogy than there is currently in most syllabuses, more time devoted to reflective and responsive activities and more flexibility for teachers and pupils to select particular topics for study, especially in relation to local circumstances and needs, as well as more opportunities for creative experiments in teaching and learning. Whatever transpires with regard to policy on syllabuses, any changes at the national level would not eliminate the need for SACREs which should continue to work in the interests of pupils at the local level. The Bradford experiment with a shadow SACRE of school students referred to above could be repeated elsewhere with benefit.

Should the subject change?

There are those, like David Hargreaves, who claim that religious education no longer has a place in the Community school, and I have argued above (Chapter 8) that Hargreaves misconceives the nature and purpose of the subject. However, the question remains as to why RE should not deal overtly with non-religious beliefs and values as well as religious ones. Of course, in practice, many teachers do give the subject this breadth, and the religious literacy, interpretive and dialogical approaches discussed above ensure that pupils apply critical and philosophical skills when examining religious claims. However, the point has been made that, by only examining ethical and values questions in relation to religions, some Agreed Syllabuses give the impression that values always have a religious basis (White forthcoming). If this is so, then perhaps there is a case for widening the scope of the subject formally to include secular points of view, as in the British Humanist Association's recommendation that the subject should continue to cover religions but should be made more inclusive:

> Renaming the subject 'Beliefs and Values Education' or something similar would convey inclusiveness and, if it were genuinely inclusive and impartial, there would be no need for any pupil to be excused from it – learning about the many beliefs held in our society ought to be part of every child's entitlement and preparation for life in a pluralist society.
>
> (BHA 2002: 11)

This proposal is different, of course, from Erricker's view that the grounds for broadening the subject are that there is no genuine distinction between religious, moral and emotional education (Chapter 4 above). New legislation would have to be introduced in order to introduce a broader subject since, currently, RE Agreed Syllabuses relate to Christianity and the other main religions represented in Britain (UK Parliament 1988: Section 8.3) and legal precedent deems that humanism cannot be regarded as a religion. However, the danger in widening the scope of the subject is that, in the view of some, expertise in the study of religions might cease to be an expectation for specialist teachers. The discussions of intercultural education, citizenship education and values education above (Chapter 8) and the accounts of international projects in this chapter show the considerable value of a specialism in religions in relation to these fields. Moreover, as the views of the young members of the Bradford shadow SACRE illustrate, learners want to be able to consult teachers who are specialists in the study of religions. There is a need to continue to supply teachers who have a depth of knowledge about a range of religious traditions and appropriate pedagogies for teaching them, but there is also a case that these teachers should be able to cover wider philosophical and ethical issues in addition to religious traditions. Such teachers (and there are many already working in the profession) would have the potential to work collaboratively with others specializing in fields such as personal, social and health education and citizenship education. The next step in religious education's response to plurality is to find agreement about the scope of the subject and the processes for producing syllabuses that give close attention to pedagogical issues.

Notes

1 Religious education in the context of plurality

1 The name Skeie is pronounced 'Shyer' in English.
2 During the twentieth century, the term 'popular culture' emerged – mass culture working through the mass media – a notion in tension with 'high culture' (i.e. the eighteenth century 'high arts' idea of culture).
3 Meijer is pronounced May-er in English.
4 In different contexts Denise Cush and David Chidester use the expression being 'epistemologically humble' in teaching religious studies and religious education. (See Chapter 10 for more on Cush's view.) Every theoretical stance, of course, has its epistemological presuppositions. However, some positions are much more open to the recognition of different stances on the nature of knowledge than others. See Chapter 2 below.
5 Keijo (pronounced Kay-o) Eriksson's work is discussed further in Chapter 6.
6 Sven Hartman's research on Swedish children (aged 5–13) shows that, in the groups of children studied, existential questions arose spontaneously in young children and were common during later childhood. Questions about loneliness, fear and social relationships were commonest. Older children asked questions about conflicts among friends, bullying, guilt and sport, but also wider social questions about injustices between rich and poor countries, war and death. Comparisons of age groups showed how the perspective widened with age and how girls seemed to produce mature responses earlier than boys. Content analysis also showed how children tried to place their questions in a larger context, developing a personal worldview reflecting their responses to the existential and social questions which they formulated.

2 Religious and cultural heritage

1 For example, in 1990 the pressure group 'Christians and Tyneside Schools', based in the city of Newcastle upon Tyne, helped to orchestrate a complaint to the Secretary of State for Education about new Agreed Syllabuses in the strongly multicultural London boroughs of Ealing and Newham, on the grounds that the syllabuses were not 'mainly Christian' and therefore, in their view, did not follow the letter of Section 8 (3) of the 1988 Act. The complaint was rejected. See Jackson (2000a) for a discussion of this case and for other examples.

Since 1988, RE has been seen by the radical right as potentially a means to regenerate moral values, and to promote 'British' cultural identity among the young and Christianity as the religion and moral force of the state. Any notion that some British citizens might learn something about personal and social values from other British citizens who are affiliated to religions other than Christianity is rejected. The radical right position is implicit in the views of the Centre for Policy Studies, which was influential on Conservative Government policy in education up to 1997, and has been expressed in general writings on education by members of small but vociferous right wing pressure groups which have targeted religious education or related fields such as collective worship, the provision of separate religious schools for religious minorities and spiritual development. Prominent in the debates are The Christian Institute, which developed from Christians and Tyneside Schools (for example, Burn *et al.* 1991; Hart 1991, 1994), the Campaign for Real Education (Flew and Naylor 1996) and the Parental Alliance for Choice in Education (PACE). For a vigorous response to Hart (1994), see Brown (1995).

2 By no means all Evangelical Christians are opposed to 'multifaith' religious education. See, for example, Cooling (1994). See Wilkins (1991) for arguments not only for the compatibility of Evangelicalism and multifaith RE teaching, but also giving reasons why Evangelical Christians can bring distinctive qualities to their professional work as teachers of religious education which covers several religious traditions.

3 Support for the view that material drawn from several traditions need not be confusing to children comes from an analysis by Stephen Orchard of HMI reports on RE published between 1985 and 1988. Orchard remarks, 'If religious education was becoming confusing or ineffective since the introduction of a multifaith approach the inspectorate seem to regard such failures as failures in competence rather than a consequence of the additional content' (Orchard 1991: 20).

4 See Chapter 8 for websites for these codes. See also the Oslo Coalition on Freedom of Religion and Belief website: http://www.oslocoalition.org/html/oslo_ declaration.html.

5 Approaches to RE that encourage dialogue and interaction are discussed in Chapter 7, while Baumann's distinction between 'dominant' and 'demotic' discourse is discussed more fully in Chapter 8.

3 State funding for religious schools?

1 Limited collaboration goes back further. There were grants from the state to the National Society and the British and Foreign Schools Society to help them found schools in the 1830s and 1840s. The history of the partnership between Church and state in English education is discussed in Chadwick (1997).

2 RI in Special Agreement schools usually followed the pattern of Aided schools. Unless parents opted to have denominational religious instruction taught by 'reserved teachers', RI in Controlled schools was identical to that in County schools.

3 The issue of religious schools within the state system was complicated by the introduction in 1988 of Grant Maintained status for schools. This legislation allowed for schools to opt out of Local Authority control in order to manage their own finances. Subsequent legislation (UK Parliament 1993) was designed to speed up the opting out process in the hope that by 1995 the majority of secondary schools, at least, would be operating outside the control of Local Education Authorities. The establishment of the Funding Agency for Schools in 1994 made it easier for religious schools to apply for Grant Maintained status. The Grant Maintained system has been dismantled by the Labour

government. Former Grant Maintained schools are now classified as Foundation schools although a clause allows for any Grant Maintained school which previously had a religious basis to opt for Voluntary Aided status (UK Parliament 1998).

4 Reasons for the failure of the venture included fears of racial divisiveness and a desire on the part of some Hindu communities to place formal religious nurture in locally run supplementary schools and classes (Kanitkar 1979).

5 Foundation schools are former Grant Maintained schools. Some Voluntary schools (those that had opted for Grant Maintained status, but who wished to revert to Voluntary status following the dismantling of the Grant Maintained system) are also former Grant Maintained schools.

6 There are nearly 7,000 state-funded schools in England with a religious character (the overwhelming majority being primary schools), accounting for about 25 per cent of the pupil population. The following figures are based on Department for Education and Employment statistics published in January 1999 and the Religious Character Order of September 1999. The figures in the first column represent the total number of *primary* schools with a religious character within each listed category while the second column gives total numbers, including secondary schools. The first Greek Orthodox Voluntary Aided school opened in 2000 and therefore is not listed in the figures. The two Sikh schools listed are the primary and secondary departments of the Guru Nanak school, Hillingdon.

Roman Catholic (RC)	1,771	2,108
RC/CE	3	11
Church of England (CE)	4,531	4,717
CE/Methodist	28	29
CE/URC	2	2
CE/Free Church	1	1
CE/Christian*	0	1
Methodist	27	27
United Reformed Church (URC)	1	1
Congregational	1	1
Christian*	13	32
Society of Friends	1	1
Seventh Day Adventist	1	1
Jewish	25	30
Muslim	2	2
Sikh	1	2
Total	6,408	6,966

Note: * The category 'Christian' covers mostly schools that were caught by the Endowed Schools Acts of the 1860s, where Church of England schools were de-denominationalized. Examples include the King Edward VI schools in various parts of England which have positively Christian but non-denominational trust deeds.

7 As an example of its confidence in the ability of religious bodies to make schools work in difficult social settings, the government, in March 2000, announced its intention to develop Inner City Academies (now called 'Academies'), catering for children of all abilities. Sponsors (including religious bodies) and the Department for Education and Skills provide the capital costs for the Academy. Running costs are met in full by the Department for Education and Skills. There will be a direct partnership between sponsors and government (not Local Education Authorities), on the model of City Technology

Colleges set up by the previous Conservative government. These Academies will be able to specialize in particular fields (e.g. the arts, sport or languages) and will be able to make their own arrangements about the length and organization of the school year and school day. All Academies are located in areas of disadvantage. Proposed Academies include Lambeth Academy in Clapham, specializing in business and enterprise, and language, and designed to take account of pupils with visual impairments. The sponsor will be the Church Schools Company which has pledged £2 million. The Academy will have a Christian ethos but selection will not be on the basis of faith. Kensington City Academy, Liverpool will be a Joint Anglican and Roman Catholic Academy with a science specialism, and will replace Our Lady's Roman Catholic School. The Diocese of Liverpool will contribute £2 million, with the Roman Catholic Archdiocese of Liverpool contributing £250,000. Further information on academies is at http:// www.standards.dfes.gov.uk/academies/what_are_academies/.

  8   'In accordance with the spirit of the Human Rights Act and to take account of the diversity of our communities, faith groups can propose to set up their own schools' (Morris 2001a).

  9   This article of the Human Rights Act is open to different interpretations. For example, in the view of Amnesty International it guarantees people the right of access to existing educational institutions; but does not require the government to establish or fund a particular type of education. In this view, the requirement to respect parents' convictions is intended to prevent indoctrination by the state (*Amnesty*, September–October 2000).

 10   I am grateful to the Research, Analysis and International Division of Ofsted for aggregated inspection data for the years 1996–9, 1999–2000 and 2000–1, as indicated in the text.

 11   The exception with regard to special measures is Church of England secondary schools during the year 2001–2. Of the 192 CE secondary schools (VA and VC), 2.1 per cent were in special measures, the same percentage as all other secondary schools with the exception of Roman Catholic schools. Of the 357 RC schools, only 0.3 per cent were in special measures.

 12   Anecdotal evidence of proselytizing motives come in a letter to *The Guardian* from a young person in Year 10 of a Church of England secondary school:

> How nice it would be if my faith school was like those described in last week's letters. I attend a Church of England state secondary. Most of our assemblies are led by either the school chaplain or a visiting vicar, and a recent series has been on 'the benefits of being a Christian'. You could say my religion is that of not having one, but this belief was dismissed by speakers, and generalisations like 'most atheists get depressed and commit suicide' were made. Not very tolerant of my faith, is it?
>
> I had assumed that the purpose of RE was to learn about religions. But in this faith school, if we tackle an issue such as 'can war be justified?', the Christian viewpoint will be discussed but not the Buddhist or Hindu or Islamic views.
>
> I'm in year 10 at one of the three faith schools chosen to act as a model for the government's 100 or so new ones. This worries me, because although the teaching quality is very good, we have never recognised Ramadan, Diwali or any non-Christian festival. If I have a human right to practise my own religion, it certainly doesn't feel that way.
>
> (*Guardian Education* 27 November 2001: 8)

13 With regard to admissions, there needs to be some flexibility from schools. However, the House of Commons debate on the proposal to amend the School Standards and Framework Act 1998 in order to require Voluntary Aided schools to provide a fixed quota of places for children from other backgrounds showed such fixed formulae to be unworkable in practice (Hansard 2002).

14 It is a pity that little interest has been shown by religious bodies in promoting the Voluntary Controlled model of a faith school, combining a distinctively religious ethos and collective worship with a broadly based religious education and flexible admissions arrangements (Brown 2003).

15 The British Humanist Association's current policy strongly supports the idea of the plural school, but argues for the phasing out of faith-based schools (BHA 2002).

4 Postmodernist approaches to religious education

1 Both Clive Erricker and Andrew Wright (whose work is discussed in the next chapter) are important contributors to the debate about spiritual education and development. Whereas Wright would argue that spiritual development takes place through faith and practice within religious traditions, Erricker takes a postmodern view that conflates spiritual, religious and moral education. My own view is that a particular view of spirituality should not be imposed on pupils; young people should be encouraged to position themselves in the debate about the nature of spirituality.

5 Religious education as religious literacy

1 The research project was carried out between 1990 and 1993 under the title 'Ethnography and Religious Education' and involved studies of children from Christian, Sikh, Jewish and Muslim backgrounds in the West Midlands. The ethnographic dimensions of the project were funded by the Economic and Social Research Council (UK) (project reference number R000232489).

2 The example of research on children from Christian backgrounds is given here. For examples of diversity of belief and practice among British children of other backgrounds see Jackson and Nesbitt 1993 on Hindu children and Nesbitt 1997a and b, 2000a, and Nesbitt and Jackson 1993 and 1995 on Sikh children. On the indeterminacy of boundaries between Hindu and Sikh traditions see Nesbitt 1991.

3 Ipgrave's classroom research on children's influence on one another also reveals processes through which children absorb, filter, criticize and rework the concepts and values of their peers from other religious backgrounds (Ipgrave 2002).

6 Interpretive approaches to religious education

1 The Americanism 'interpretive' is a term used internationally in social anthropology and has been adopted in favour of 'interpretative'.

2 The terms 'individual' and 'person' are not intended only to be interpreted narrowly in Western terms (cf. Geertz 1983: 55–70). The model is intended to accommodate the

portrayal of different conceptions of 'self', for example more integrative community-based senses of self-identity (e.g. Murray 1991) or more fluid and changeable conceptions of self.

3 See also Østberg (1999) for discussion of the concept of integrated plural identity in relation to her Pakistani interviewees in Oslo.

4 Selected Warwick RE Project materials are available directly from Warwick Religions and Education Research Unit. For details contact Ursula McKenna, on u.mckenna@warwick.ac.uk.

5 Approximately 20 per cent of children in English and Welsh schools are categorized as having special educational needs (SEN). This umbrella term covers children with a range of difficulties whether learning, physical or sensory, or emotional and behavioural. About 18 per cent of these children receive education in mainstream schools. The other 2 per cent have needs which mainstream classrooms cannot meet. These children are educated in special schools which range from those that deal with mild/moderate learning difficulties and/or behavioural problems, to those that deal with more severe difficulties, to those that deal with profound and multiple difficulties.

6 Keijo is pronounced Kay-o in English.

7   Dialogical approaches to religious education

1 Her first piece of research was a study of the Muslim pupils who formed the majority (over 85 per cent) of her school (Ipgrave 1999; Jackson 1999).

2 This project on 'Inter-faith Dialogue in the Classroom as a Tool for Religious Education', based at Warwick Religions and Education Research Unit, was funded by the All Saints Educational Trust.

3 The email project has now been extended to involve groups of schools from Leicester and East Sussex, under the title 'Building E Bridges'. A study by members of WRERU at the University of Warwick is being conducted during 2003–4 to evaluate this project and to make recommendations for extending the work to schools in other locations.

8   Religious education's contribution to intercultural education

1 Until September 1999 (when the School Standards and Framework Act 1998 was implemented), 'common schools', that is schools *fully* funded by the state, were designated by law as 'county schools'. Such schools are now known as 'community schools'.

2 Jackson (1997, Chapter 3) discusses some of the literature challenging conventional representations of religions as bounded systems with a core of essential beliefs.

3   … research by the Professional Council for RE has found that among secondary pupils aged 11–18, those who enjoy the subject and see benefit for their own lives from studying religion, outnumber those who are negative about RE by four to one.

(Blaylock 2001)

4 Although RE is an entitlement of all children, it is a part of the basic curriculum and not the national curriculum. The national curriculum plus RE makes up the basic curriculum.

9 The relevance of research to religious education

1 There is also a good deal of sense in Hargreaves' view that educational researchers could benefit from a sideways look at research in other academic fields where one of the key goals of research is to improve professional practice, and he discusses medical research in particular (e.g. Hargreaves 1997).

2 ISREV had its first meeting in Birmingham in 1978. Since then it has met biennially, usually alternately at a European or North American venue.

3 Kay also discusses the contributions of Harold Loukes and Colin Alves.

4 See Kay 1996 for a brief review of Loukes' research reported in *Teenage Religion* (1961).

5 The Frangoulis *et al.* study referred to above is also a model of dissemination. In addition to publication of the results in the *British Journal of Religious Education*, a shorter and less technical account appeared in the professional journal *Bereavement Care*. In this case, the editor of *Bereavement Care* saw the possibilities for useful dissemination and produced the abbreviated version herself in conjunction with the researchers (Lansdown *et al.* 1997). Perhaps the editors of the professional RE magazines might learn something from this.

6 One study by an ENRECA member, Professor Heinz Streib, uses video analysis in some German primary classrooms to test the *Gift to the Child* approach developed by John Hull and his colleagues at the University of Birmingham. Streib plans to extend this study to other countries.

7 For example, at the time of writing, Warwick has ten doctoral students working in religious education and related fields.

10 Towards a pluralistic religious education

1 Denise Cush and Dave Francis list 11 characteristics of RE that exhibit positive pluralism:

- Plurality is welcomed as an opportunity for learning rather than a problem. It is possible to learn from the views and practices of others without necessarily losing your own religious and cultural roots.
- Epistemological humility means that one's own views may well be opposed to those of others, but can be held in a provisional way which is respectful rather than arrogant and is open to further learning.
- Positive pluralism implies an adoption of a non-confessional approach to religious education where all children are taught together rather than in separate faith groups, and where no tradition is specially promoted or privileged in terms of its truth claims.
- RE should respect the backgrounds of all pupils, whether religious or not, and be inclusive of the full diversity of worldviews – at least those represented in the school or locality ...

- Positive pluralism teaches neither that all views are equally valid like the negative pluralist, nor that all paths lead to the same goal like the universalist, thus avoiding the concern of many that a pluralist RE is necessarily indoctrinating children into either what is sometimes called 'relativism' or into a 'no-name', universalist brand of religion.
- It thus allows for a critical thinking and a 'philosophical approach' where students can explore and develop their own beliefs and values in relation to the challenging questions with which religions deal.
- Positive pluralism recognizes plurality within traditions and thus avoids constructing normative versions. It also holds that dividing human beliefs and values into labelled religious traditions is artificial as religions have interacted throughout the centuries, and particularly in the contemporary globalized situation where many hold multiple or hybrid allegiances.
- As in the 'phenomenological' approach RE should attempt to be as far as possible both academically impartial and empathetic towards the believers' experience.
- As in the 'existential' approach religious education should make connections with and illuminate the interests, needs and concerns of pupils.
- As in the 'experiential' approach, religious education should 'transcend the informative', engaging student attitudes by being affective as well as cognitive, providing opportunities for reflective exercises, creative expression and engaged action.
- As in the 'interpretive approach' students should have the opportunity to engage in a dialogue, if only at a distance, with members of the traditions studied in order to enhance their understanding both of religion and of their own experiences and beliefs. (Cush and Francis 2002).

2 As a result of her research in schools, Joy White has produced the following questions for consideration by those formulating inclusive school policies:

- Timing of parents' consultations: do they conflict with set prayer times?
- Exam schedules: do they conflict with important religious festivals?
- Bereavement procedures: do school procedures and entitlements take account of the customs and requirements of individuals?
- Policies for critical incidents: do they represent the preferences of faith groups?
- Food and dietary requirements: are they respected within catering procedures? Are staff informed and aware of these requirements?
- Extra-curricular events: do they take into account pupil and staff attendance at supplementary schools and places of worship?
- Use of ICT: can the learning objectives be achieved without the use of technology when such use conflicts with believers' belief systems?
- Resources accepted for the library: does the policy clearly indicate and explain from which religious traditions resources will be accepted in the library and which will not?
- Visiting speakers: is the rationale clear for deciding which faiths will be represented and which will not?
- Use of school facilities for outside agencies: is the rationale clear for deciding which faiths will be accepted and which will not?

- Methods of fund-raising: are pupils/parents being expected to show support for the school by taking part in methods of fund-raising that conflict with their beliefs and values?
- Charities supported: are they inclusive of a range of faith traditions?
- Displays: are they inclusive of a range of faith traditions?
- Uniform and dress-code: do they take account of the requirements of the faith traditions represented in the school?
- End of term staff celebrations: do the celebrations conflict with the values and beliefs of faith traditions represented in the school?
- Recognition of faith specific achievement by staff and pupils: are they acknowledged and affirmed?
- Bullying and harassment policies: do these cover faith/religious harassment?
- Facilities for prayer and reflection: are appropriate facilities, including access to water for ablutions, provided?
- Faith supplementary schools: are these included in the school's programmes of consultation and liaison? (White 2003: Appendix A).

3   This group also recommended that states should:

- Encourage schools to develop policies with respect to diversity (including religious diversity) promoting equity based on the national and local situation and within the legal framework of the country.
- Collect and disseminate examples of good practice of school policies.
- Encourage schools to develop curricula that reflect cultural diversity, including religious and linguistic diversity.
- Provide initial and continuing teacher education that reflects the reality and needs of teachers preparing children for participation in an open society and of teachers working in multicultural schools.
- Encourage schools to develop a critical attitude towards textbooks and electronic means of information and to develop criteria for the selection and use of resources.

4   The project's website is at http://www.oslocoalition.org/html/project_school_education.
5   The reports of the different faith working groups were also published (SCAA 1994c).

References

Ainsworth, D. (nd) 'Religion and the intellectual capacities of young children', Occasional Papers, Oxford: Farmington Institute for Christian Studies.

Altizer, J.J. and Hamilton, W. (1968) *Radical Theology and the Death of God*, Harmondsworth: Penguin.

Alves, C. (1991) 'Just a matter of words? The religious education debates in the House of Lords', *British Journal of Religious Education*, 13 (3): 168–74.

Andree, T., Bakker, C. and Schreiner, P. (eds) (1997) *Crossing Boundaries: Contributions to Interreligious and Intercultural Education*, Münster: Comenius Institut.

Anon. (1988) *Education in a Multicultural Society*, Labour Party Consultative Document, London: House of Commons.

Archbishop's Council (2001) *The Way Ahead: Church of England Schools in the New Millennium*, London: Church House Publishing.

Arweck, E. and Nesbitt, E. (forthcoming a) 'Values education in a Hindu-related new religious movement', *British Education Research Journal*.

—— (forthcoming b) 'From textbook to classroom: how values education is applied in schools', *British Journal of Religious Education*.

Ashenden, C. (1995) 'Christianity and the primary school: the contribution of anthropology to teaching about Christianity', unpublished PhD thesis, University of Brighton.

Ashton, E. (1997) 'Readiness for discarding? An examination of the researches of Ronald Goldman concerning children's religious thinking', *Journal of Education and Christian Belief*, 1 (2): 127–44.

Astley, J., Francis, L.J., Burton, L. and Wilcox, C. (1997) 'Distinguishing between aims and methods in RE: a study among secondary RE teachers', *British Journal of Religious Education*, 19 (3): 171–84.

Bailey, S.H., Harris, D.J. and Jones, S.L. (1991) *Civil Liberties: Cases and Materials*, 3rd edn, London: Butterworth.

Bakhtin, M. (1981) 'Discourse in the novel', in M. Holquist (ed.) *The Dialogic Imagination*, Austin: University of Texas Press.

Ballard, R. (ed.) (1994) *Desh Pardesh: The South Asian Presence in Britain*, London: Hurst and Co.

Barratt, M. (1994a) *An Egg for Babcha*, 'Bridges to Religions' series, The Warwick RE Project, Oxford: Heinemann.

—— (1994b) *Lucy's Sunday*, 'Bridges to Religions' series, The Warwick RE Project, Oxford: Heinemann.

—— (1994c) *Something to Share*, 'Bridges to Religions' series, The Warwick RE Project, Oxford: Heinemann.

—— (1994d) *The Buddha's Birthday*, 'Bridges to Religions' series, The Warwick RE Project, Oxford: Heinemann.

—— (1994e) *The Seventh Day is Shabbat*, 'Bridges to Religions' series, The Warwick RE Project, Oxford: Heinemann.

Barratt, M. and Price, J. (1996a) *Meeting Christians: Book One*, 'Bridges to Religions' series, The Warwick RE Project, Oxford: Heinemann.

—— (1996b) *Teacher's Resource Book: Meeting Christians: Book One*, 'Bridges to Religions' series, The Warwick RE Project, Oxford: Heinemann.

Barth, F. (ed.) (1969) *Ethnic Groups and Boundaries*, London: Allen and Unwin.

—— (1981) 'Ethnic groups and boundaries', in F. Barth (ed.) *Process and Forms in Social Life: Selected Essays*, London: Routledge and Kegan Paul.

—— (1994) 'A personal view of present tasks and priorities in cultural and social anthropology', in R. Borofsky (ed.) *Assessing Cultural Anthropology*, New York: McGraw Hill.

—— (1996) 'How features of the encompassing society set parameters for local multiculturalism', unpublished paper, conference on Multicultural Competence: A Resource for Tomorrow, Bergen University College, Norway, August.

—— (2000) 'Boundaries and connections', in A. Cohen (ed.) *Signifying Identities: Anthropological Perspectives on Boundaries and Contested Values*, London: Routledge.

Bassey, M. and Constable, H. (1997) 'Higher education research in education 1992–1996: fields of enquiry reported in the HEFC's RAE', *Research Intelligence*, 61: 6–8.

Bates, D. (1992) 'Secularity, agape and religious education – a critical appreciation of the work of J.W.D. Smith', *British Journal of Religious Education*, 14 (3): 132–44.

—— (1994) 'Christianity, culture and other religions (Part 1): the origins of the study of world religions in English education', *British Journal of Religious Education*, 17 (1): 5–18.

Bates, D., Durka, G. and Schweitzer, F. (eds) (forthcoming) *Religion, Reconciliation and Inclusion in a Pluralistic World: Essays in Religious Education and Practical Theology in Honour of John M. Hull*, London, RoutledgeFalmer.

Bauer, J. (1997) 'Muslim children in Birmingham: interviews with Muslim children', *Warwick Religions and Education Research Unit Occasional Papers I*, University of Warwick, Institute of Education.

Baumann, G. (1996) *Contesting Culture: Discourses of Identity in Multi-Ethnic London*, Cambridge: Cambridge University Press.

—— (1999) *The Multicultural Riddle: Rethinking National, Ethnic and Religious Identities*, London: Routledge.

Baumfield, V. (2002) *Thinking Through Religious Education*, Cambridge: Chris Kington Publishing.

Beck, U. (1992) *Risk Society: Towards a New Modernity*, London: Sage.

Beckett, F. (2001) 'Holier than thou', *The Guardian*, 13 November.

Beckford, J.A. (1985) *Cult Controversies: The Societal Response to the New Religious Movements*, London: Tavistock.

—— (ed.) (1986) *New Religious Movements and Rapid Social Change*, London: Sage.

Beckford, J. and Gilliat, S. (1998) R*eligion in Prisons: Equal Rites in a Multi-Faith Society*, London: Cambridge University Press.

Benedict, R. (1935) *Patterns of Culture*, London: Routledge and Kegan Paul.

Bennett, J.A. (1994) 'An exploration of the philosophy and interrelationship between personal, social, moral and religious education, and the implications of recent educational reforms on their position, philosophies and methodologies', unpublished PhD thesis, University of Hull.

Blaylock, L. (2001) 'Answers and clues', *Times Educational Supplement*, Curriculum Special, June 29.

Brannen, J. (ed.) (1992) *Mixing Methods: Qualitative and Quantitative Research*, Aldershot: Avebury.

British Humanist Association (2002) *A Better Way Forward: BHA Policy on Religion and Schools*, London: British Humanist Association.

Brown, A. (1989) 'Religious education and worship in schools: flexibility, frustration, foibles and fallacies', *Resource*, 12 (1): 1–3.

—— (1995) 'Changing the agenda: whose agenda?', *British Journal of Religious Education*, 17 (3): 148–56.

—— (2003) 'Church of England schools: politics, power and identity', *British Journal of Religious Education*, 25 (2): 103–16.

Brown, K.M. (1991) *Mama Lola: A Vodou Priestess in Brooklyn*, Berkeley: University of California Press.

Burn, J. and Hart, C. (1988) *The Crisis In Religious Education*, London: Educational Research Trust.

Burn, J., Hart, C. and Holloway, D. (1991) *From Acts to Action*, Newcastle-upon-Tyne: The Christian Institute.

Burtonwood, N. (1998) 'Liberalism and communitarianism: a response to two recent attempts to reconcile individual autonomy with group identity', *Educational Studies*, 24 (3): 295–310.

Castles, S. and Kosack, G. (1973) *Immigrant Workers and Class Structure in Western Europe*, London: Oxford University Press for the Institute of Race Relations.

Chadwick, P. (1997) *Shifting Alliances: Church and State in English Education*, London: Cassell.

Chantepie de la Saussaye, P. (1891) *Manual of the Science of Religion* (English translation of *Lehrbuch der Religionsgeschichte*, Freiburg, 1887), extract reprinted in Waardenburg, J. (1973) *Classical Approaches to the Study of Religion*, Vol. 1, The Hague: Mouton.

Chater, M. (1997) 'A new vision for religious education: the evolution of divergent models of religious education towards a convergence based upon new metaphors', unpublished PhD thesis, University of Edinburgh.

Chidester, D. (1992) *Religions of South Africa*, London: Routledge.

—— (1996) *Savage Systems: Colonialism and Comparative Religion in Southern Africa*, Charlottesville: University Press of Virginia.

—— (1997) 'Man, god, beast, heaven, light, burning fire', in T. Andree, C. Bakker and P. Schreiner (eds) *Crossing Boundaries: Contributions to Interreligious and Intercultural Education*, Münster: Comenius Institut.

—— (1999) 'Embracing South Africa, internationalizing the study of religion', in D. Chidester, J. Stonier and J. Tobler (eds) *Diversity as Ethos: Challenges for Interreligious and Intercultural Education*, Cape Town: Institute for Comparative Religion in Southern Africa.

—— (2003a) 'Global citizenship, cultural citizenship, and world religions in religion education', in R. Jackson (ed.) *International Perspectives on Citizenship Education and Religious Diversity*, London: RoutledgeFalmer.

—— (2003b) 'Religion education in South Africa: teaching and learning about religion, religions and religious diversity', *British Journal of Religious Education*, 25 (4): 261–78.

Chidester, D., Mitchell, G., Phiri, I. and Omar A.R. (1992) *Religion in Public Education: Options for a New South Africa*, Cape Town: Institute for Comparative Religion in Southern Africa.

Chidester, D., Stonier, J. and Tobler, J. (eds) (1999) *Diversity as Ethos: Challenges for Interreligious and Intercultural Education*, Cape Town: Institute for Comparative Religion in Southern Africa.

Christian Aid (2000) *An RE Curriculum for Global Citizenship*, London: Christian Aid in association with the Association of Religious Education Inspectors, Advisers and Consultants, CAFOD, the ClearVison Trust, the Development Education Association and the Department for International Development.

Clifford, J. (1986) 'Introduction: partial truths', in J. Clifford and G. Marcus (eds) *Writing Culture: The Poetics and Politics of Ethnography*, Berkeley: University of California Press.

Cohen, A. (1982a) 'Belonging: the experience of culture', in A. Cohen (ed.) *Belonging: Identity and Social Organization in British Rural Cultures*, Manchester: Manchester University Press.

—— (ed.) (1982b) *Belonging: Identity and Social Organization in British Rural Cultures*, Manchester: Manchester University Press.

—— (ed.) (1986) *Symbolizing Boundaries: Identity and Diversity in British Cultures*, Manchester: Manchester University Press.

Cole, W.O. (1972) *Religion in the Multifaith School*, 1st edn, Yorkshire Committee for Community Relations.

Colson, I. (2004) 'Their churches are at home: the communication and definition of values in four aided Church of England secondary schools', *British Journal of Religious Education*, 26(1): 73–83.

Connolly, C. (1992) 'Religious schools: refuge or redoubt?', in M. Leicester and M. Taylor (eds) *Ethics, Ethnicity and Education*, London: Kogan Page.

Cooling, T. (1990) 'Evangelicals and modern religious education', in L. Francis and A. Thatcher (eds) *Christian Perspectives for Education*, Leominster: Gracewing.

—— (1994) *A Christian Vision for State Education*, London: SPCK.

—— (1997a) 'In defence of the common school', in J. Shortt and T. Cooling (eds) *Agenda for Educational Change*, Leicester: Apollos.

—— (1997b) 'Theology goes to school: the story of the Stapleford Project', *Journal of Christian Education*, 40 (1): 47–60.

—— (2002) unpublished letter to the British Humanist Association.

Cooling, T. and Cooling, M. (1987) 'Christian doctrine in religious education', *British Journal of Religious Education*, 9 (3): 152–9.

Coombs, A. (1988) 'Diluting the faith', *Education*, 26 August.

—— (1991) Letter, *The Times*, 12 April.

Copley, T. (1997) *Teaching Religion: Fifty Years of Religious Education in England and Wales*, Exeter: University of Exeter Press.

Cox, C. (1988) 'Foreword', in J. Burn and C. Hart (eds) *The Crisis In Religious Education*, London Educational Research Trust.

Cox, E. (1966) *Changing Aims in Religious Education*, London: Routledge and Kegan Paul.

—— (1967) *Sixth Form Religion*, London: SCM.

Cox, H. (1965) *The Secular City*, London: Penguin.

Crapanzano, V. (1980) *Tuhami, Portrait of a Moroccan*, Chicago: University of Chicago Press.

Crick, B. (1969) *The Teaching of Politics*, Harmondsworth: Penguin.

—— (2000) 'Introduction to the new curriculum', in D. Lawton, J. Cairns and R. Gardner (eds) *Education for Citizenship*, London: Continuum.

Crick, B. and Porter, A. (eds) (1978) *Political Education and Political Literacy*, London: Longman.

Cush, D. (1999) 'Models of religious education in a plural society: looking to the future', in I. Borowik (ed.) *Church–State Relations in Central and Eastern Europe*, Krakow: Nomos.

Cush, D. and Francis, D. (2002) '"Positive pluralism" to awareness mystery and value: a case study in religious education curriculum development', *British Journal of Religious Education*, 24 (1): 52–67.

Dashefsky, A. (1972) 'And the search goes on: religio-ethnic identity and identification', *Sociological Analysis*, 33 (4): 239–45.

Davies, G. (2002) Speech in the House of Commons, 5 February, reproduced in *Hansard*, 6 February: Columns 887–8.

Debray, R. (2002) *L'Enseignment du Fait Religieux dans L'École Laïque: Rapport au Ministre de l'Éducation Nationale*, Paris: Odile Jacob.

DfEE (2000) *Developing a Global Dimension in the School Curriculum*, London: Department for Education and Employment in collaboration with Department for International Development, Qualifications and Curriculum Authority, Development Education Association and The Central Bureau.

DfEE/QCA (1999) *The National Curriculum for England: Citizenship*, London: Department for Education and Employment and Qualifications and Curriculum Authority.

DfES (2001) *Schools Achieving Success*, London: The Stationery Office. Online. Available HTTP: http://www.dfes.gov.uk/achievingsuccess/chap5.shtml (accessed June 2002).

Donald, J. and Rattansi, A. (eds) (1992) *Race, Culture and Difference*, London: Sage.

Downey, M. and Kelly, A.V. (1978) *Moral Education: Theory and Practice*, London: Harper and Row.

Du Toit, C.W. and Kruger, K.S. (eds) (1998) *Multireligious Education in South Africa: Problems and Prospects in a Pluralistic Society*, Pretoria: Research Institute for Theology and Religion, University of South Africa.

Edwards, S. (1999) 'RE and emancipation: a critical approach to cultural development in the comprehensive school', unpublished MA dissertation, Institute of Education, University of Warwick.

Eriksson, K. (1999) *På Spaning Efter Livets Mening*, Malmö: Intitutionen för Pedagogik, Lärarhögskolan, Malmö (includes a summary of the research in English).

—— (2000) 'In search of the meaning of life: a study of the ideas of senior compulsory school pupils on life and its meaning, in an experiential learning context', *British Journal of Religious Education*, 22 (2): 115–27.

Erricker, C. (2001) 'From silence to narration: a report on the research method(s) of the Children and Worldviews Project', *British Journal of Religious Education*, 23 (3): 156–64.

Erricker, C. and Erricker, J. (1996) 'Where angels fear to tread: discovering children's spirituality', in R. Best (ed.) *Education, Spirituality and the Whole Child*, London: Cassell.

—— (2000a) *Reconstructing Religious, Spiritual and Moral Education*, London: RoutledgeFalmer.

—— (2000b) 'The Children and Worldviews Project: a narrative pedagogy of religious education', in M. Grimmitt (ed.) *Pedagogies of Religious Education*, Great Wakering: McCrimmons.

Erricker, C., Erricker, J., Ota, C., Sullivan, D. and Fletcher, M. (1997) *The Education of the Whole Child*, London: Cassell.

Everington, J. (1996a) 'A question of authenticity: the relationship between educators and practitioners in the representation of religious traditions', *British Journal of Religious Education*, 18 (2): 69–77.

—— (1996b) *Meeting Christians: Book Two*, 'Bridges to Religions' series, The Warwick RE Project, Oxford: Heinemann.

—— (1996c) *Teacher's Resource Book: Meeting Christians: Book Two*, 'Bridges to Religions' series, The Warwick RE Project, Oxford: Heinemann.

—— (2001) 'Dreams, difficulties and dilemmas: the relationship between citizenship and religious education in English schools', unpublished paper,

International Seminar on Citizenship and Education, International Perspectives on Cultural and Religious Diversity, University of Warwick, September.

Everington, J. and Sikes, P. (2001) ' "I want to change the world": the beginning RE teacher, the reduction of prejudice and the pursuit of intercultural understanding and respect', in H.-G. Heimbrock, P. Schreiner and C. Scheilke (eds) *Towards Religious Competence: Diversity as a Challenge for Education in Europe*, Münster: Lit Verlag.

Farrer, F. (2000) *A Quiet Revolution: Encouraging Positive Values in Our Children*, London: Rider.

Felderhof, M. (2000) 'Religious education and human rights', in N. Holm (ed.) *Islam and Christianity in School Religious Education*, Åbo (Finland): Åbo Akademi University.

Ferguson, R. (1999) 'Strategies for teaching religion in colleges of education', unpublished MEd thesis, University of Stellenbosch.

Fischer, M.M.J. (1986) 'Ethnicity and the post-modern arts of memory', in J. Clifford and G. Marcus (eds) *Writing Culture: The Poetics and Politics of Ethnography*, Berkeley: University of California Press.

Fitzgerald, T. (1990) 'Hinduism and the "world religion" fallacy', *Religion*, 20: 101–18.

Flew, A. and MacIntyre, A. (1955) *New Essays in Philosophical Theology*, London: SCM.

Flew, A. and Naylor, F. (1996) *Spiritual Development and All That Jazz*, Paper 25, York: Campaign for Real Education.

Flutter, J. and Rudduck, J. (2004) *Consulting Pupils: What's in It for Schools?*, London: RoutledgeFalmer.

Foucault, M. (1971) *Madness and Civilisation*, London: Tavistock.

Francis, L.J. (1979) 'School influence and pupil attitude towards religion', *British Journal of Educational Psychology*, 49: 107–23.

—— (1984) *Teenagers and the Church*, London: Collins.

—— (1992) 'Monitoring attitudes towards Christianity: the 1990 study', *British Journal of Religious Education*, 14 (3): 178–82.

—— (1996) 'Religious education', in P. Gordon (ed.) *A Guide to Educational Research*, London: The Woburn Press.

—— (2000a) 'Research in religious education and church schools studies: part one', in W.K. Kay and L.J. Francis (eds) *Religion in Education (3)*, Leominster: Gracewing.

—— (2000b) 'Research in religious education and church schools studies: part two', in W.K. Kay and L.J. Francis (eds) *Religion in Education (3)*, Leominster: Gracewing.

Francis, L.J., Astley, J. and Robbins, M. (2001) *The Fourth R for the Third Millennium: Education in Religion and Values for the Global Future*, Dublin: Lindisfarne.

Francis, L.J., Greer, J.E. and Gibson, H.M. (1991) 'Reliability and validity of a short term measure of attitude towards Christianity among secondary school pupils in England, Scotland and Northern Ireland', *Collected Original Papers in Education*, 15 (3), fiche 2, G09.

Francis, L.J., Kay, W.K. and Campbell, W.S. (eds) (1996) *Research in Religious Education*, Leominster: Gracewing.

Frangoulis, S., Jordan, N. and Lansdown, R. (1996) 'Children's concepts of an afterlife', *British Journal of Religious Education*, 18 (2): 114–23.

Gadamer, H.-G. (1975) *Truth and Method*, New York: Seabury Press.

Gardner, P. (1991) 'Personal autonomy and religious upbringing: the "problem"', *Journal of the Philosophy of Education*, 25 (1): 69–81.

Gates, B. (1976) 'Religion in the developing world of children and young people', unpublished PhD thesis, University of Lancaster.

—— (1996) 'Research in religious education', *Journal of Beliefs and Values*, 17 (1): 42–3.

Gay, J. (2001) 'The future of religious education', letter in *The Church Times*, 16 February.

Gay, J., Kay, B., Lazenby, D., Lord, E. and Peacocke, R. (1992) *Religious Education and Collective Worship in Primary Schools*, Abingdon: Culham College Institute.

Gearon, L. (2002) 'Religious education and human rights: some postcolonial perspectives', *British Journal of Religious Education*, 24 (2): 140–51.

—— (ed.) (2003a) *Human Rights: Religion*, Brighton: Sussex Academic Press.

—— (2003b) *Citizenship through Secondary Religious Education*, London: RoutledgeFalmer.

Geaves, R. (1998) 'The borders between religions: a challenge to the world religions approach to religious education', *British Journal of Religious Education*, 21 (1): 20–31.

Geertz, C. (1973) *The Interpretation of Cultures*, New York: Basic Books.

—— (1983) *Local Knowledge*, New York: Basic Books.

—— (1988) *Works and Lives: The Anthropologist as Author*, Cambridge: Polity Press.

Giddens, A. (1990) *The Consequences of Modernity*, Cambridge: Polity Press.

—— (1993) *Sociology*, 2nd edn, Cambridge: Polity Press.

—— (with U. Beck and S. Lash) (1994) *Reflexive Modernisation*, Cambridge: Polity Press.

Goldman, R.J. (1964) *Religious Thinking from Childhood to Adolescence*, London: Routledge and Kegan Paul.

—— (1965) *Readiness for Religion*, London: Routledge and Kegan Paul.

—— (1966–8) (ed.) *Readiness for Religion series*, London: Hart Davis.

Grace, G. (2002) *Catholic Schools: Mission, Markets and Morality*, London: RoutledgeFalmer.

Greer, J.E. (1972) 'The child's understanding of Creation', *Educational Review*, 24: 94–110.

—— (1984a) 'Fifty years of the psychology of religion in religious education', *British Journal of Religious Education*, 6 (2): 93–7.

—— (1984b) 'Fifty years of the psychology of religious education (part two)', *British Journal of Religious Education*, 7 (1): 23–8.

—— (1985) 'Edwin Cox and religious education', *British Journal of Religious Education*, 8 (1): 13–19.

Grimmitt, M.H. (1981) 'When is "commitment" a problem in RE?', *British Journal of Educational Studies*, 29 (1): 42–53.

—— (1987) *Religious Education and Human Development: The Relationship Between Studying Religions and Personal, Social and Moral Education*, Great Wakering: McCrimmons.

—— (ed.) (2000a) *Pedagogies of Religious Education: Case Studies in the Research and Development of Good Pedagogic Practice in RE*, Great Wakering: McCrimmons.

—— (2000b) 'The captivity and liberation of religious education and the meaning of pedagogy', in M. Grimmitt (ed.) *Pedagogies of Religious Education: Case Studies in the Research and Development of Good Pedagogic Practice in RE*, Great Wakering: McCrimmons.

Groome, T. (1980) *Christian Religious Education: Sharing Our Story and Vision*, San Francisco: Harper and Row.

Haakedal, E. (2001a) 'Contextual teaching and learning in religious education: a discussion of practices and reflections of an Eastern and a Western Norwegian primary school teacher', in H.-G. Heimbrock, P. Schreiner and C. Scheilke (eds) *Towards Religious Competence: Diversity as a Challenge for Education in Europe*, Münster: Lit Verlag.

—— (2001b) 'From Lutheran catechism to world religions and humanism: dilemmas and middle ways through the story of Norwegian religious education', *British Journal of Religious Education*, 23 (2): 88–97.

Habermas, J. (1972) *Knowledge and Human Interests*, London: Heinemann.

Halbfass, W. (1988) *India and Europe: an Essay on Understanding*, Albany: State University of New York Press.

Halstead, J.M. and Taylor, M. (2000) *The Development of Values, Attitudes and Personal Qualities: A Review of Recent Research*, Slough: National Foundation for Educational Research.

Hammer, R. (1982) 'The Christian and World Religions', in R. Jackson (ed.) *Approaching World Religions*, London: John Murray.

Hammond, J., Hay, D., Moxon, J., Netto, B., Raban, K., Straughier, G. and Williams, C. (1990) *New Methods in RE Teaching: An Experiential Approach*, London: Oliver and Boyd/Longman.

Hanlon, D. (2000) 'The effectiveness of primary religious education in-service training', *British Journal of Religious Education*, 22 (2): 103–14.

Hansard (2002) Columns 867–957, 6 February.

Hargreaves, D.H. (1986) 'Curriculum for the future', in G. Leonard and J. Yates (eds) *Faith for the Future*, London: National Society/Church House Publishing.

—— (1994) *The Mosaic of Learning: Schools and Teachers for the Next Century*, Demos Paper 8, London: Demos.

—— (1996) 'Teaching as a research-based profession: possibilities and prospects', The Teacher Training Agency Annual Lecture, London: Teacher Training Agency.

—— (1997) 'In defence of research for evidence-based teaching: a rejoinder to Martyn Hammersley', *British Educational Research Journal*, 23 (4): 405–19.

Hart, C. (1991) *Religious Education: From Acts to Action*, Newcastle-upon-Tyne: CATS Trust.

—— (1994) *RE: Changing the Agenda*, Newcastle: The Christian Institute.

Hartman, S.G. (1986) *Children's Philosophy of Life*, Stockholm: Gleerup.

—— (1994) 'Children's personal philosophy of life as the basis for religious education', *Panorama: International Journal of Comparative Religious Education and Values*, 6 (2): 104–28.

Hawke, R.A. (1982) 'Moral education in a multi-religious society', in R. Jackson (ed.) *Approaching World Religions*, London: John Murray.

Hay, D. (1982) *Exploring Inner Space*, Harmondsworth: Penguin (revised edition 1987, London: Mowbray).

—— (1990) 'The bearing of empirical studies of religious experience on education', *Research Papers in Education*, 5 (1): 3–28.

Hay, D. and Hammond, J. (1992) ' "When you pray, go to your private room": a reply to Adrian Thatcher', *British Journal of Religious Education*, 14 (3): 145–50.

Hay, D. and Nye, R. (1998) *The Spirit of the Child*, London: HarperCollins.

Heelas, P. (1996) *The New Age Movement: The Celebration of Self and the Sacralization of Modernity*, Oxford: Blackwell.

Heimbrock, H.-G. (2001) 'Beyond globalism and relativism: religious education, plurality and life-world orientation', in H.-G. Heimbrock, C. Scheilke and P. Schreiner (eds) *Towards Religious Competence: Diversity as a Challenge for Education in Europe*, Münster: Lit Verlag.

—— (2004 forthcoming) 'Beyond secularisation: experiences of the sacred in childhood and adolescence as a challenge for RE development theory', *British Journal of Religious Education*.

Heimbrock, H.-G., Scheilke, C. and Schreiner, P. (eds) (2001) *Towards Religious Competence: Diversity as a Challenge for Education in Europe*, Münster: Lit Verlag.

Hick, J. (1990) *Philosophy of Religion*, 4th edn, Englewood Cliffs, NJ: Prentice Hall.

Hillage, J., Pearson, R., Anderson, A. and Tamkin, P. (1998) *Excellence in Research on Schools*, London: Department for Education and Employment.

Hirst, P. (1974) *Moral Education in a Secular Society*, London: Hodder and Stoughton.

Hobson, P.R. and Edwards, J.S. (1999) *Religious Education in a Pluralist Society*, London: Woburn Press.

Home Office (2001a) *Community Cohesion: A Report of the Independent Review Team chaired by Ted Cantle*, December, London: Home Office.

—— (2001b) *Building Cohesive Communities: A Report of the Ministerial Group on Public Order and Community Cohesion*, December, London: Home Office.

Hookway, S. (2002) 'Mirrors, windows, conversation: RE for the millennial generation', *British Journal of Religious Education*, 24 (2): 99–110.

Hull, J.M. (1982) 'Open minds and empty hearts?', in R. Jackson (ed.) *Approaching World Religions*, London: John Murray.

—— (1991) *Mishmash: Religious Education in Multi-Cultural Britain: A Study in Metaphor*, Birmingham Papers in Religious Education, Derby: Christian Education Movement.

—— (1996a) 'Freedom and authority in religious education', in B.E. Gates (ed.) *Freedom and Authority in Religions and Religious Education*, London: Cassell.

—— (1996b) 'Religious education and the conflict of values in modern Europe', in A. Lande and W. Ustorf (eds) *Mission in a Pluralist World*, Sonderuck: Peter Lang.

—— (1996c) 'A gift to the child: a new pedagogy for teaching religion to young children', *Religious Education*, 91 (2): 172–88.

—— (1997) 'Encounter with religion and responding to religion', Address given to celebrate the inauguration of the Cheshire Agreed Syllabus on 13 May 1996, Cheshire County Council Education Services.

—— (2002) 'Understanding contemporary European consciousness: an approach through geo-politics', *Panorama: International Journal of Comparative Religious Education and Values*, 14 (2): 123–40.

Humanist Philosophers' Group (2001) *Religious Schools: The Case Against*, London: British Humanist Association.

Human Rights Act (1998) Human Rights Act, 'Right To Education, Schedule 1 – The First Protocol, Part II, Article 2', London: HMSO, Chapter 42. Online. Available HTTP: http://www.hmso.gov.uk/acts/acts1998/19980042.htm (accessed May 2003).

Hyde, K.E. (1990) *Religion in Childhood and Adolescence*, Birmingham, AL: Religious Education Press.

ICCS (2001) Intereuropean Commission on Church and School Newsletter 24, Münster: ICCS, 2–3.

ICE (1954) *Religious Education in Schools: The Report of an Inquiry made by the Research Committee of the Institute of Christian Education into the working of the 1944 Education Act*, London: National Society and SPCK.

Ipgrave, J. (1998) 'The religious education of Muslim students', London: Teacher Training Agency.

—— (1999) 'Issues in the delivery of religious education to Muslim pupils: perspectives from the classroom', *British Journal of Religious Education*, 21 (3): 147–58.

—— (2001) 'Pupil to pupil dialogue in the classroom as a tool for religious education', *Warwick Religions and Education Research Unit Occasional Papers II*, University of Warwick, Institute of Education.

—— (2002) 'Inter faith encounter and religious understanding in an inner city primary school', unpublished PhD thesis, University of Warwick.

—— (2003) 'Dialogue, citizenship and religious education', in R. Jackson (ed.) *International Perspectives on Citizenship, Education and Religious Diversity*, London: RoutledgeFalmer.

Jackson, R. (1982) 'Commitment and the teaching of world religions', in R. Jackson (ed.) *Approaching World Religions*, London: John Murray.

—— (1987) 'Changing conceptions of Hinduism in timetabled religion', in R. Burghart (ed.) *Hinduism in Great Britain: Religion in an Alien Cultural Milieu*, London: Tavistock.

—— (1990) 'Religious studies and developments in religious education in England and Wales', in U. King (ed.) *Turning Points in Religious Studies*, Edinburgh: T. and T. Clark.

—— (1996a) 'The construction of "Hinduism" and its impact on religious education in England and Wales', *Panorama: International Journal of Comparative Religious Education and Values*, 8 (2): 86–104.

—— (1996b) 'Ethnographic research and curriculum development', in L.J. Francis, W.K. Kay and W.S. Campbell (eds) *Research in Religious Education*, Leominster: Gracewing.

—— (1997) *Religious Education: An Interpretive Approach*, London: Hodder and Stoughton.

—— (1999) 'The inter-relatedness of subject, pedagogy and research approaches: theology, religious studies and religious education in England and Wales', in D. Chidester, J. Stonier and J. Tobler (eds) *Diversity as Ethos: Challenges for Inter-religious and Intercultural Education*, Cape Town: Institute for Comparative Religion in Southern Africa.

—— (2000a) 'Law, politics and religious education in England and Wales: some history, some stories and some observations', in M. Leicester, C. Modgil and S. Modgil (eds) *Spiritual and Religious Education*, London: Routledge. [*Education, Culture and Values*, 5].

—— (2000b) 'The Warwick Religious Education Project: the interpretive approach to religious education', in M. Grimmitt (ed.) *Pedagogies of Religious Education: Case Studies in the Research and Development of Good Pedagogic Practice in RE*, Great Wakering: McCrimmons.

—— (ed.) (2003a) *International Perspectives on Citizenship, Education and Religious Diversity*, London: RoutledgeFalmer.

—— (2003b) 'Citizenship, religious and cultural diversity and education', in R. Jackson (ed.) *International Perspectives on Citizenship, Education and Religious Diversity*, London: RoutledgeFalmer.

Jackson, R. and Nesbitt, E. (1992) 'The diversity of experience in the religious upbringing of children from Christian families in Britain', *British Journal of Religious Education*, 15 (1): 19–28.

—— (1993) *Hindu Children in Britain*, Stoke-on-Trent: Trentham.

Jackson, R., Barratt, M. and Everington, J. (1994) *Bridges to Religions: Teacher's Resource Book*, The Warwick RE Project, Oxford: Heinemann.

Jacobson, J. (1997) 'Religion and ethnicity: dual and alternative sources of identity among young British Pakistanis', *Ethnic and Racial Studies*, 20 (2): 238–56.

James, A. and Prout, A. (1997) *Constructing and Reconstructing Childhood: Contemporary Issues in the Sociological Study of Childhood*, 2nd edn, London: Falmer Press.

Johns, E.L. (ed.) (1985) *Religious Education Belongs in the Public Schools: Theory for a Multi-cultural, Inter-faith Approach*, Toronto: Ecumenical Study Commission on Public Education.

Jones, R. and Welengama, G. (2000) *Ethnic Minorities in English Law*, Stoke-on-Trent: Trentham.

Kanitkar, V.P. (1979) 'A school for Hindus?', *New Community*, 7 (2): 178–83.

Kassam, N. (ed.) (1997) *Telling It Like It Is: Young Asian Women Talk*, London: Livewire.

Kay, W.K. (1996) 'Historical context: Loukes, Goldman, Hyde, Cox and Alves', in L.J. Francis, W.K. Kay and W.S. Campbell (eds) *Research in Religious Education*, Leominster: Gracewing.

Kay, W.K. and Linnet-Smith, D. (2000) 'Religious terms and attitudes in the classroom (Part 1)', *British Journal of Religious Education*, 22 (2): 81–90.

Kierkegaard, S. (1962) *Philosophical Fragments*, Princeton, NJ: Princeton University Press.

King, R. (1999) *Orientalism and Religion: Postcolonial Theory, India and 'The Mystic East'*, London: Routledge.

King, U. (2002) *Spirituality and Postmodernism*, Farmington Papers, Philosophy of Religion 11, Oxford: Farmington Institute for Christian Studies.

Knauth, T. (1999) 'From reconstruction to interpretation: steps for analyzing RE lessons multiperspectively', in D. Chidester, J. Stonier and J. Tobler (eds) *Diversity as Ethos: Challenges for Inter-religious and Intercultural Education*, Cape Town: Institute for Comparative Religion in Southern Africa.

Kotzé, M. (1997) 'Looking at the Namibian syllabi', in T. Andree, C. Bakker and P. Schreiner (eds) *Crossing Boundaries: Contributions to Interreligious and Intercultural Education*, Münster: Comenius Institut.

Krisman, A. (1997) *Speak from the Heart: Exploring and Responding to RE in the Special School*, Oxford: Farmington Institute for Christian Studies. Online. Available: http://www.farmington.ac.uk/documents/reports/framed/teaching_training.html (accessed June 2003).

—— (1999) 'Building up to the sky', *Resource*, 21 (2): 6–9.

Kwami, R. (1996) 'Music education in and for a multicultural society', in C. Plummeridge (ed.) *Music Education: Issues and Trends*, London: Institute of Education.

Kwenda, C., Mndende, N. and Stonier, J. (1997) *African Religion and Culture Alive!*, Hatfield (SA): Collegium.

Kymlicka, W. (1999) 'Education for citizenship', in J.M. Halstead and T.H. McLaughlin (eds) *Education in Morality*, London: Routledge.

Lansdown, R., Frangoulis, S. and Jordan, N. (1997) 'Children's concept of an afterlife', *Bereavement Care*, 16 (2): 16–19.

Larsen, L. and Plesner, I.T. (eds) (2002) *Teaching for Tolerance and Freedom of Religion or Belief*, Oslo: The Oslo Coalition on Freedom of Religion and Belief, University of Oslo.

van der Leeuw, G. (1938) *Religion in Essence and Manifestation*, London: Allen and Unwin.

Leganger-Krogstad, H. (1998) 'Ethnic minority in conflict with Norwegian educational ideals', *Panorama: International Journal of Comparative Religious Education and Values*, 10 (1): 131–45.

—— (1999) 'A contextual approach to RE within the Norwegian school system', unpublished paper presented to a conference on 'The Concrete, the Particular and the General: The Relevance of Life-world, Subject and Contextual Orientation for Reforming Religious Education in Europe', 1–3 September, Frankfurt am Main, Germany.

—— (2000) 'Developing a contextual theory and practice of religious education', *Panorama: International Journal of Comparative Religious Education and Values*, 12 (1): 94–104.

—— (2001) 'Religious education in a global perspective: a contextual approach', in H.-G. Heimbrock, P. Schreiner and C. Scheilke (eds) *Towards Religious Competence: Diversity as a Challenge for Education in Europe*, Münster: Lit Verlag.

—— (2003) 'Dialogue among young citizens in a pluralistic religious education classroom', in R. Jackson (ed.) *International Perspectives on Citizenship, Education and Religious Diversity*, London: RoutledgeFalmer.

Leicester, M. (1992) 'Antiracism versus the new multiculturalism: moving beyond the interminable debate', in J. Lynch, C. Modgil and S. Modgil (eds) *Cultural Diversity and the Schools: Equity or Excellence? Education and Cultural Reproduction*, London: Falmer Press.

Leutner-Ramme, S. (1999) 'Religious education in the multiperspective view of the participants', in D. Chidester, J. Stonier and J. Tobler (eds) *Diversity as Ethos: Challenges for Inter-religious and Intercultural Education*, Cape Town: Institute for Comparative Religion in Southern Africa.

Lewis, A. and Lindsay, G. (eds) (2000) *Researching Children's Perspectives*, Buckingham: Open University Press.

Lewis, P. (1997) 'Arenas of ethnic negotiation: co-operation and conflict in Bradford', in T. Modood and P. Werbner (eds) *The Politics of Multiculturalism in the New Europe: Racism, Identity and Community*, London: Zed Books.

Linnet-Smith, D. and Kay, W.K. (2000) 'Religious terms and attitudes in the classroom (Part 2)', *British Journal of Religious Education*, 22 (3): 181–91.

Lister, R. (1997) 'Citizenship: towards a feminist synthesis', *Feminist Review*, 57: 28–48.

Lombard, C. (1997) 'Contextual and theoretical considerations in the Namibian curricular process', in T. Andree, C. Bakker and P. Schreiner (eds) *Crossing Boundaries: Contributions to Interreligious and Intercultural Education*, Münster: Comenius Institut.

Loukes, H. (1961) *Teenage Religion: An Enquiry into Attitudes and Possibilities among British Teenagers*, London: SCM Press.

—— (1965) *New Ground in Christian Education*, London: SCM Press.

—— (1973) *Teenage Morality*, London: SCM Press.

Lyotard, J.-F. (1984) *The Postmodern Condition: A Report on Knowledge*, trans. G. Bennington and B. Massumi, Manchester: Manchester University Press.

Mager, R. (2002) 'Religion in the public realm in Quebec: forty years of debate over the presence of religion in the public school system (1960–2000)', *British Journal of Religious Education*, 24 (3): 183–95.

Malone, P. (1998) 'Religious education and prejudice among students taking the course "studies of religion"', *British Journal of Religious Education*, 21 (1): 7–19.

Marks, J. (2001) 'Standards in Church of England, Roman Catholic and LEA Schools in England', in J. Burn, J. Marks, P. Pilkington and P. Thompson (eds) *Faith in Education*, London: Civitas.

Marshall, P.J. (ed.) (1970) *The British Discovery of Hinduism in the Eighteenth Century*, Cambridge: Cambridge University Press.

Mavor, I. (1989) 'Religion in Australian schools', *Religion and Public Education*, 16 (1): 83–90.

May, S. (ed.) (1999) *Critical Multiculturalism: Rethinking Multicultural and Antiracist Education*, London: Falmer Press.

McIntyre, J. (1978) 'Multi-culture and multifaith societies: some examinable assumptions', *Occasional Papers*, Oxford: Farmington Institute for Christian Studies.

McKenna, U. (2002) 'Towards an inclusive pedagogy for religious education in primary schools', *Warwick Religions and Education Research Unit Occasional Papers III*, University of Warwick: Institute of Education.

McPhail, P., Ungoed-Thomas, J. and Chapman, H. (1972) *Moral Education in the Secondary School*, London: Methuen.

Meijer, W.A.J. (1995) 'The plural self: a hermeneutical view on identity and plurality', *British Journal of Religious Education*, 17 (2): 92–9.

—— (2004) 'Tradition and reflexivity in religious education', in H. Lombaers and D. Pollefeyt (eds) *Hermeneutics and Religious Education*, Leuven: BETL (Bibliotheca Epheridum Theologicarum Lovaniensium).

Mercier, C. (1996) *Muslims*, 'Interpreting Religions' series, The Warwick RE Project, Oxford: Heinemann.

Miller, J. (2003a) 'Using the visual arts in religious education: an analysis and critical evaluation', *British Journal of Religious Education*, 25 (3): 200–16.

—— (2003b) 'Faith and belonging in Bradford', *RE Today*, 20 (3): 34.

—— (2003c) 'Out of the shadows', *Times Educational Supplement*, 28 February, the 'Teacher' section: 34.

Milot, M. and Ouellet, F. (eds) (1997) *Religion, Education et Démocratie: Un Enseignement Culturel de la Religion est-il Possible?* Montreal: Harmattan.

Mitchell, G., Mndende, N., Phiri, I.A. and Stonier, J. (1993) *The End of the Tunnel: Religion Education for a Non-Racial South Africa*, Cape Town: Institute for Comparative Religion in Southern Africa.

Modood, T. (1992) 'On not being white in Britain: discrimination, diversity and commonality', in M. Leicester and M. Taylor (eds) *Ethics, Ethnicity and Education*, London: Kogan Page.

—— (1997) '"Difference", cultural racism and antiracism', in P. Werbner and T. Modood (eds) *Debating Cultural Hybridity*, London: Zed Books.

Modood, T. and Werbner, P. (eds) (1997) *The Politics of Multiculturalism in the New Europe: Racism, Identity and Community*, London: Zed Books.

Morris, E. (2001a) Personal communication, 13 August.

—— (2001b) Speech at the Church of England General Synod, 14 November.

—— (2002) Speech in the House of Commons, *Hansard*, 6 February, Column 898.

Mullard, C. (1984) *Anti-Racist Education: The Three O's*, Cardiff: National Association for Multiracial Education.

Murphy, R. (1977) 'The development of religious thinking in children in three easy stages?', *Learning for Living*, 17: 16–19.

Murray, V. (1991) 'Catholic and Sikh sixth formers: education for different identities', *Sikh Bulletin*, 8: 1–6.

NCC (1990) *Education for Citizenship* (Curriculum guidance 8), York: National Curriculum Council.

Nesbitt, E.M. (1990a) 'Pitfalls in religious taxonomy: Hindus, Sikhs, Ravidasis and Valmikis', *Religion Today*, 6 (1): 9–12.

—— (1990b) 'Religion and identity: the Valmiki community in Coventry', *New Community*, 16 (2): 261–74.

—— (1991) *'My Dad's Hindu, My Mum's Side are Sikhs': Issues in Religious Identity*, Charlbury: National Foundation for Arts Education.

—— (1993a) 'The transmission of Christian tradition in an ethnically diverse society', in R. Barot (ed.) *Religion and Ethnicity: Minorities and Social Change in the Metropolis*, Kampen (The Netherlands): Kok Pharos.

—— (1993b) 'Children and the world to come: the views of children aged eight to fourteen on life after death', *Religion Today*, 8 (3): 10–13.

—— (1993c) 'Drawing on the ethnic diversity of Christian tradition in Britain', *Multicultural Teaching*, 11 (2): 9–12.

—— (1995a) 'Celebrating and learning: the perpetuation of values and practices among Hindu Punjabi children in Coventry, UK', *Indo-British Review*, 20 (2): 119–31.

—— (1995b) 'The religious lives of Sikh children in Coventry', unpublished PhD thesis, University of Warwick.

—— (1997a) ' "Splashed with goodness": the many meanings of Amrit for young British Sikhs', *Journal of Contemporary Religion*, 12 (1): 17–33.

—— (1997b) ' "Sikhs and proper Sikhs": young British Sikhs' perceptions of their identity', in P. Singh and N.G. Barrier (eds) *Sikh Identity: Continuity and Change*, Delhi: Manohar.

—— (1998a) 'British, Asian and Hindu: identity, self-narration and the ethnographic interview', *Journal of Beliefs and Values*, 19 (2): 189–200.

—— (1998b) 'Bridging the gap between young people's experience of their religious traditions at home and school: the contribution of ethnographic research', *British Journal of Religious Education*, 20 (2): 102–14.

—— (2000a) *The Religious Lives of Sikh Children: A Coventry Based Study*, Monograph Series, Leeds: University of Leeds, Community Religions Project.

—— (2000b) 'Researching 8–13 year olds' perspectives on their experience of religion', in A. Lewis and G. Lindsay (eds) *Researching Children's Perspectives*, Buckingham: Open University Press.

—— (2001) 'Religious nurture and young people's spirituality', in J. Erricker, C. Ota and C. Erricker (eds) *Spiritual Education, Cultural, Religious and Social Differences: New Perspectives for the 21st Century*, Brighton: Sussex Academic Press.

Nesbitt, E.M. and Henderson, A. (2003) 'Religious organisations in the UK and values education programmes for schools', *Journal of Beliefs and Values*, 24 (1): 75–88.

Nesbitt, E.M. and Jackson, R. (1993) 'Aspects of cultural transmission in a diaspora Sikh community', *Journal of Sikh Studies*, 18 (1): 52–66.

—— (1995) 'Sikh children's use of "God": ethnographic fieldwork and religious education', *British Journal of Religious Education*, 17 (2): 108–20.

Norcross, P. (1989) 'The effects of cultural conditioning of multifaith education in the monocultural primary school', *British Journal of Religious Education*, 11 (2): 87–91.

Oberoi, H. (1994) *The Construction of Religious Boundaries: Culture, Identity and Diversity in the Sikh Tradition*, Delhi: Oxford University Press.

Ofsted (1995) *Religious Education: A Review of Inspection Findings 1993/94*, London: Her Majesty's Stationery Office.

—— (1997) *The Impact of New Agreed Syllabuses on the Teaching and Learning of Religious Education*, London: Her Majesty's Stationery Office.

—— (1999) *Primary Education: A Review of Primary Schools in England 1994–98*, London: The Stationery Office.

—— (2000) *Evaluating Educational Inclusion*, London: The Stationery Office.

O'Grady, K. (2003) 'Motivation in religious education: a collaborative investigation with year eight students', *British Journal of Religious Education*, 25 (3): 214–25.

Orchard, S. (1991) 'What was wrong with religious education? An analysis of HMI Reports 1985–1988', *British Journal of Religious Education*, 14 (1): 15–21.

Orfield, G. and Gordon, N. (2001) 'Schools more separate: consequences of a decade of resegregation', paper presented at The Civil Rights Project conference, Harvard University, Cambridge, MA, July.

Ouseley, H. (ed.) (2001) *Community Pride Not Prejudice: Making Diversity Work in Bradford*, Bradford: Bradford Vision.

Outka, G. and Ramsey, P. (eds) (1968) *Norm and Context in Christian Ethics*, London: SCM.

Oxfam (no date) *Curriculum for Global Citizenship*, Oxford: Oxfam.

Paludan, P. and Prinds, E. (1999) *Evaluation of Education in Citizenship and Moral Judgement*, Copenhagen: Danish Ministry of Education.

Plesner, I.T. (2002) 'Religio-political models and models for religious and moral education', *Panorama: International Journal of Comparative Religious Education and Values*, 14 (2): 111–22.

Pocock, C. (2000) *An Investigation into the Contribution of RE to Citizenship and Preparation for Adult Life*, Oxford: Farmington Institute. Online. Available HTTP: http://www.farmington.ac.uk/ (accessed July 2003).

Prelot, P.-H. (2002) 'Schools and religion in France', unpublished paper, forum on 'The new intercultural challenge to education: religious diversity and dialogue in Europe', Strasbourg: Council of Europe.

Price, L.M. (1988) 'The role of story in the religious education of the First School child', unpublished MA thesis, University of Warwick.

Priestley, J. (1985) 'Towards finding the hidden curriculum: a consideration of the spiritual dimension of experience in curriculum planning', *British Journal of Religious Education*, 7 (3): 112–19.

QCA (1998) *Guidelines for Schools: The Promotion of Pupils' Spiritual, Moral, Social and Cultural Development*, London: QCA.

—— (2003) *A Non-Statutory Framework for Religious Education: Report of a Feasibility Study*, London: Qualifications and Curriculum Authority.

Rattansi, A. (1992) 'Changing the subject: racism, culture and education', in J. Donald and A. Rattansi (eds) *Race, Culture and Difference*, London: Sage in association with The Open University.

—— (1999) 'Racism, postmodernism and reflexive multiculturalism', in S. May (ed.) *Critical Multiculturalism: Rethinking Multicultural and Antiracist Education*, London: Falmer Press.

REC (1988) *Religious Education: Supply of Teachers for the 1990s*, Lancaster: The Religious Education Council of England and Wales.

—— (1990) *What Conspired Against RE Specialist Teacher Supply?*, Lancaster: The Religious Education Council of England and Wales.

Richards, N. (1986) 'The history of post war religious education with particular reference to the relationship between religious and moral education: a study of pluralism', unpublished PhD thesis, University of Sheffield.

Ricoeur, P. (1988) *Time and Narrative*, vol. 3. Chicago/London: University of Chicago Press.

Robinson, E. and Lealman, B. (1980) *The Image of Life*, London: CEM.

Robinson, W. (1988) 'The skills of thinking and the religious education teacher', *British Journal of Religious Education*, 10 (2): 79–85.

Robson, G. (1995) *Christians*, 'Interpreting Religions' series, The Warwick RE Project, Oxford: Heinemann.

—— (1996) 'Religious education, government policy and professional practice, 1988–95', *British Journal of Religious Education*, 19 (1), 13–23.

Rorty, R. (1980) *Philosophy and the Mirror of Nature*, Oxford: Blackwell.

Rossiter, G. (1981) *Religious Education in Australian Schools*, Canberra: Curriculum Development Centre.

Roux, C. (2000) 'Multi-religious education: an option for South Africa in the new education system', *British Journal of Religious Education*, 22 (3): 173–80.

Rudge, L. (1998) ' "I am nothing – does it matter?" A critique of current religious education policy and practice in England on behalf of the silent majority', *British Journal of Religious Education*, 20 (3): 155–65.

Runnymede Trust (2000) *The Future of Multi-Ethnic Britain: The Parekh Report*, London: Profile Books.

Rüpell, G. and Schreiner, P. (eds) (2003) *Shared Learning in a Plural World: Ecumenical Approaches to Intercultural Education*, Münster: Lit Verlag.

Sacks, J. (1994) *Will We Have Jewish Grandchildren?*, London: Valentine Mitchell.

Said, E. (1978) *Orientalism*, London: Routledge and Kegan Paul.

Schagen, S., Davies, D., Rudd, P. and Schagen, I. (2002) *The Impact of Specialist and Faith Schools on Performance*, Slough: NFER.

Scheilke, C. (2001) 'Protestant schools: the new role, new results, new tasks', in H.-G. Heimbrock, C. Scheilke and P. Schreiner (eds) *Towards Religious Competence: Diversity as a Challenge for Education in Europe*, Münster: Lit Verlag.

Schools Council (1971) *Religious Education in Secondary Schools, Schools Council Working Paper 36*, London: Evans/Methuen.

Schools Curriculum and Assessment Authority (SCAA) (1994a) *Model Syllabuses for Religious Education: Model 1: Living Faiths Today*, London: School Curriculum and Assessment Authority.

—— (1994b) *Model Syllabuses for Religious Education: Model 2: Questions and Teaching*, London: School Curriculum and Assessment Authority.

—— (1994c) *Model Syllabuses for Religious Education: Faith Communities' Working Group Reports*, London: School Curriculum and Assessment Authority.

Schreiner, P. (2001) 'Towards a European oriented religious education', in H.-G. Heimbrock, C. Scheilke and P. Schreiner (eds) *Towards Religious Competence: Diversity as a Challenge for Education in Europe*, Münster: Lit Verlag.

Schweitzer, F. (2001) 'Religious education beyond the nation state: the challenge of supranational and global developments', in L.J. Francis, J. Astley and M. Robbins (eds) *The Fourth R for the Third Millennium: Education in Religion and Values for the Global Future*, Dublin, Lindisfarne.

Schweitzer, F. and Boschki, R. (2004) 'What children need: co-operative religious education in German schools: results from an empirical study', *British Journal of Religious Education* (forthcoming).

Scruton, R., Ellis-Jones, A. and O'Keeffe, D. (1985) *Education and Indoctrination*, London: Education Research Centre.

Sheridan, L. (2002) 'Discrimination and racism, post September 11', University of Leicester website: Online. Available HTTP: http://www.le.ac.uk/press/press/discriminationandracism.html (accessed 29 October 2002).

Short, G. (2003) 'Faith schools and social cohesion: opening up the debate', *British Journal of Religious Education*, 25 (2): 129–41.

Short, G. and Carrington, B. (1995) 'Learning about Judaism: a contribution to the debate on multi-faith religious education', *British Journal of Religious Education*, 17 (3): 157–67.

Short, G. and Lenga, R.-A. (2002) 'Jewish primary schools in a multicultural society: responding to diversity?', *Journal of Beliefs and Values*, 23 (1): 43–54.

Sikes, P. and Everington, J. (2001) 'Becoming an RE teacher: a life history approach', *British Journal of Religious Education*, 24 (1): 8–20.

—— (forthcoming a) '"I'm a woman before I'm an RE teacher": managing religious identity in secondary schools', *Gender and Education*.

—— (forthcoming b) '"RE teachers do get drunk you know": becoming an RE teacher in the twenty-first century', *Teachers and Teaching: Theory and Practice*.

Skeie, G. (1995) 'Plurality and pluralism: a challenge for religious education', *British Journal of Religious Education*, 25 (1): 47–59.

—— (2001) 'Citizenship, identity, politics and religious education', in H.-G. Heimbrock, C. Scheilke and P. Schreiner (eds) *Towards Religious Competence. Diversity as a Challenge for Education in Europe*, Münster: Lit Verlag.

—— (2002) 'The concept of plurality and its meaning for religious education', *British Journal of Religious Education*, 25 (2): 47–59.

—— (2003) 'Nationalism, religiosity and citizenship in Norwegian majority and minority discourses', in R. Jackson (ed.) *International Perspectives on Citizenship, Education and Religious Diversity*, London: RoutledgeFalmer.

Skutnabb-Kangas, T. (1987) *Are the Finns in Sweden an Ethnic Minority? Finnish Parents Talk about Finland and Sweden*, Roskilde: Roskilde University Centre Institute.

Slee, N. (1986) 'Goldman yet again: an overview and critique of his contribution to research', *British Journal of Religious Education*, 8 (2): 84–93.

—— (1989) 'Conflict and reconciliation between competing models of religious education: reflections on the British scene', *British Journal of Religious Education*, 11 (3): 126–35.

Smart, N. (1967) 'A new look at religious studies: the Lancaster idea', *Learning for Living*, 7 (1): 27–9.

—— (1968) *Secular Education and the Logic of Religion*, London: Faber.

—— (1971; US edn 1969) *The Religious Experience of Mankind*, London: Fontana.

Smith, W.C. (1978) *The Meaning and End of Religion*, London: SPCK.

—— (1981) *Towards a World Theology: Faith and the Comparative History of Religion*, London: Macmillan.

Starkings, D. (ed.) (1993) *Religion and the Arts in Education: Dimensions of Spirituality*, London: Hodder and Stoughton.

Stenhouse, L. (1970) 'Controversial value issues in the classroom', in W.G. Carr (ed.) *Values and the Curriculum: A Report of the Fourth International Curriculum Conference*, Washington: National Education Association.

Sterkens, C. (2001) *Interreligious Learning: The Problem of Interreligious Dialogue in Primary Education*, Leiden: Brill.

Steyn, H.C. (2003) 'The good South African citizen: then and now', in R. Jackson (ed.) *International Perspectives on Citizenship, Education and Religious Diversity*, London: RoutledgeFalmer.

Stonier, J. (1996) 'Oral into written: an experiment in creating a text for African religion', unpublished MA dissertation, University of Cape Town.

—— (1997) 'A chorus of voices', in T. Andree, C. Bakker and P. Schreiner (eds) *Crossing Boundaries: Contributions to Interreligious and Intercultural Education*, Münster: Comenius Institut.

—— (1999) 'A new direction for religious education in South Africa? The proposed new RE policy', in D. Chidester, J. Stonier and J. Tobler (eds) *Diversity as Ethos: Challenges for Interreligious and Intercultural Education*, Cape Town: Institute for Comparative Religion in Southern Africa.

Streib, H. (2001) 'Inter-religious negotiations: case studies on students' perception of and dealings with religious diversity', in H.-G. Heimbrock, C. Scheilke and P. Schreiner (eds) *Towards Religious Competence: Diversity as a Challenge for Education in Europe*, Münster: Lit Verlag.

—— (2003) 'Strangeness and familiarity of religious phenomena: their interplay in religious education classroom communication', unpublished paper, Conference of the European Network for Religious Education through Contextual Approaches, Schönberg, Germany, March.

Stringer, M.D. (2002) 'Introduction: theorizing faith', in E. Arweck and M.D. Stringer (eds) *Theorizing Faith: The Insider/Outsider Problem in the Study of Ritual*, Birmingham: Birmingham University Press.

Sullivan, J. (2000) *Catholic Schools in Contention*, Dublin: Veritas.

—— (2001) *Catholic Education: Distinctive and Inclusive*, Dordrecht: Kluwer Academic Publishers.

Swedish Ministry of Education and Science (1994) *Curriculum for Compulsory Schools* [Lpo 94], Stockholm.

—— (1995) *Syllabi for the Compulsory School*, Stockholm.

Tate, N. (1995) 'Cultural identity and education', address to Shropshire Secondary Heads Conference, 13 July, London: School Curriculum and Assessment Authority.

Taylor, M. (1991) *SACREs: Their Formation, Composition, Operation and Role on RE and Worship*, Slough: NFER.

Thatcher, A. (1991) 'A critique of inwardness in religious education', *British Journal of Religious Education*, 14 (1): 22–7.

Thompson, P. (2004) 'Whose confession? Which tradition?', *British Journal of Religious Education*, 26(1): 61–72.

Tickner, M.F. and Webster, D.H. (eds) (1982) 'Religious education and the imagination', *Aspects of Education*, 28, University of Hull.

Timms, S. (2001) Speech in the House of Commons, 15 October.

Tobler, J. (2003) 'Learning the difference: religion education, citizenship and gendered subjectivity', in R. Jackson (ed.) *International Perspectives on Citizenship, Education and Religious Diversity*, London: RoutledgeFalmer.

Tomlinson, S. and Craft, M. (eds) (1995) *Ethnic Relations and Schooling: Policy and Practice in the 1990s*, London: The Athlone Press.

Tooley, J. and Darby, D. (1998) *Educational Research: A Critique: A Survey of Published Educational Research*, London: Office for Standards in Education.

Trevathan, A. (2002) Contribution to a policy briefing on faith-based education, University of Warwick (Westminster Office), 28 May.

Troyna, B. (1983) 'Multiracial education: just another brick in the wall?', *New Community*, 10: 424–8.

Troyna, B. and Carrington, B. (1990) *Education, Racism and Reform*, London: Routledge.

UK Parliament (1988) *Education Reform Act 1988*, London: HMSO.

—— (1993) *Education Act*, London: Her Majesty's Stationery Office.

—— (1998) *School Standards and Framework Act*, London: Department for Education and Employment.

Valins, O. (2000) 'Institutionalised religion: sacred texts and Jewish spatial practice', *Geoforum*, 31 (4): 575–86.

—— (2003) 'Defending identities or segregating communities? Faith based schooling and the UK Jewish community', *Geoforum*, 34 (2): 235–47.

Valins, O., Kosmin, B. and Goldberg, J. (2001) *The Future of Jewish Schooling in the United Kingdom: A Strategic Assessment of a Faith-based Provision of Primary and Secondary School Education*, London: Institute for Jewish Policy Research.

Waardenburg, J. (1973) *Classical Approaches to the Study of Religion*, vol. 1, The Hague: Mouton.

Walford, G. (1995) *Educational Politics: Pressure Groups and Faith Based Schools*, Aldershot: Avebury.

—— (2000) *Policy and Politics in Education: Sponsored Grant-maintained Schools and Religious Diversity*, Aldershot: Ashgate.

Wardekker, W. and Miedema, S. (2001) 'Religious identity formation between participation and distanciation', in H.-G. Heimbrock, P. Schreiner and C. Scheilke (eds) *Towards Religious Competence: Diversity as a Challenge for Education in Europe*, Münster: Lit Verlag.

Watson, G. (1990) *The Report of the Ministerial Inquiry on Religious Education in Ontario Public Elementary Schools*, Toronto: Government of Ontario.

Wayne, E., Everington, J., Kadodwala, D. and Nesbitt, E. (1996) *Hindus*, 'Interpreting Religions' series, The Warwick RE Project, Oxford: Heinemann.

Webster, D. (1984) 'Research in RE', in J.M. Sutcliffe (ed.) *A Dictionary of Religious Education*, London, SCM Press.

Weisse, W. (1996a) 'An intercultural approach to religious instruction in Hamburg: construction, reform and curriculum planning', *Scriptura: International Journal of Bible, Religion and Theology*, 55 (4): 291–301.

—— (1996b) 'Christianity and its neighbour-religions: a question of tolerance?', *Scriptura: International Journal of Bible, Religion and Theology*, 55 (4): 263–76.

—— (1996c) 'Approaches to religious education in the multicultural city of Hamburg', in W. Weisse (ed.) *Interreligious and Intercultural Education: Methodologies, Conceptions and Pilot Projects in South Africa, Namibia, Great Britain, the Netherlands and Germany*, Münster: Comenius Institut.

—— (ed.) (1996d) *Interreligious and Intercultural Education: Methodologies, Conceptions and Pilot Projects in South Africa, Namibia, Great Britain, the Netherlands and Germany*, Münster: Comenius Institut.

—— (1999) 'Religious education in the multiperspective view of the participants: introduction', in D. Chidester, J. Stonier and J. Tobler (eds) *Diversity as Ethos: Challenges for Inter-religious and Intercultural Education*, Cape Town: Institute for Comparative Religion in Southern Africa.

—— (2003) 'Difference without discrimination: religious education as a field of learning for social understanding?', in R. Jackson (ed.) *International Perspectives on Citizenship, Education and Religious Diversity*, London: RoutledgeFalmer.

Weisse, W. and Knauth, T. (1997) 'Dialogical religious education: theoretical framework and conceptual conclusions', in T. Andree, C. Bakker and P. Schreiner (eds) *Crossing Boundaries: Contributions to Inter-religious and Intercultural Education*, Münster: Comenius Institute.

Weller, P., Feldman, A. and Purdam, K. (2001) *Religious Discrimination in England and Wales*, London: Home Office.

Werbner, P. (2000) 'Divided loyalties, empowered citizenship? Muslims in Britain', *Citizenship Studies*, 4 (3): 307–24.

White, John (forthcoming) 'Should religious education be a compulsory school subject?', *British Journal of Religious Education*.

White, Joy (2003) 'An exploration of the significance of faith group identification for non-denominational schools', unpublished MA dissertation, University of Warwick.

Wilde, J. (1998) 'Religious education in further education: a study in under-provision', *British Journal of Religious Education*, 21 (1): 44–54.

Wilkins, R. (1991) 'How can an Evangelical Christian teach multi-faith RE?', *Resource*, 13 (3): 1–3.

Wilson, J. (1971) *Education in Religion and the Emotions*, London: Heinemann.

Wilson, J., Williams, N. and Sugarman, B. (1967) *Introduction to Moral Education*, Harmondsworth: Penguin.

Winston, J. (1998) *Drama, Narrative and Moral Education*, London: Falmer Press.

—— (1999) 'Theorising drama as moral education', *Journal of Moral Education*, 28 (4): 459–71.

Wintersgill, B. (2000) 'Task-setting in religious education at Key Stage 3: a comparison with history and English', *Resource*, 22 (3): 10–17.

Woodward, W. (2001) 'Cross purposes', *Guardian Education*, 25 September: 2.

Wright, A. (1993) *Religious Education in the Secondary School: Prospects for Religious Literacy*, London: David Fulton.

—— (1996a) 'Language and experience in the hermeneutics of religious understanding', *British Journal of Religious Education*, 18 (3): 166–80.

—— (1996b) 'Postmodernism and religious education: a reply to Liam Gearon', *Journal of Beliefs and Values*, 17 (1): 19–25.

—— (1998) *Spiritual Pedagogy: A Survey, Critique and Reconstruction of Contemporary Spiritual Education in England and Wales*, Abingdon: Culham College Institute.

—— (1999) *Discerning the Spirit*, Abingdon: Culham College Institute.

—— (2001) 'Dancing in the fire: a deconstruction of Clive Erricker's postmodern spiritual pedagogy', *Religious Education*, 96 (1): 120–35.

—— (2003) 'The contours of critical religious education: knowledge, wisdom, truth', *British Journal of Religious Education*, 25 (4): 279–91.

Young, I.M. (1990) *Justice and the Politics of Difference*, Princeton, NJ: Princeton University Press.

Østberg, S. (1997) 'Religious education in a multicultural society: the quest for identity and dialogue', in T. Andree, C. Bakker and P. Schreiner (eds) *Crossing Boundaries: Contributions to Interreligious and Intercultural Education*, Münster: Comenius Institut.

—— (1999) 'Pakistani children in Oslo: Islamic nurture in a secular context', unpublished PhD thesis, Institute of Education, University of Warwick.

—— (2000a) 'Islamic nurture and identity management', *British Journal of Religious Education*, 22 (2): 91–103.

—— (2000b) 'Punjabi, Pakistani, Muslim and Norwegian? Self-perceptions and social boundaries among Pakistani children in Oslo', *International Journal of Punjab Studies*, 7 (1): 133–59.

—— (2003a) 'Cultural diversity and common citizenship: reflections on ethnicity, religion, nationhood and citizenship among Pakistani young people in Europe', in R. Jackson (ed.) *International Perspectives on Citizenship, Education and Religious Diversity*, London: RoutledgeFalmer.

—— (2003b) *Pakistani Children in Norway: Islamic Nurture in a Secular Context*, Monograph Series, Leeds: University of Leeds, Community Religions Project.

—— (2003c) 'Norwegian-Pakistani adolescents: negotiating religion, gender, ethnicity and social boundaries', *Young: Nordic Journal of Youth Research*, 2: 161–81.

Index